Early Medieval Italy

Central Power and Local Society 400–1000

Chris Wickham

D1233009

Ann Arbor Paperbacks
The University of Michigan Press

First edition as an Ann Arbor Paperback 1989
First published in the United States of America by
The University of Michigan Press 1989
First published 1981 by
The Macmillan Press Ltd

1998 1997 1996 1995   7 6 5 4

Library of Congress Cataloging-in-Publication Data
Wickham, Chris, 1950–
    Early Medieval Italy: central power and local society, 400–1000
Chris Wickham.
        p.   cm.—(Ann Arbor paperbacks:AA198)
    "First published 1981 by the Macmillan Press LTD"—T.p. verso.
    Bibliography: p.
    Includes index.
    ISBN 0–472–08099–7
    1. Italy—History—476–1268. I.Title. II. Series.
DG503.W52   1989
945—dc20   89–32476
                                                          CIP

Contents

CONTENTS

LIST OF MAPS

The illustration on the front of the book shows the Tempietto del Clitunno near Spoleto, a Roman temple reused as an early medieval church. It is reproduced with the permission of the Mansell Collection.

Acknowledgements

I should like to thank the general editor of this series, Denis Bethell, who invited me to write this book and has greatly helped its writing, despite illness. Ralph Davis and Rodney Hilton have also read the whole book and commented on it, and Tom Brown, Wendy Davies, Michael Hendy, Rosamond McKitterick and Rosemary Morris have commented on sections; I have followed most of their suggestions. Tom Brown and Brian Croke let me look at work in advance of publication, to my great profit. For ideas, discussion and other help, I am indebted to all my colleagues at Birmingham University, and also, among many, Beryl Clark, John Gillingham, Ceri Lloyd-Morgan, Christina Lord, Crispin Shoddy, Bryan Ward-Perkins, my parents, Ian Wood and Patrick Wormald. I am also grateful to Rosaleen Darlington, who did all the typing, Kyle Rae who compiled the index, and Harry Buglass, who drew the maps.

C. J. W. January 1980

Chronological Table

725	Pope Gregory II refuses to pay land tax; beginning of break with Byzantium
726	Liutprand invades Exarchate
733–42	Liutprand gains supremacy in southern Italy
746	Laws of Ratchis
750–5	Laws of Aistulf
751	Aistulf takes Ravenna
754 or 5–756	Pippin III invades Italy. Exarchate given to Pope Stephen II
772	Desiderius moves on Rome
773–4	Charlemagne conquers Italy
774	Arichis II of Benevento takes on the title of prince
787–8	Charlemagne establishes temporary hegemony over Benevento
800	Charlemagne crowned emperor in Rome
817	Revolt of Bernard of Italy
827	Arab invasion of Sicily
c.839	Amalfi establishes independence from Naples
839–49	Civil war in Benevento
843	Treaty of Verdun; Carolingian Empire split up
849	Benevento divided; independent principality of Salerno
850	Louis II crowned emperor and begins sole rule in Italy
867–71	Siege and fall of Bari
875	Death of Louis II; disputed succession in the North
876	Byzantines begin reconquest of South
888	Berengar I elected king; civil wars (889–905) against him
892–5	Byzantines hold Benevento
894	Invasion of Arnulf of Germany
898	Last Frankish capitulary
899	First Hungarian invasion
900	Atenulf I unifies Capua and Benevento
902	Arabs take Taormina, last Byzantine stronghold in Sicily
903	First royal diploma for *incastellamento*
915	Death of Adalbert II of Tuscany. Arabs driven out of Garigliano
924	Hungarians sack Pavia; murder of Berengar I

927	Plot by Pavese officials against King Hugh
928–32	Marozia sole ruler in Rome
931	Hugh gains hegemony in Tuscany
932–54	Alberic II sole ruler in Rome
941	Fall of house of Ivrea; Hugh supreme in Spoleto
945	Fall of Hugh; end of effective hegemony of Italian kings
962	Otto I of Germany, king of Italy and emperor
967	Capitulary of Verona
968–70	Otto I attempts to conquer Byzantine Italy
996–1002	Otto III ruling in Italy
999–1003	Pope Sylvester II (Gerbert of Aurillac)
1002	Death of Hugh of Tuscany; break-up of Tuscan march
1002–c.1015	Arduin of Ivrea maintains himself as king against Henry II
1005	Death of Nilus of Rossano (born c.910) at Grottaferrata near Rome
1009–18	Revolts in Apulian cities; first use of Norman mercenaries
1012–28	Pope Benedict VIII; aristocratic papacy reaches its peak
1024	Pavesi sack royal palace; end of central government of the Italian kingdom

Map 1

Map 2

Map 3

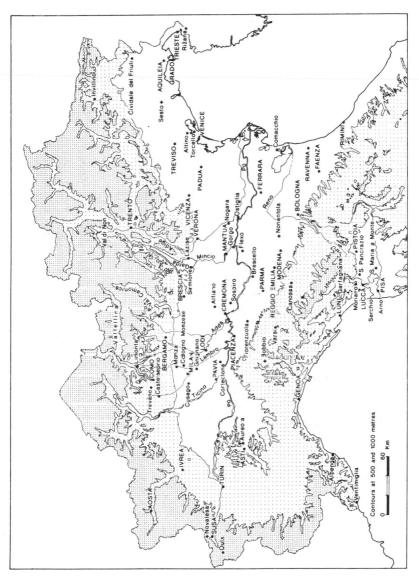

Map 4 Northern Italy

Contours at 500 and 1000 metres

0   60 Km

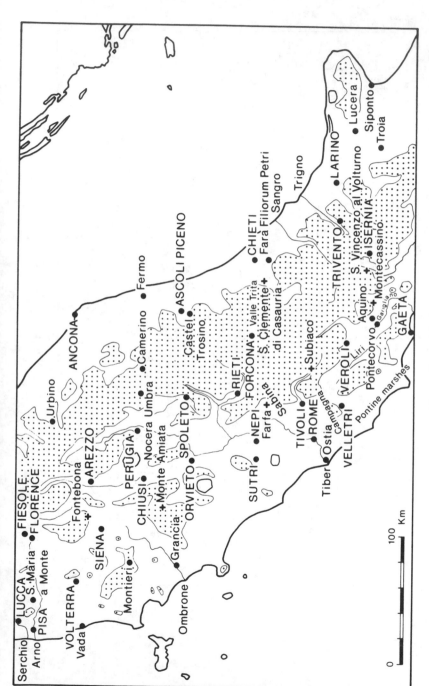

Map 5 Central Italy

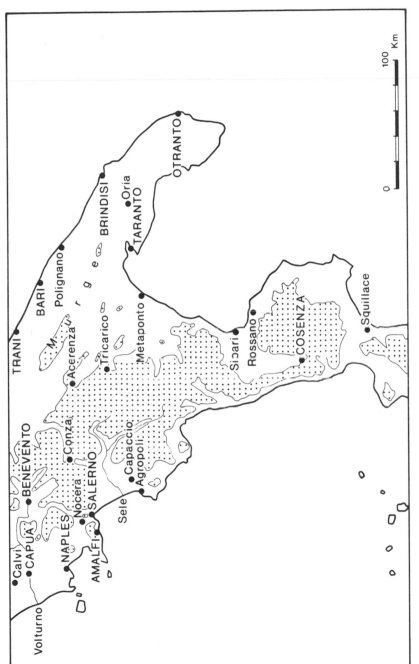

Map 6 Southern Italy

Introduction

ITALY is a geographical unity, at least in name; the Alpine mountain barrier makes certain of that. But it is not a homogeneous unit. Italy is and always has been a collection of regions, and each region is a collection of smaller units. Some of these are very ancient, and have kept their identity and loyalties even under the strongest governments, such as the Roman Empire and the twentieth-century Italian state. Even now, Italian is a second language that most Italian children have to learn; the dialect they speak at home is so different in some parts of Italy that it can be classified as a separate language altogether. An Italian is Milanese or Neapolitan before he is Italian; or, very often, he identifies being Italian *with* being Milanese or Neapolitan. That this is a fundamental Italian problem is symbolised by the fact that the Italian Communist Party does not call its newspaper 'Humanity', or 'Forwards', or 'Truth', as elsewhere in Europe, but 'Unity', *L'Unità*, representing, at least in part, a necessity to make Italian unification a reality alongside any advances to socialism.

It is in this context that the study of early medieval Italy may be of interest even to contemporary historians. For the period c.500–1000 is the period of the only serious attempts made between the Roman Republic and 1815 to make Italy into any sort of independent political unit at all, and indeed sees the ultimate total failure of such attempts, which foundered eventually on the same rocks that exist today: the continuing crucial importance of local identities and problems. For only a few decades was the whole of Italy part of a single independent state: from the 460s (say) until the 530s; but the bulk of the mainland – say two-thirds – was in some sense part of the same state for most of the early medieval period, and the kings of Italy, Ostrogothic, Lombard, and Frankish, were both powerful and rich. The kingdom they ruled, however, was no more a coherent unit than modern Italy, and for the same reasons, vastly increased by an underdeveloped economy and bad communications: the localities of Italy were totally dissimilar and had their own separate histories and developments. These problems are common to all Europe in the Middle Ages; the interest of the Italian experience lies in the relative *success* that many of these kings had. The break-up of Italy was in no sense inevitable, except perhaps the separation from it of the South, still the most intractable problem of

Italian politics; and there were several points in the eighth and ninth centuries when the centralising attempts of kings looked as if they were going to be successful – as if, indeed, they *were* successful. Their failure, therefore, has to be explained too, and is as interesting as their success. Early medieval Italy has not been traditionally seen in terms of these problems. Italy between the fall of the Roman Empire in the West and the rise of the communes is certainly not a simple field for study, and at times it has been treated with some embarrassment. The invasion of Italy by the Lombards in 568, not long after the Eastern Empire had with difficulty conquered it from the Ostrogoths, did indeed break the political unity of Italy as a whole. The other 'natural' political form in Italy, the independent city-state, did not make its reappearance until the rise of Amalfi and Naples in the ninth century and the better-known northern and central Italian cities in the eleventh. To older historians, the intervening period did not seem to conform to any clear rules. Italy, the fount of culture and civilisation, showed very little of either across these centuries, except a considerable legal sophistication, and the occasional pretentious stylist, either with real literary ability (as with Paul the Deacon) or without it (as with Liutprand of Cremona). Italy, the mercantile centre of the ancient and medieval Mediterranean, seemed to have temporarily lost contact with the sea, as port after port along the Tyrrhenian and Adriatic coasts was abandoned or silted up. Instead, it appeared, Italy was controlled by the rough warriors of the German north, who introduced their own social forms: the closed economy, the manor, feudalism. Italy seemed to have become part of northern Europe, to develop along northern European lines, until freed by the founders of the communes and the first entrepreneurs of merchant capitalism. The Belgian historian Henri Pirenne provided the classic economistic analysis of a Europe whose centre of gravity had moved from the Mediterranean to the Rhine, following the closure of the Mediterranean by the Arabs – though Italian writers of the generation before Pirenne had already painted a grim picture of a closed feudal Italy, where the country had become independent of the city, although and because the city was now as rural as the country. Though such a picture might have been expected to allow at least for a sympathetic analysis of those parts of Italy not in the hands of the Germans, such areas were scarcely studied, except for the Rome of the popes. Legal history and institutional history were the major sorts of history-writing to flourish before the Second World War, and their special concerns served further to distort the image.

These tendencies reached their extreme in the fascist era in Italy, with its strong, if to us ironic, element of anti-Germanism. At this time few people studied early medieval Italy at all. Gabriele Pepe could write in 1941, in his *Il Medioevo Barbarico d'Italia*, still in print today, of the period of the Lombard kings, always the worst sufferers from this historiographical tradition:

> The two hundred years which run from 568 to 774 . . . exactly constitute one of those ages which Vico called 'unhappy', if not the most unhappy in our history; neither the iron 10th century, nor the Counter-reformation, nor the reaction between 1821 and 1848, give us such sorrow, such an impression of death, as these two hundred years. After the death of Gregory I, the shadows are even deeper; even that light of political and economic life which came from the Byzantine cities is dimmed by savage spirits of blood, by cruelty, by anarchic tendencies.

Nobody now could describe early medieval Italy, or any part of it, as baldly as this. We have lost the moralistic contempt for the period of which Pepe was a late, if forceful, rhetorician. Since the war Italian early medieval history has undergone something of a renaissance, starting in 1948 with Gianpiero Bognetti's historical contribution to a joint historical and architectural analysis of the little Lombard church of S. Maria di Castelseprio, between Milan and Varese, which put the church against a broad and detailed backcloth of the political and religious history of the fifth to seventh centuries.[1] There is now no shortage of excellent work on the period, mostly of course in Italian, but also greatly helped by a revival of the traditional German interest in the history of Italy – British and French scholars are very much less numerous but have also made a number of very important contributions. A number of general syntheses based on recent work are also beginning to appear, of which the most notable is that contained in the contributions by Giovanni Tabacco and Philip Jones to the vast collaborative *Einaudi Storia d'Italia* published in 1974; there has not yet been an attempt, however, to present a single account of the development of Italy in these years. Still less has there been any attempt in English; the English-speaking student of early medieval Italy has to try to construct his own image of Italian development as a whole from a small number of studies, mostly articles, on very specialised topics, as the bibliography to this book shows.

There are more fruitful ways of seeing Italian early medieval history than in the reflected brilliance of its past and future. There will be few historians who try to deny that Italian high culture had few major luminaries between Gregory the Great and Peter Damiani, or that there are few great works of architecture between S. Vitale in Ravenna and the cathedral at Pisa; but the period lasted five centuries, centuries of development and experiment like all centuries, and not as obscure in Italy as in many other parts of contemporary Europe.

The first way has already been outlined. Though seldom wholly united, the Italian state survived the collapse of the Roman Empire in the West. Italy remained a conceptual whole. Paul the Deacon, writing in the 790s, listed its eighteen provinces, from the Alps to Corsica, Sicily, and Sardinia.[2] It was as if nothing had changed in three centuries. It is true that the impression is so given largely because Paul's terminology was very antique: it could easily have come from the sixth century, or even earlier (though even by sixth-century standards it was inaccurate). In this passage, Paul studiously ignored developments of any kind since that time, save for brief references to Bobbio (Columbanus's monastery, founded in 612) and Pavia, the new name for *Ticinum*, which only replaced the old name after the city had become the capital of Lombard Italy. But nevertheless he had a conception of the unity of Italy that existed despite its political division. That it was a conception shared by the kings can be easily seen in the activities of the strongest of them, from Liutprand (712–44) to Louis II (844–75), whose intentions of occupying it all are very visible.

This conception of Italy as an entity that could still be defined is emphasised by the underlying similarity of the political units of the peninsula. The most important of these units was the kingdom of Italy, centred on the Po valley and extending as far south as kings could manage; but there was also a whole range of minor states scattered up and down Italy after 568, the Exarchate around Ravenna (until 750), the lands ruled by the popes, the cities around the Bay of Naples, and the Lombard states in the South, which a number of kings tried to integrate into the kingdom of Italy, but which usually remained independent. All of these entities retained a public position and consciousness, which in most cases was based on the same foundations as the kingdom of Italy: the network of cities.

Cities were old. Many of them, indeed, predated the Roman Empire itself. They were the repository of basic public consciousness and responsibility in the Empire, and the Italian cities retained these features right through the early Middle Ages. There are, therefore, direct lines of descent from the Roman Republic to the communes. The Italian state retained the cellular structure of the Empire. The implications of this were initially good for the state, for the Empire had been strong and centralised. But when the state began to collapse in the tenth century, its structure came to be a disadvantage, for the interests of each city were not by any means totally tied up in the central government; Italy was ultimately a congeries of localities with, furthermore, local interests mostly crystallised around individual cities. There was already in existence a viable network of city states long before the centralised state departed from the Italian political scene.

The themes that will be developed in this book are four fold. First, the inheritance of the late Roman state, its continuation under the Germanic kings, and its final collapse in the tenth century. Second, the localities that formed the real spontaneous basis for Italian historical development; their regional differences, geographical, economic, and social, and their interrelationship on the economic level. Third, the city and its own development, also a Roman inheritance, but also based on a local society and changing with that society; its relationship to its territory; and the aspects of society peculiar to the city, such as literacy and the importance of written law. Fourth, the overwhelming importance in Italian economy and society, even politics, of the holding of land, a well-known fact and common to all Western Europe in the Middle Ages but worth stressing nonetheless. Even cities were largely dependent on the landowning of their inhabitants, rather than on, for example, commerce (see below, pp. 85ff). It is this dependence of aristocratic society on land, and, more exactly, dependent tenant cultivation that I will take as characteristic of 'feudal' society, rather than the more limited precision of the existence of fiefs and vassal homage; fiefs, at least, were in fact comparatively rare in Italy in our period. I would add a fifth, the relationship between urban Italy and the unurbanised mountain tracts that occupy the interior of peninsular Italy, as an illustration of the institutional force of the cities of the plains. The study of this is in its infancy, however, and cannot be dealt with as fully as it deserves.

These themes do not, of course, subsume all the elements of Italian historical development in this period. This is partly for reasons of space. The South of Italy will not, therefore, receive as much attention as the North; though other reasons here are a comparative lack of historical material, and my own comparative ignorance of many of the early medieval developments in Italy south of Naples. Similar reasons, plus a very real difference in their historical experiences, preclude consideration of the islands, Sicily and Sardinia (and indeed Corsica, in most ways more Italian than either of these).

The other major gap is a detailed consideration of the Church as an independent institution and of cultural development in its traditionally accepted medieval forms: ecclesiastical culture, fine arts and architecture. I prefer to view the Church in its social context, and it will appear as such here. The papacy, however, which has often, rather improperly, been seen in the past as the true symbol of the Italian Church and Italian culture (to the considerable detriment of the reputations of worthy and able men such as John X and Benedict VIII), has been largely excluded. As an international symbol, its history does not lie inside the scope of this book; as the focus for the local development of Rome and the Campagna, it suffers from the extreme atypicality of the development of Rome as a city; as the office of many of the great spiritual leaders of early medieval Europe, such as Gregory I, Hadrian I, Nicholas I, and Sylvester II, it would distort the framework of a book that aims primarily at an analysis of men inside their time rather than outside it. The papacy is, furthermore, unique in early medieval Italian history in being adequately covered in English.

The themes of this book are also conditioned in another way: by the nature of the evidence for the period. The Italians of our period were not good writers of history; in fact they were almost uniquely bad at it. Even the near-illiterate Anglo-Saxons are better served by contemporary histories and chronicles than the Italians. Between the 550s when Procopius's histories cease (and Procopius was scarcely Italian) and the eleventh century there is barely enough history-writing to fill a single volume. In the *Monumenta Germaniae Historica*, the famous repository of historical sources, texts for Merovingian Gaul fill eight volumes. The one volume for Italy, however, the *Scriptores Rerum Langobardicarum et Italicarum* covers the whole period from the sixth to the tenth century, and to the authors contained in it (Paul the Deacon, Agnellus, Andreas of Bergamo, Erchempert, John of Naples, and some even shorter works) one could scarcely add more than the papal biographies in the *Liber Pontificalis*, the *Chronicon Salernitanum*, and Liutprand of Cremona's *Antapodosis*. Except the *Liber Pontificalis*, dealing mostly with Rome, none of these works is long. And some of them, most notably Andreas of Bergamo, show a most unsophisticated use of the historical past (see below p. 51). Italy, furthermore, receives very little informed coverage from abroad, after Procopius, except for the Frankish annals of the eighth to ninth centuries.

By contrast with this dearth of narrative, we are very well provided with charter material. It does not start as early as that in France and the Rhineland (apart from the fifth to seventh-century series of still-surviving Ravenna papyri), but it allows a good coverage of certain areas in Italy at least from the late eighth century onwards (Lucca, Farfa, Brescia), and many others from the ninth century (Milan, Verona, most of Emilia, the Val Volturno, Naples), and increases in volume all the time. The intensely particular purpose of individual charters and their entirely regional context emphasises the local side of Italian history, of course. It is possible to reconstruct an intricate society on a local level from a range of charters. By contrast, to assess the activities of kings on the basis of nothing but royal diplomas, as is often necessary for us, gives a very barren impression of central government; and to see precisely how the two interact is often very inferential. This is an insoluble problem in our period.

We are lucky, on the other hand, to have a good quantity of legislation surviving from the seventh, eighth and ninth centuries, amplified rather inconsistently by the occasional German emperor thereafter; and, furthermore, in several hundred court cases from the eighth century onwards, we can see how such legislation affected certain kinds of disputes. This at least can show how deep the state penetrated into some aspects of society: in fact awareness by ordinary people of the legislative activity of the state was considerable.

This completes the list of the three basic types of literary evidence for the history of early medieval Italy. Other types exist, but are not significant in quantity. The exception is the group of collections of papal letters, most particularly those of Gregory I (590–604) and John VIII (873–82), but stretching from the 560s onwards fairly consistently, with at least one or two letters each reign, and sometimes, as with Hadrian I (772–95), a substantial number. Not all of these relate to Italy (as opposed to Rome and its immediate area on the one hand, and the rest of Europe on the other), but many of them do, and in the case of the three above-named popes, form a major element in the evidence for Italy as a whole in their periods.

Archaeology, finally, is beginning to become a significant element in the evidence for our period. It is no longer possible to dismiss Italian medieval archaeology as insignificant and appallingly conducted. Important excavations have recently been undertaken and are already producing results, allowing us to add Luni, Genoa, a number of other sites in Liguria and Lombardy, Capaccio Vecchia in Campania, and several sites in Lazio, Molise and Sicily to the classic excavations of before the 1970s, Ventimiglia, Castelseprio, Torcello, and the run of very early cemetery sites like Castel Trosino and Nocera Umbra. Though comprehensive and comprehensible excavations in an important city and a major village are still lacking for the seventh to tenth centuries, thus reducing the amount of evidence that sheds light on strictly historical problems in our period, I shall use archaeological material wherever the two disciplines meet.

That a survey of this kind can be undertaken at all shows in itself how far Italian historiography has advanced in the last three decades, above all in the development of early medieval regional studies to match the well-established tradition of local studies in communal Italy and later. But even more than Kenneth Hyde's study of Italy, *Society and Politics in Medieval Italy, 1000–1350,* in the same series, this book must inevitably confront many gaps in research. Much of the argument in this book is therefore and can only be still speculative, particularly when I come to the complexities of the tenth century and the night of the eleventh, which, besides being the first century when Italian charters are in large part still unedited, is still short of good local studies (exceptions include Violante's classic study of Milan, Schwarzmaier's on Lucca, and Toubert's on Latium).[3] And here and elsewhere, it must be emphasised, the need to generalise in a book this size means that many details will be lost, and many exceptions ignored. But the survey needs to be made. Italian history in the early Middle Ages remains almost unknown in the English-speaking world, although Italy and Italian history were then of formative importance in Europe, and although the development of Italy often ran counter to some of the cherished traditions and formulations of northern European historians. When Italy is studied, it is usually as an appendage of the North. Here, it will be seen on its own. I hope this will make the themes of its history clearer than they usually appear in English.

1. The Roman Legacy

MOST of the features of early medieval Italy were in some way inherited, legitimately or illegitimately, from Rome; throughout this book we shall be discussing them. Two, however, should be dealt with at the start as a stage and a backcloth to what follows: first, the landscape; second, the political and administrative history of the late Empire and the Ostrogothic kingdom, from whose structure the whole framework of the early medieval states of Italy developed.

The Italian landscape cannot be claimed by the Romans as a product of their history; its fundamental patterns are prior to all societies. The Romans, nevertheless, altered it more than any society before at least the sixteenth century and probably the nineteenth. Not that the Romans had the techniques to counter the deep intractabilities of their environment – often enough we still have not today – but they had 800 years or so to make an impression by main force, and many of the most lasting features of Italy are theirs in great part: the deforested and eroded hills of the South, centuriation (the still surviving squared patterns of fields in many of the Italian plains), the intercultivation of cereals, vines, and olives ('promiscuous cultivation' to the Italians), and, perhaps above all, the network of roads and cities that is still for the most part in use today.

The landscape was not fully tamed as a result of the Roman impact, as we shall see, but one might well feel when reading Roman writers that the Romans chose to think so. Italy, in common with the rest of the Mediterranean, tends to look suspiciously homogeneous in Roman texts. The itinerary lists delineate it as nothing but a network of lines and dots – roads and cities, the common currency of the Empire. Regional differences in Roman Italy have to be built up from fragmentary references in Strabo's *Geography* and Pliny's *Natural History*; descriptions of the countryside are normally entirely conventional. Even a narrative as detailed as Procopius's *History of the Gothic Wars*, written in the 550s, barely makes reference to mountains and forests (despite their considerable strategic importance); one might believe, and it sometimes has been believed, that the forests of the early Middle Ages were in some way a new invention, a reversion to a pre-Roman world. This would be an exaggeration. The Roman literary classes, our chief sources of evidence, were primarily an urban élite; they liked to idealise the countryside, and go there as seldom as possible.[1] Our early medieval texts, on the other hand, are largely records of transactions of land, with bald descriptions of their contents and boundaries – stylised, but not idealised. Their uncleared and uncultivated land, like their mountains and rivers, were mostly Roman too. It is in this context that it is most useful to record the Roman achievements in building, clearance, and hydraulics: that of a deeply differentiated environment – fertile and barren, agricultural and pastoral, mountain and plain, the cold winters of the North and the arid summers of the South.

Of these the most important contrast is that between mountain and plain. The prosperity of the various regions of Italy in pre-industrial times was virtually a mathematical function of their average height above sea level. The Romans left Italy an urban society, a chequer-board of hundreds of city territories, but they could not prevent the contrast between the rich and important cities of the Po plain and the tiny closely-spaced cities of the Appennines.

Italy is made up of the great plain of the North, surrounded by mountains, and the long Appennine ridge of the peninsula, central and southern Italy, edged by plains and hills (see the map section, pp. xiiiff). The northern plain is that of the valleys of the Po, Adige, and Reno, scarcely separable at their mouths, and of the smaller rivers of the Veneto. It has long been the richest area of Italy, and has been its political centre, the eye of the tadpole, since the fifth century AD, even when the capital has been at Rome. Its cities were, from the late Empire onwards, the major cities of Italy too – Milan, Pavia, Verona, Ravenna – only Rome and Naples in the peninsula could compete with or surpass them by the start of our period. The Alps tower over the plain, apparently impassable. Their steep slopes mask a number of easy passes, however, and these are still easier on the other side where the Alps slope up much more gently. Italy was often invaded in our period across these passes, and their existence accounts for some of the importance of the cities that lay on the plain at their mouths – Turin and later Ivrea for the western passes, Milan and Verona for the central ones, Aquileia and Cividale del Friuli for the east.

More important for the internal history of Italy, however, are the Appennines on the southern edge of the Po plain, for these block the North off from the rest of Italy. The Appennines look much less impressive than the Alps on the map, and are, for the most part, only around half the height. They were a major barrier, nonetheless. Even at their lowest, north of Genoa and Perugia, they separated totally different societies. The histories of Pavia and Genoa, for example, though the cities are only 100 kilometres apart, had almost nothing in common in our period. Control of the Appennine passes was as important as it was in the Alps, and explains the significance of such central Italian cities as Lucca and Spoleto, or further south, Benevento. The Appennines, as much as the Alps, gave unity to the Po plain. The plain had its own contrasts – the rich lands around Milan and Verona, the remote uplands of Piedmont, and the Po marshes, which split off Emilia and gave security and isolation to Ravenna – but it remained the nucleus for the kingdom of Italy right up to the end of our period, when the peninsula had long split up into separate states.

The peninsula is dominated by the Appennines. Its contrasts are so great that generalisation is nearly impossible: on the east, a thin strip of fertile coast running all the way down Italy from Rimini to the plains and pastoral plateaux of Apulia. On the west, a series of river valleys, fertile arrows pointed into the interior – in Tuscany the valleys of the Serchio, Arno, Ombrone; in Lazio the Tiber and Garigliano; in Campania the Volturno and Sele; every one with their different histories, slowly becoming more and more explicit, and becoming eventually the nuclei for the tenth-century states of the peninsula. The mountain ridge keeps to the east coast, and has always relegated it to the margins of history, with the exception of Apulia. At its widest, it touches the west coast too, between Lazio and Campania, the classic divide between central Italy and the South. But the valleys and uplands of Tuscany and Lazio, north of this divide, do not form a single unit. The valleys here are separated by empty hill-country and scrub, the mineral-rich hills west of Siena, Monte Amiata to its south, and so on. No one has ever made much impression on this country, and it keeps the richer, more urbanised areas of central Italy apart as effectively as the Appennines themselves do. The South has even greater contrasts, as will be seen in chapter 6, pp. 147 ff. This sort of differentiation is the starting-point for the oppositions in the history of lowland Italy. The hills and mountains themselves are different again.

Barring a few in the Po marshes and Adriatic lagoons, every city in Italy is within sight of the mountains. Mountain inhabitants tended not to conform to the social and political rules of the plains, though plainsmen, above all the Romans, usually wished to ignore such a tendency, and did what they could to keep it under control. Less easy to control were economic unconformities: the mountains were the stronghold of pastoralism, and the agricultural plains were usually short of meat. In the days of the *pax Romana*, and before, the transhumant herds crossed the plains to summer pastures in the coastal marshes. They may have slackened off in the troubled periods of the early Middle Ages, but the routes remained open until the fourteenth to seventeenth centuries, the second great age of transhumance.[2] Only parts of the Appennines were totally given over to pasture (probably the upper valleys of the Sangro and Trigno, for example); but the primitive subsistence farming of the rest of the mountains was even more damaging to the rule of the lowlands, for it existed without recourse to the plains at all. Real control over such people by the men of the plains could only come with the ownership of land, and it is unlikely that lowland landowners ever extended their property-holding into the mountains on a large scale until the foundation of the great seventh to ninth-century Benedictine monasteries – Bobbio, Monte Amiata, Farfa, Montecassino, S. Vincenzo al Volturno, S. Clemente in Casauria.

The mountains were, and are, wild. Even the plains were not wholly tame in the Roman period. The Romans cleared them of forest, very largely: Pope Gregory the Great in 598 had to ask his Lombard enemies in Benevento for building-timber from Bruttii when he repaired the basilicas of St Peter and St Paul in Rome.[3] They had more trouble clearing them of marsh, a hazard along much of the Italian coastal plain and many rivers. Hydraulics and river-banking needed constant maintenance, and riverspates slowly became worse as the mountain valley-bottoms began to be deforested. Many of the great Italian rivers were anyway untamable with Roman techniques. The Po plain was never cleared of swamp and scrub woodland. Sidonius Apollinaris, sailing down the Po to Ravenna in 467, waxed lyrical on its animal-life and vegetation:

> I inspected the sedgy Lambro, the sky-blue Adda, the swift Adige, the slow Mincio, . . . turning slightly upstream into their waters in each case; their banks were all adorned with oak and maple groves. Here sweetly sang a harmony of birds . . . ; all the bushes had sprouted in tumult along the river-edges on the warming moisture of the water-filled soil.[4]

The Po does not now run to Ravenna; nor is the Adige one of its tributaries; even the modern Italians have not fully controlled it. But the Romans certainly had not finished clearing the accessible marshes of the plains by the end of the Roman period. We find reclamation projects in Ostrogothic texts as late as 507–11, not, it seems, very successful, in the plain north of Spoleto and in the Pontine Marshes between Rome and Naples.[5] Roman settlement tended to avoid valley-bottoms, and seems to have been normally thickest in the upper plains and hills on the edges of mountain country.

What is unclear is how much the marshlands and scrubland of the plain expanded at the end of the Roman period, when (we can assume) the complex hydraulic engineering of the Empire began to be neglected, and (as is often said) the population began to decline. They must have done to some extent, but it is difficult to prove how much. Apart from some artificially-drained areas, like the Ferrarese and the plain of Florence, there is little secure evidence of the abandonment of large tracts of land at the end of the Empire. The coastland of Tuscany and Lazio, for example, was inhabited in the Etruscan period and deserted by 1100; but its southern stretches were already in part depopulated (and perhaps malarial) before the late Empire, and its northern parts were still prosperous as late as the eighth century, only losing their inhabitants, perhaps, with the Arab attacks of the ninth.[6] The rhythm of rural abandonment does not correspond very exactly to political changes; it is difficult to see why it should. And if the clearance and rural control of the Roman period has been exaggerated, so has the agricultural decline and abandonment of the early medieval countryside.

The Romans confronted the Italian landscape most effectively and permanently, in fact, by building roads; if the natural obstacles of Italy could not be controlled, they could at least be bypassed and ignored. The great consular roads remained the major land routes of Italy until the railway age almost without addition, apart from the Via Francigena between Piacenza and Rome, a new inland route that replaced the coastal Aurelia when the Tuscan coast was abandoned after 800. Armies used these roads, and could move about Italy with great ease and convenience (to themselves). So did the imperial administration, by means of a complex state-funded network of post-horses and stabling (the *cursus publicus*), that extended to the commandeering of boats on major rivers as well (Sidonius was using it on the Po). Officials and official instructions could cross Italy at some speed. Carolingian administrators later did the same in a less organised way. Private traffic, however, was less common on these roads, apart from the senatorial friends of Roman officials, illegally exploiting the *cursus publicus*, and merchants with easily transportable goods, especially luxuries. Most people, when they had to travel, found it cheaper and more convenient to go by sea, where they could. And large-scale traffic, such as food, was prohibitively expensive by road. It had always to be taken by ship where possible, and was thus only conveniently available along the coast and in the Po valley where many rivers are navigable – Brescia, Mantua, Cremona, and Parma all had ports. Local famines were a norm in Italy, as elsewhere in the Roman world, and even the administrative organisation of the late Empire could do little to relieve them – though Theoderic made great efforts to do so in the early sixth century. Grain speculators often made windfall profits.[7] In winter both land and sea traffic more or less ceased, with snow blocking the Appennines and storms throughout the Mediterranean. Geography here has been determinant in Italian history. States can perform their essential functions without too much hindrance from the geography (except perhaps in the southern Appennines), but the regions of Italy they have ruled have been almost wholly localised, with few permanent links with each other. This was true even under the Roman Empire, and has been ever since, until the middle of the present century. When states have weakened, they have tended to lose control of everything that keeps Italy together as a single entity. When the state falls, Italy itself springs apart.

This tendency is crystallised in the other great Roman socio-economic legacy, the city. The Roman constitution was traditionally one of semi-independent city-states or *municipia*, run by their own *curiae* or city councils. Though by 400 this was no more than an oppressive myth (the 'independence' of city councils resting in their responsibility to underwrite the heavy taxation of the late Empire), the local identity of the cities persisted, and acted as a permanent focus for their traditional territories. Some of these territories remain nearly unaltered within modern provincial boundaries. When the Italian state in the North eventually fell, in the tenth and eleventh centuries, the network of cities survived and replaced it. City-states also replaced many of the regional states of the peninsula, where the cities were strong enough. Italy itself did not survive, but the persistence and permanence of Italian cities is one of the crucial and particular features of the history of the early medieval period. As we shall see, it is a constituent element of almost every theme that here follows.

THE year 476, the traditional date for the 'fall of the Western Roman Empire', marked no important break in the history of Italy, still less the

Western Empire. To say so now is almost commonplace, though still necessary. The deposition of Romulus Augustulus, the last emperor of the West, in that year by Odoacer merits no editorial comment in any western chronicler. In the chronicles of the *Consularia Italica*, for example, the only difference is in terminology – the succession of emperors now becomes a succession of (barbarian)kings.[8] Only writers in the capital of the Eastern Empire, Constantinople – and not all of them – saw the change in the apocalyptic way that the imagery of the 'fall of the Western Empire' implies. The Italians, nearer to the experience, were not greatly moved. The holocaust in Italy came in the great age of wars, 535–605: the shifts of the balance under the German rulers, first Odoacer (476–93) and then the Ostrogothic kings (490–553) were trivial by contrast.

There were, of course, new elements. Instead of a Roman ruler of the whole West, the Italians were now subject to a German ruler of Italy only (including Dalmatia, and the Central Alps, Roman Rhaetia), like their kin in Visigothic Spain and Gaul, or Vandal Africa. Odoacer and his great successor, the Ostrogoth Theoderic (490–526), certainly saw themselves as the equivalents of the other German kings. But by 476 the Western Empire itself had become restricted to Italy and its dependent territories, and political subjection to barbarian military leaders was no novelty. Since Arbogast in the 380s there had been a steady succession – Stilicho, Sarus, Ricimer, Gundobad – interspersed with Roman military leaders like Constantius, Aetius, and Orestes, distinguishable from the Germans in their race, but in no other respect. And the barbarian takeover in Italy was fundamentally different from that elsewhere. The Visigoths and Vandals conquered the edges of the Western Empire, breaking the Roman network of government; Odoacer, however, took power in the centre in a near-bloodless army coup, apparently continuing to recognise a refugee Western Emperor in Dalmatia, Julius Nepos (d. 480), and also seeking recognition from the Eastern Emperor Zeno as his viceroy in the West (Zeno temporised, but did not grant it).[9] The political life of Italy went on unaffected.

This political life was by the fifth century concentrated in two places: Rome and Ravenna. Rome was the symbol of Empire, the home of the Senate; Ravenna in 401 replaced Milan as the seat of the civil administration. The emperors usually lived in Ravenna, though several (particularly between 450 and 476) preferred Rome. The German kings kept themselves strictly to Ravenna, save for ceremonial visits. Theoderic celebrated his *decennalia* in Rome in 500, with all the imperial trimmings, games, a triumph, rebuilding, and free grain.[10] Rome and Ravenna existed in more or less permanent opposition: the past and the present, authority and power, the geographical realisation of the old tension between Senate and emperor – though after 400 the emperor's person was less important than his executive arms, the civil administration and the army. The army, by the middle of the fifth century mostly German, tended to favour an effective civil administration, as it relied on the capacity of the government to collect taxes for its livelihood. It had no permanent geographical base, but its centres lay in the northern cities (the North being most liable to invasion) and its relationship with Ravenna was close.

The underlying opposition between the Senate and the administration was twofold. First, the Senate tended to regard itself as the legitimate source of authority in the Late Roman state, subject only to the emperor. By one definition, it still was: the holding of administrative office was almost the only qualification that admitted aspirants to the Senate at all, and indeed the period between 425 (at the latest) and 490, especially the reign of Odoacer, saw the major offices of state under the near-permanent control of the great senatorial families, particularly the Decii, Anicii, and Petronii. Such senators even sometimes briefly achieved the imperial office itself, with Petronius Maximus (455) and Anicius Olybrius (472). Nevertheless, the two hierarchies were not identical. The praetorian prefect, the chief administrative office-holder, was not necessarily the highest-ranking senator, for rank in the Senate depended on the holding of consulships and the title of patrician, formal traditions that stretched right back to the Roman Republic. The prefect did not have the status that this tradition gave; he was, nevertheless, infinitely more powerful. Theoderic, whose strength rested firmly on his own Ostrogothic army, revived the fourth-century tradition of appointing able parvenus to high office, and sometimes gave offices to Goths. In 510 he even appointed a non-Roman to the office of prefect of Rome (the influential easterner, Artemiodorus).[11] Those of the Senate who were not in the administration must have found this rather overt. Senators, as we shall see, continued to be prominent in Ravenna, but the rules there were different from those at Rome.

Secondly, and more important, the interests of the two hierarchies were in conflict. The civil administration was responsible for collecting the land tax from Italy, including from senatorial estates. The unwillingness of the rich and powerful to pay this tax was one of the basic weaknesses of the fifth-century Empire, for it was needed to pay for defence in a century when barbarians were occupying Gaul, Spain and Africa. When the Empire became restricted to Italy, the army did not become smaller by the same proportion, and the other main drains on expenditure, the central bureaucracy itself and the provisioning of Rome, remained an Italian responsibility. The tax was heavy, but not effectively collected (except from the poor). Supplementary taxes on commercial transactions were inadequate for expenditure. As a result, the army finally revolted over pay in 476, propelling Odoacer to power, and demanded a third of the estates of Italy instead.[12] The resistance of the Senate was largely responsible for this, for the landed power of senators was considerable; but barbarian settlement was rather less easy to avoid than taxation. Senatorial estates were probably not, on the other hand, in the areas of greatest barbarian settlement.

The influence of the Senate seems to be particularly high in the fifth century. It was, however, on the wane. The greatest senators of the early fifth century, like the Symmachi and Petronius Maximus, averaged incomes of over 5000 pounds of gold a year – Petronius's father spent 4000 pounds on seven days of his son's praetorian games in the 420s. This wealth, though, was dependent on possession of land right across the Mediterranean, particularly in Africa and Sicily. German conquest made such widespread ownership increasingly difficult. The Vandals were in Africa. Between 467 and 477 they were even in Sicily, until Odoacer got it back by treaty. Senators were still rich, but on into the Ostrogothic period they were increasingly overshadowed by the civil administration, which under Theoderic was beginning to collect its taxes successfully again. It is perhaps significant that Faustus, probably the most prestigious pro-Gothic senator of the early sixth century, and praetorian prefect of Italy in 507–12, is not, like Petronius, known for his extravagance, but for the (equally traditional) senatorial characteristics of corruption and greed.[13] We know little about the details of senatorial income, but senatorial expenditure was certainly lessening. Senators were less and less prepared to spend money in building and rebuilding public monuments to embellish Rome. One of the exceptions, the traditionalist Symmachus, who rebuilt the theatre of Pompey in c. 510, was reimbursed by a grateful Theoderic. Most new building in Rome was now the work of the kings (Odoacer, for example, refurbished the Colosseum) and increasingly the Church.[14] By comparison with them, the Senate was certainly losing ground. It was becoming more and more difficult for Italy to support two separate civilian hierarchies.

The Church has not so far appeared in this account. We have been dealing so far only with Rome and Ravenna. In both cities politics remained decidedly secular. Not that churchmen were unimportant there, particularly not the bishop of Rome. Some of the fifth-century bishops, or popes, achieved international stature, above all Leo I (440–61) and Gelasius I (492–6). But the popes did not control Rome – the Senate still did that. The ecclesiastical bureaucracy was only just beginning to acquire the coherence that underlay its power in the centuries to follow. Only in the 540s, as the Senate was decimated by war and emigration to Constantinople, did the pope (then Vigilius, son and brother of praetorian prefects) begin to be a major moving force. In this respect though, Rome was not necessarily characteristic of all Italy. We can say fairly little in this period about regional differences in social structure across Italy, but the homes of the Senate and the civil government were obviously atypical. Parts of northern Italy at least, especially Milan and Pavia, are clearly enough documented to show contrasts.

Senators were the aristocracy of Rome; they were not the aristocracy of Italy. Every city had its own nobility but outside Rome they were not normally as influential or rich. This generalisation was partially self-fulfilling, in that the rich tended to buy their way into the Senate. But the best-known example of this, the Cassiodorii, provincials from Bruttii (now Calabria), spent most of their time in Rome and Ravenna by the time of their greatest representative, Cassiodorus Senator (c. 487–582). New senatorial families became deracinated, absentee landlords: Cassiodorus only went to his home town Squillace to retire. In the North, there were fewer such rising families. Local aristocrats probably only owned land inside small areas, seldom outside the Po plain. The Church, however, was long-established and influential in the northern cities, and was already in the fifth century accumulating property through pious donations. In Milan, it had benefited particularly when Milan was the capital and Ambrose its bishop in the late fourth century: the Milanese Church was very rich. In Pavia, too, bishops were influential, at least from the time of Epiphanius (467–97). These two, and others like Ennodius of Pavia (513–21) and Datius of Milan (c. 528–52) became spokesmen for their cities, true political leaders – defenders of the people against excessive taxation, injustice, even enemy armies. They were used as arms of the state, as well. Epiphanius went on embassies for several emperors and kings; Ennodius wrote panegyrics for Theoderic; Datius sold grain for the state in the 535 famine, being the only man the praetorian prefect Cassiodorus could trust. Price-fixing was a traditional obligation of city councils, but bishops in general were becoming responsible for it alongside them.[15] The Church was acquiring a status equal to the city council, the body representing the entire landholding community of the city. The collectivity of urban aristocrats of, say, Milan, could of course command far greater wealth than the bishops, but the episcopal Church had become a rather greater landowner than any individual layman, and its power reflected that, Milan and Pavia are probably typical in this of the leading cities of the Italian North – and of much of Gaul too. Whether the cities of the Centre and South were similar cannot be said; bishops may not yet have accumulated enough land to support such a role outside the Po plain. But in the future, all cities in Italy would be represented by their bishops. Episcopal power suffered a temporary setback in the Lombard invasion, but city councils were given a mortal blow. With the major exception, it seems, of Naples, they seldom saw the seventh century. Bishops were left institutionally supreme. Their secular rivals after the seventh century, dukes, gastalds, and counts, were usually local nobles, but their official statuses were representative of central, not local, government. The only office left that represented the city was that of the bishop.

Against the tensions of these social structures, the politics of the later Empire played themselves through, mostly in the interplay between ambitious emperors and ambitious army leaders, which after 408 (when Stilicho, *magister militum* for the Emperor Honorius, fell) was always resolved in favour of the army. This is scarcely surprising – the army always determined Roman politics. The only novelty of the fifth century is that the emperor no longer commanded the army. The last soldier-emperor, Theodosius I, died in 395. His successors, with brief exceptions in the 450s and 460s, did not intervene in military matters. (Ostrogothic kings later would also suffer a fatal haemorrhage of power in the decade 526–36 when they did not command the army.) These emperors were all somewhat shadowy figures, if we except the short-lived verve of Majorian's reign (457–61). We can see the period best through the careers of the army leaders Aetius and Ricimer, ascendant in 429–54 and 456–72 respectively. Aetius was the last man to be prominent in both Gaul and Italy, and the last man to be an effective opponent of the barbarian invaders of the Empire, using Hunnic mercenaries against the Visigoths and Gothic allies against the Huns. His assassination in 454 shocked the chroniclers, as they would not be in

476. The politics of Aetius's ascendancy have not yet been finally sorted out, but there is force in the argument that he supported a Gallic faction of the Senate against at least some groups of Italian senators who did not wish to bear the cost of his wars.[16] Certainly there was rivalry between the two regions in the confused period after his death, particularly during the brief reign of the Emperor Avitus (455-6), a leading Gallic senator, supported by a Gallic army and eventually deposed after losing a skirmish at Piacenza to an Italian army under Ricimer. We cannot trace this rivalry much beyond 456, but Gaul and Italy were already drifting apart. After Majorian's fall in 461 their histories no longer had much connection. The Visigoths and Burgundians were expanding their territories in Gaul; the Empire was already almost exclusively Italian.

Ricimer was Aetius's old officer, and the grandson of a Visigothic king. He tried for fifteen years to maintain himself stably in Italy with a quiescent emperor, being unable to assume the throne himself, as a German and (probably) an Arian heretic. Despite several attempts, he never found one that was both unambitious and acceptable to the emperor in the East. Significantly, he twice (456-7 and 465-7) ruled alone as *patricius*, as direct representative of the Eastern emperor, the position Odoacer sought in 476.[17] Odoacer was refused, and ruled as king instead; the more romanised Ricimer would probably never have been able to bring himself to this resort, and was thus permanently under pressure to accept emperors that were, in Ricimer's state, a cause of instability. In many ways the political history of the fifth century in Italy was that of a constant unsuccessful search for a stable political system that was both legitimate and militarily effective. Odoacer brought fourteen years' peace to Italy. His solution was at least more permanent than Ricimer's. But only Theoderic, who obtained recognition from the Eastern emperor, fully solved the problem, and his solution, being dependent on the East, was itself negated when the East withdrew recognition in 535 and initiated the Gothic wars.

Odoacer was effective but he was weak. The army was solidly with him, for with a third of the lands of Italy it had a firm material backing for the first time in a century, but it was small. Odoacer courted the Senate very solicitously and gave high office to many of its leaders. Some stayed with him until the end, but most of his support disappeared when the Ostrogoths, under Theoderic, invaded Italy in 489 with the encouragement of the Emperor Zeno. The bishops of Milan and Pavia, as representatives of the North, went over to Theoderic immediately. In

493, after four years of war, Theoderic took Ravenna and killed Odoacer. Theoderic had with him a people numbering perhaps 100–120,000, represented by a standing army of 25–30,000, on recent guesses:[18] a small number in proportion to the total population of Italy, which was several millions, but large enough to give Italy a strong military base. Theoderic, unlike Odoacer, did not need senatorial support, though he desired it. The same was true to a lesser extent for Eastern recognition, though this was granted in 497 when Anastasius I accepted that Italy was no longer part of the Empire. Theoderic's models were Trajan and Valentinian I, two of the greatest military emperors, and his political activities closely resembled those of the latter.[19] He was certainly the strongest ruler in Italy since Valentinian's death in 375. Far from a break in continuity, he often seems like the restoration of a continuity broken for a century.

This impression is enhanced by the documentation of the reign, for the Ostrogothic period is the first to be well-documented since Valentinian's death. This is very largely through the remarkable collection of official letters known as the *Variae*, written by Cassiodorus Senator while he held various offices between 507 and 537, but also through an array of other material – histories, saints' lives, letters, philosophical works. It is clear from the *Variae* that Theoderic's rule was effective: that taxes were collected, even (though with some difficulty) from senators; that some instances, at least, of the gross corruption typical of the late Roman state were corrected; that internal peace was maintained; and that wars were both successful and foreign. Procopius, who fought in the Byzantine army against Theoderic's heirs, regarded him as the moral equivalent of an emperor, and several sources remark on his popularity with Goths and Romans. He seems to have promised the Senate and people of Rome in 500 that he would not interfere with their laws; and this sort of scrupulosity for the maintenance of Roman traditions is the major reason why the Ostrogoths, when overthrown in the Gothic Wars, left almost no trace at all of their rule in Italy, except perhaps for Theoderic's monumental tomb in Ravenna.[20]

Theoderic courted the Senate's talent. There was, certainly, always a senatorial group who preferred to avoid the Arian barbarian court, but very few of its known members kept out of administrative office altogether. In 522 the philosopher Boethius, one of the leaders of this traditionalist group, was honoured with the unheard-of privilege of both consulships (East and West) for his infant sons, and accepted the office of *magister officiorum* in Ravenna. Rightly or wrongly, he seems to have used his position to defend the interests of the Senate against the rest of the administration, and in 523–4 he was imprisoned and executed; Theoderic, consciously or unconsciously, again imitated Valentinian in his violent rejection of traditionalist senatorial opposition. Boethius was accused of intrigues with the Eastern emperor, and whether this was true or not in his case, in the decade or so following his death it began to be true for other senators. The Senate began to be split into actively pro- and anti-Gothic tendencies; when the Goths too began to split after Theoderic's death in 526, the kingdom was decisively weakened.

The pro-Gothic section in the Senate is the most interesting. It is the best documented, for its members took the most active part in the civil administration and figure in the *Variae*. It was also by no means a homogeneous group, and the contrasted careers of some of its members show up the currents in the politics of the Ostrogothic kingdom very clearly. We must start with Liberius (*c*. 465–555), extraordinarily long-lived, like his younger contemporary Cassiodorus, and holder of administrative offices for some sixty-five years. He first held office under Odoacer, and was one of the last administrators to leave him. Theoderic at once made him praetorian prefect (493–500), and put him in charge of settling the Goths on the third-portions of the estates of Italy vacated by the rather less numerous followers of Odoacer. We have two separate panegyric descriptions of his success, by Ennodius and Cassiodorus, in which it would appear that this was accomplished in peace and amity. 'the victors desired nothing more, and the conquered felt no penalty'. However this may be, we certainly have no record of discord in any of our numerous sources, except possibly in Samnium, where a particularly large number of Goths were settled. Liberius seems to have performed the crucial element in any barbarian occupation, the expropriation of estates for the Gothic land settlement, with remarkable sleight of hand. This is especially impressive when we remember that the Ostrogothic conquest was the first proper barbarian conquest that Italy had undergone, decades later than most of the other provinces of the West. He remained influential after leaving the prefecture, and in about 510 became praetorian prefect of Gaul (that is to say Provence, which Theoderic occupied in 508). In this rather more military office he seems to have been equally successful. He held it until about 533–4, thus remaining out of the way in the crisis of Boethius's arrest, and over the reign of Athalaric, Theoderic's grandson and successor (526–34). During Athalaric's reign, tensions were beginning among the Goths, for

Athalaric was a minor, and his regent, his mother Amalasuntha, was too romanised to satisfy the more military of the Goths. At Athalaric's death, Amalasuntha married her cousin Theodahad (king, 534–6) to bolster up her power as reigning queen, but Theodahad was an old enemy, and imprisoned her. In 535 he had her killed. He sent an embassy to the Eastern emperor, Justinian, to explain his actions, and chose Liberius among others to lead it. Liberius denounced him and stayed in the East. The years 534–5 were the second crisis of the Ostrogothic kingdom. If Theoderic lost the support of the traditionalists in the Senate in 523–4, Theodahad lost that of the legitimists in the administration in 534–5. Significantly, Liberius moved directly into East Roman official posts. He was prefect in Alexandria in the late 530s, and at the age of eighty-five headed armies in Sicily and Spain in 550–2. He returned to Italy in 554 at the end of the war and died at Rimini, where his epitaph survives.[21]

Cassiodorus Senator stayed longer than Liberius. His father, the elder Cassiodorus, had held office under Odoacer and moved over to Theoderic as early as 490, becoming praetorian prefect in c. 503–7; Cassiodorus Senator was *quaestor* in 507–11, *magister officiorum* in 523–7, succeeding Boethius, and praetorian prefect in 533–8. The family, as we have seen, was provincial and perhaps (though it is difficult to tell) somewhat parvenu, at any rate, Senator is, though not unique as a name, a little self-conscious as a given name for a member of the Senate. Cassiodorus's cultural values were certainly those of any educated late Roman noble, as a reading of the *Variae* easily shows. The term *civilitas*, to name only the most prominent example, is a constant touchstone in his rhetoric – he uses it and variants over forty times in the *Variae*. But Boethius's successor in office is unlikely to have stood particularly close to Boethius's group, and we must note too that Cassiodorus was praetorian prefect at the time Liberius departed, and remained so for the first three years of the war. The Roman aristocracy had not yet fully abandoned the Goths. Only after 538 did Cassiodorus leave Italy for Constantinople. Justinian offered him no offices. He returned, like Liberius, at the end of the war, and retired to Bruttii. Here he founded Vivarium, one of the most important monastic centres of the early Middle Ages for the copying of classical literature, in its short period of existence (the 550s–590s).[22]

Theoderic seems to have believed that the best way to preserve Roman civilisation was to let it continue unaltered. He believed the same about Gothic culture, particularly its warrior traditions, and did his best to keep the Goths from becoming romanised.[23] In this too he was apparently successful. Goth and Roman were to be linked only at the political level, despite Cassiodorus's claims in his panegyric on Liberius that 'both nations, while living together, will combine as one'. But Theoderic did not forbid his own kin from absorbing Roman values, and both Amalasuntha and Theodahad were highly educated. Theoderic remained a warrior hero, but his successors were not. The Goths became restless, not unreasonably, for their rulers were so alienated from Gothic society that they were, it seems, secretly planning to hand Italy over to the emperor. When Amalasuntha was killed, Justinian declared war, inaugurating the twenty years of the Gothic wars (535–54). As his army under Belisarius marched up from Sicily in 535–6, Theodahad was deposed and replaced by a fighter, Witigis (536–40). Every new king henceforth seemed more and more obviously a rough untutored barbarian. Cassiodorus, as we have seen, only lasted two more years – already before his departure the Goths were reputedly killing Roman senators in Ravenna. Some remained, even now. Cethegus, head of the Senate, was regarded as a Gothic supporter and forced to flee Rome as late as 545. And we do not know what happened to Cyprian, Boethius's accuser, who had had his sons brought up among the Goths, or his brother Opilio, who pleaded Theodahad's case in Constantinople in 534 when Liberius opposed it, though Opilio may have died in Rome some time after the mid-540s. But as the war increased in ferocity, the split became complete. Totila, the last great king of the Ostrogoths (541–52), is only known to have had one Roman official, his *quaestor* Spinus, an obscure figure from Spoleto.[24]

This characterisation of the relationship and growing split between Goths and Romans has one major flaw, though a traditional one: it only describes the attitude of the aristocracies of Rome and Ravenna. Other aristocracies may well have been similarly divided; major Neapolitan nobles opposed Belisarius in 536, but Datius of Milan begged for his help in 537.[25] The bulk of the population will make their appearance as the main actors in later chapters, but the impact of the Goths on them is best discussed here. Not that it is easy to detect. The Goths certainly did not settle evenly across Italy. They seem to have been concentrated in the area north of the Po, particularly around Verona and Pavia (the locations of Theoderic's two palaces outside Ravenna), and in the central Appennines, Picenum and northern Samnium (modern Marche and Abruzzo).[26] The rest of the peninsula paid the *tertia*, the Gothic third-share, as a tax. There is no reason why the Gothic presence should have physically impinged on most Italians at all. They may merely in Theoderic's time have felt relief at the peace he brought, tempered, no doubt justifiably, by resentment at the burden of taxes he imposed. At least, though, the Goths reduced taxation in times of dearth. When the Byzantines (as I shall call the East Romans, to avoid confusion) began to reoccupy Italy, they did nothing to reduce taxation, and Procopius claims that in 541 they even claimed back tax not paid to the Gothic government during the first part of the war and before. Neither the Goths nor their Byzantine supplanters made any significant changes to the structures of society. Perhaps not surprisingly, therefore, popular enthusiasm about the war, when it came, seems to have been somewhat muted. The Neapolitan people were totally uncertain as to which side they supported in 536. The inhabitants of Rome were rather unwilling participants in the siege of Rome by the Goths in 536–7, the first of four.[27] The Goths and Byzantines seem to have fought over a population of non-combatants for all the twenty years of the war. It is doubtful whether any of them were interested in anything except peace. This they did not get.

The impact of the Gothic wars on society was certainly greater than that of the Gothic peace, and it is in this context that the one social shift attributable to the Ostrogoths has been placed. Slaves were often prone to flee their estates in the late Roman period; in the war, though, they had somewhere to flee to, and numbers of them in the 540s found their way into Totila's army. Totila willingly received them. In 546, a Lucanian senator, Tullianus, armed slaves as an adjunct to the Byzantine army; Totila promised them their owners' estates if they disbanded. These actions have been claimed as Totila's 'social revolution' against the Senate. Short-term responses to the impact of war are, however, a better explanation. Normally the Ostrogoths had no interest in disturbing the social hierarchies of Italy. Their aristocrats owned land too, probably as a direct result of the original settlement. In 553 Ranilo, a Gothic noblewoman, gave land near Urbino and Lucca to the Church of Ravenna, including slaves, 'if in this barbaric time those who have fled can be brought back'. There is no reason to suppose that Totila thought differently: normally when he controlled senatorial estates he took their rents directly and left the peasants as they were.[28]

The course of the war fills nearly four volumes of Procopius's histories, and cannot be recorded here except in brief outline. Belisarius fought his way systematically up Italy in 535–40 as far as the Po, and occupied Ravenna, Witigis retiring to the East as an imperial patrician.

But the Goths in the north elected new kings, the third of whom, Totila, in effective lightning campaigns between 542 and 550, reconquered the whole of Italy and Sicily except for a number of coastal towns (including Ravenna) reinforced by the Byzantine fleet. Only a massive army led by Narses eventually destroyed Totila in 552, his successor Teias in the same year, and a supporting Franco-Aleman army in 554. Even then the Byzantines did not control the lands north of the Po, which had been for the most part under the rule of the Franks, expanding out of Gaul, since the early 540s, with Gothic garrisons remaining in Pavia, Verona and Brescia. By 561 Narses had reoccupied the North as well, but this shadowy Frankish rule should not be forgotten. It is the beginning of a long tradition of Frankish intervention in Italy.

The wars devastated Italy. Conquest and counter-conquest left not a single part of Italy untouched, though Tuscany seems to have got off fairly lightly, and probably also the lands north of the Po (except Milan), if the Franks did not do too much damage. The most severely-fought areas were Emilia, Picenum, Umbria, and the Roman Campagna, the strategic keys to an Italy governed from Rome and Ravenna (exactly these areas became, later, the Byzantine territories remaining in Lombard north Italy). Procopius describes appalling famines as early as 538. In 556 Pope Pelagius I describes his Italian estates as desolated.[29] The Goths disappeared as a nation. Most of them must, of course, still have been there, and particularly in Ravenna Gothic nomenclature and probably landowning survived a long time. As late as 769 the Brescian landowner Staviles described himself as 'living by the law of the Goths'.[30] But the Goths never again appeared as a political grouping, and their archaeological culture vanished without trace; the Lombards settling in the same areas picked up almost none of it. In other respects, however, Italy may have recovered fairly fast. The area of Ravenna was a major war zone, but the Ravennate papyrus charters of the 550s–60s show very little evidence of destruction. The total desolation of Italy in these years has certainly been exaggerated. Still, war had only just begun. The years 554–68 are a brief interlude in seventy years of war, which started again in 568 with the Lombard invasions and continued, on and off, to 605. Though Italy recovered after 605, as it was beginning to in the 560s, there is no doubt that it was severely affected. We will see in the next chapters how much.

The period 554–68 is a useful half-way mark for assessing some of the crucial political changes of the age of wars at a time when evidence is still fairly good. In 554 Justinian issued a Pragmatic Sanction, measures to restore Italy in its new and proper place as the westernmost province of the Empire.[31] All Ostrogothic concessions were to be observed except Totila's. All property-holding was to be re-established as it had been in 490, with particular concern for the reversal of the measures of the 540s. Slaves were to return to their former masters. Tax arrears were to be halved, and not to be claimed for five years. Civil judges were to run civil courts instead of the army; they were to be elected by the bishops and nobles of each region. We should note this last, for it had particularly little force. In reality, the army had run those parts of Italy it controlled ever since the 530s; civilian administrators were entirely subordinate to it, and continued to be. There were praetorian prefects in Italy in 554–68, but we do not even know their names. Italy was ruled by Narses, as commander-in-chief. We have already seen that Italy could not easily support two civilian hierarchies, and what remained of the Senate disappeared by 600 as a separate body. Many senators never returned from Constantinople, now the capital, and the rest sank back into the more anonymous ranks of the Italian aristocracy. But in the late sixth century even the civil administration began to decline in importance, and became swallowed up in the military administration. The Goths could never have done this, with their ethnically distinct army. The ascendancy of the Byzantine army after the reconquest was anyway greater than the control of the Gothic army over the administration had ever been. Impoverished Italy could by now only support one hierarchy at all, whether civil or military, and into the seventh century the army gradually, both in Lombard and Byzantine territories, became the landowning aristocracy as well. Early medieval Italy was a very much simpler world than late Roman Italy, even if (as we shall see) not wholly different.

2. The Kingdom of Italy, 568–875: Survival and Consolidation in the North

The Lombard Kingdom

THE Lombards dominate early medieval Italian history, and their sudden appearance in Italy from Pannonia (modern Hungary) in 568 marks one of the traditional breaks in Italian history. From 568 onwards, Italy was to undergo nearly fourteen centuries of disunity, for the Lombards never conquered the whole peninsula. They stand, therefore, at the beginning of the long history in Italy of particularism and of occupation by foreign powers. On the other hand, after c.600, they had occupied some two-thirds of the whole peninsula, and by the late seventh century perhaps three-quarters; and from the reigns of Grimoald (662–71), and especially Liutprand (712–44), the compact Lombard kingdom, comprising most of northern Italy and Tuscany, was politically pre-eminent over both the Lombard duchies of the southern Appennines, Spoleto and Benevento, and the Roman–Byzantine outposts, centring on Ravenna, Rome, Naples and the southern extremities of the Italian mainland (see Map 2). Lombard political institutions were preserved virtually *in toto* by the Franks after Charlemagne's conquest of 774, and these institutions were Lombard in a way that the Ostrogothic state was never Ostrogothic. In origin, certainly, many of them were Roman, even some with Germanic names, as we shall see, but they were assembled out of fragments by the Lombards themselves (with Roman help), rather like the Emperor Constantine's construction of the church of S. Lorenzo fuori le mura in Rome out of sections of demolished temples. Most developments in Italian medieval history can be traced back somehow to the Lombard period, and it will reappear throughout this book as in some sense a starting-point.

Far more than an historical break, though, the Lombard invasion marks a historiographical break. After 568, and still more after the 610s, our evidence becomes extremely sparse, only recovering again with the beginning of our sequences of medieval documents in the 710s. (The exception to this void is Ravenna, with its seventh-century papyrus charters and competent local chronicle by Andreas Agnellus. For this, see chapter 3.) Our dominant source is the Lombard history of Paul the Deacon, written in the 790s, but he too was faced with sparse evidence, and his work is in consequence fairly short (some 140 pages of folio text).[1] Paul was an intelligent critic and an attractive stylist, and he could correct the Latin of his sources – including Gregory of Tours – but he had a fairly simplistic sense of the past. What passes for such in his history is mostly pride in past Lombard prowess, touched up with a desire to make the pagan Lombards as violent as possible to contrast with their Christian successors, culminating in King Liutprand. Embarrassing phenomena, like Lombard Arianism, or the papal opposition to his hero Liutprand, he obscured or painted out. His reliability is often suspect, and his evidence has always to be weighed with considerable caution. Apart from him, the major source is the Lombard law code, particularly Rothari's Edict of 643 (388 chapters) and Liutprand's legislation (152 chapters). Where, as with the late sixth century, we have a certain amount of other evidence, it is generally in contradictory and confusing fragments, nearly all from outside the Lombard kingdom and hostile to it. As a result of this paucity, Lombard historiography consists, far more than in any other period of Italian history, of a minefield of opposing theories by modern historians. Almost every conceivable contrasting interpretation of the late sixth and seventh centuries has been posed by some historian of the last 150 years, usually working from a very generous interpretation of the rules of evidence. Historians of the Ostrogothic period tend to have convergent overall attitudes to their material. In the Lombard period, however, history itself tends to become, rather more overtly than elsewhere, the theories of individual historians. A high proportion of what follows is necessarily speculative.

The early history of the Lombards, before 568, is not of direct relevance to Italy. It suffices to say that they were a West Germanic people, like the Franks, speaking a language related to Old High German. They were first recorded by Tacitus on the Lower Elbe, subsequently moving to what is now Bohemia, then to Lower Austria; finally, in the early sixth century (c.527) settling in the Roman frontier province of Pannonia. They had kings for as far back as they remembered, mostly from the Lething family, at least until 547, when the last king of that line, Walthari, was succeeded by his tutor Audoin, Alboin's father. Procopius records them as being Catholic in 548, when

Audoin solicited Byzantine help against the Arian Gepids, whom the Lombards finally overcame in 567 with Avar support.[2] This early Catholicism was doubtless restricted to the court and its supporters, and by 568 the king had become Arian, and thus, from the Byzantine standpoint, a heretic; but nonetheless it is a genuine indication that the Lombards in the age of Justinian were part of the Byzantine orbit. The marriage alliances of the sixth century kings down to Alboin also seem to show them in a large central-European framework of mutual support under the hegemony of the Franks. The Lombards did not arrive from nowhere, nor were they simple barbarian savages in the pure state. They had occupied a Roman province for forty years. They had, too, absorbed into their political system a whole series of Roman military titles, such as *dux* and *comes*, and probably acted in a formal sense as Roman federates. Narses, when he destroyed Totila, asked for and obtained a military contingent from Audoin, but he found it too violent and undisciplined and soon sent it home.[3] Alboin, on the other hand, when he invaded Italy, seems to have kept his large and disparate army and people under his control between 568 and 572, the date of his murder. Military discipline is not, of course, a particularly useful or significant index of romanisation (still less civilisation), but the Lombards are in the early years depicted almost exclusively in military terms. We have no other criteria.

Gianpiero Bognetti saw in Alboin's invasion a 'grand plan', a strategy on the largest scale. Alboin had Austrasian Frankish connections through his first wife, and, with a tactical conversion to Arianism in c.565, hoped to gain support from the Arian Goths of northern Italy too, who had only been overcome by Narses in 561. Alboin proceeded slowly and apparently without opposition across the Po plain in 568–9, leaving dukes in the major cities, particularly his nephew Gisulf in Cividale del Friuli, and then besieged Pavia, the first city to resist him, for three years (569–72). During these three years, complications began, for contingents of marauding Lombards began to spill over the Alps into Frankish Burgundy (in 569–75), and by 571 Lombards are found forming duchies a long way down the peninsula in Spoleto (under Faroald) and Benevento (under Zotto), apparently without having occupied any of the intermediate territory. Bognetti had answers for this, however: the invasions of Burgundy resulted from Alboin's alliance with Sigebert of Austrasia, whereas the peninsular duchies were in fact set up by the Byzantines as garrisons *against* Alboin at strategic points, for both Spoleto and Benevento control major Appennine passes. The latter theory seems quite likely, less so the former; but anyway Alboin's murder, perhaps with Byzantine involvement, put an end to the 'grand plan', and for the rest of the century we have chaos.[4]

Alboin's successor Cleph was also murdered in 574, and for the next ten years, the so-called interregnum, the Lombards had no kings at all. Paul the Deacon says they were governed by thirty-five dukes, though that is certainly too many.[5] He names only five, those of Pavia, Bergamo, Brescia, Trento, and Friuli (Cividale), most of the nearest dukes to the Trentino, where one of his principal sources lived, Secundus of Non. We can add Turin, Spoleto, and Benevento for certain, but can guess at only a handful of others. By the eighth century, the Lombards certainly had dukes or their equivalent in all the Roman cities of the North and of Tuscany, but we cannot say yet that every city had been given one. We cannot even, for that matter, be very sure what the Lombards controlled, for the Byzantines certainly maintained garrisons at a number of important points in northern Italy: on Lake Como until 588, in Susa (on the major route into Burgundy) until the Franks occupied it in the 570s, in the Val di Non until the late 580s, and in Cremona until 603.

The interregnum is one of the cruxes of Lombard historiography. It is usually seen as the index of the barbarism and atavism of the Lombards, that they should be so weakly attached to kingship that they should actually abandon it, an act almost without parallel in the history of the Romano-Germanic kingdoms. It was, however, not exactly normal for Germans even of Tacitus's time to abandon kingship in the middle of a war, which in this case still continued after Cleph's death – the first Byzantine counter-attack came under Baduarius in 575, failing disastrously. Other explanations for the interregnum may be better. Many have been offered. The most satisfactory is again that of Bognetti, who suggested that the Lombard dukes may have been subverted and dispersed by Byzantine bribes. Menander, the principal Byzantine chronicler for the late 560s and 570s, records that in 577 the Emperor Tiberius II paid to the Franks 30,000 pounds of gold to fight the Lombards, and to the Lombards to make peace. In 579, too, he sent money to individual Lombard dukes to get them to defect. And in fact in our sixth century sources, particularly the letters of Gregory the Great, we know the names of almost as many Lombards fighting for the Byzantines as against them. One, Droctulf, even had a tomb inscription erected in Ravenna, celebrating his heroic deeds: 'terrible of aspect but of kindly mind, he had a long beard and a brave heart. He ever loved the honours and the name of Rome; he was the exterminator of his own people'. Droctulf was ethnically a Sueve, and the Lombard confederation included a large number of different ethnic groups – Saxons, Gepids, Bulgars, Sarmatians, Sueves, Thuringians, Pannonian Romans – and the Saxons can actually be seen acting as a homogeneous group in our sources. Such a mix cannot have helped Lombard political cohesion in the period. By now, Spoleto and Benevento had certainly turned against Byzantium, and could spread havoc in the peninsula. On the other hand, the Byzantines by 580 had bought the duke of Friuli, Grasulf, probably the most powerful duke in the North. At least it must be possible that the 570s and 580s were a time of so much confusion, for Lombards as well as Romans – Byzantines, that the intelligent use of Byzantine money could well have been the cause of the temporary abandonment of Lombard kingship.[6] But if so, it was only temporary. In 584, in the face of Austrasian Frankish invasions from the North, the Lombards as well as Romans–Byzantines, that the intelligent use of king. They had in this a definite political intention, too, for (if Paul is to be believed) they each gave half of their *substantiae*, wealth and possessions, to give him a strong foundation for kingship. Certainly kings in Italy ever after had a firm landed base, which could be drawn on as late as the twelfth century. Darmstadter reckoned that in Lombardy and Piedmont, at least, it consisted of over 10 per cent of the total land area.[7]

Authari is presented as a romantic, young, energetic king, but we know little about him. He survived three Frankish invasions in six years, and died in 590 having recently established an alliance with the Bavarians through his marriage with the Bavarian princess Theodelinda. Immediately before his death, he promulgated an anti-Catholic edict. Gregory the Great, elected pope in the same year, found this to be divine justice, but God is more likely to have been a friend of Authari's: the last Frankish invasion, in 590, was a two-pronged attack co-ordinated with the Byzantines, which ought to have swept the Lombards away, but did not. The Lombards shut themselves up in cities, not resisting, but the Franks and Byzantines missed each other, and the Franks soon returned home. The Byzantines were outraged, but the Franks probably had no real desire to annihilate the Lombards. Instead, they almost certainly obtained overlordship over northern Italy, following the traditions of the 540s–550s. Authari certainly paid them tribute, and though one source says that his successor Agilulf (590–616) paid a lump sum to free himself from it, the Lombards as late as the 620s are to be found in the Frankish army against the Slav king Samo, alongside the Alemans, who were certainly a tributary people.[8]

After 590 the Byzantines resigned themselves for the moment to the continuing existence of the Lombards, and began to consolidate themselves in the geographical areas to which they were confined. Their military élites finally established themselves there as politically and tenurially dominant, alongside the episcopal hierarchies of Ravenna, Rome, and Naples (cf. chapter 3, pp. 74–9). After 590 the Lombards, too, begin to achieve a firmer sense of political cohesion. Authari was largely on the defensive, but Agilulf, with no Frankish threat, went on to the attack, occupying or reoccupying several cities along the Po, and threatening Rome in 593–4. By 605, a series of truces between the two sides was crystallised into a permanent peace, which was broken only twice by any Lombard king for the next 120 years. From this point, the recovery of Italy was possible. Agilulf saw this in terms of the establishment of the centralised power of the Lombard state, and Paul describes him overthrowing or obtaining the submission of at least eight dukes (Paul's source Secundus was at Agilulf's court, making Paul a reliable witness for this reign). By 603 even Gisulf II of Friuli, the most politically self-sufficient duchy of the North, came to terms. Further south, Agilulf was either less ambitious or less successful. He seems to have established himself in Tuscany by the end of his reign, though still in 603 Gregory the Great shows us an independent Lombard duke there, Cillanis, who was at war with briefly autonomous Pisa. Spoleto and Benevento, on the other hand, had completely independent policies, despite Paul's claim that Duke Arichis I of Benevento (591–641) was a Friulian set up by Agilulf: so, for example, Duke Ariulf of Spoleto, who threatened Rome on his own account in 592, refrained from helping Agilulf do the same in 593.[9] Agilulf certainly conceded the southern duchies *de facto* autonomy, and in this respect fixed the political situation for a century and a half, with the brief exception of Grimoald's reign. The Lombard kingdom did not include the South, and its history is different, as we will see in chapter 6. In the North, though, Agilulf at least achieved recognition of his supremacy from all other Lombard power groups, and on this basis he began to consolidate his state, which for the first time begins to take shape in our evidence. He did so with a careful eye to the imitation of Roman and Byzantine forms and ceremonies, and certainly used

Roman advisers and ministers, of which Secundus of Non was one. A representation of him, flanked by Lombard warriors, but also with angels bearing signs saying *victuria*, survives on a gold helmet-fitting found in Tuscany. An inscription showed him with the Roman-influenced titles of *grat(ia) d(e)i, vir glor(iosissimus), rex totius Ital(iae)*. And, following Authari, he certainly used the Roman and Ostrogothic title *flavius*. In 604 he had his son Adaloald, already baptised a Catholic, presented as king in the Roman circus of Milan (as were the emperors in Constantinople) in the presence of ambassadors from Francia.[10]

Agilulf, clearly, was concerned to establish, through a fairly eclectic set of images, a late Roman aura for his kingship. Bognetti saw him as a heroic figure, the Arian (or pagan) warrior concerned to romanise and catholicise his court and inheritance, in many ways paralleling Theoderic a century before, and, like Theoderic, drawing down nationalist German wrath on his heirs, thus initiating a series of religious coups d'etat and civil wars lasting on and off between 626 and 690.[11] This latter idea, to me, is very unlikely. The whole question of Lombard religious history needs discussion, however, at least briefly.

The Lombards were certainly for the most part pagan when they entered Italy in 568, though we know little about their practices – sacrificing to a goat's head, as Gregory the Great says, or at a woodland shrine, following Jonas of Bobbio (writing in the 640s), or firing at a hide hung on a tree, as in the ninth-century life of Barbatus, bishop of Benevento, who lived in the 670s.[12] Superimposed on this, the religion of at least some of the aristocracy was Christian. They were largely Catholic in the 540s, but from Alboin onwards beginning to be Arian, at least in the royal entourage. Authari we know was actively Arian. Agilulf may have been – he was at least not Catholic, though much of his court was; Arioald (626–36) and Rothari (636–52) were certainly Arian. Thereafter, we cannot show any king to have been Arian, though Grimoald (662–71) should probably be included in the list. Adaloald (616–26), Aripert I (652–61), and Grimoald's successors were all Catholic. Bognetti saw a large-scale break between 'progressive' elements, who wished to introduce Catholicism into the Lombard court and society, and traditionalist nationalist warrior groups, who used Alboin's and Authari's Arianism as a touchstone. Agilulf could surround himself with Catholics, like his wife Theodelinda, or Agrippinus bishop of Como, or the Irishman Columbanus (who founded the monastery of Bobbio in 613), because Catholicism in northern Italy had been attached to the schism of the Three Chapters (an abstruse debate over the orthodoxy of three theological tracts) ever since 551, and was therefore opposed to the papacy and to the Byzantines. When, however, under Adaloald and his mother-regent Theodelinda, there were movements to end this schism, the nationalist Lombards became perturbed. And when in 626 the Eastern emperor Heraclius began to win in his wars against the Persians, thus making the Byzantine menace seem a little more present, the alarmed Lombards quickly replaced Adaloald with an Arian, Arioald. Thereafter, every time the Lombards had a Catholic king, his whole range of activities was weakened by the danger of revolt by the traditionalists, as occurred in 661–2, and again in c. 688 when the rebel duke of Trento, Alahis, was briefly brought to the throne.

Some of the problems involved in this picture are extremely detailed, and not relevant to this narrative. But the picture Bognetti presents is one of clearly defined groups attached to conscious political ideologies and would be crucial for our analysis if it were true. There are problems about it, however. The first is the absence of evidence for any particular fervency for religion along the Lombards at all. Authari's anti-Catholic edict we have already referred to: it was limited to refusing to Lombards the right to baptise their children Catholic. Authari certainly had Catholic followers, however; Gregory tells us about one.[13] Arioald and Rothari can be seen in surviving actions to respect at least the rights of the Church of Rome over Catholics in Lombard territory. Of Grimoald's religious sensibilities we know nothing whatsoever – though Paul, our major source here, never admitted any of his kings to be Arian with the sole exception of Rothari. The late seventh and eighth-century kings, by now clearly Catholic, are no more zealous than the Arian kings were. Even the use of the Church as a political force to support the state, a commonplace among early medieval monarchies, is almost wholly absent until the Frankish conquest.[14] Alboin converted to Arianism for transparently political reasons, and the last king to support Arianism militantly died in 590, only twenty-five years later. This is not enough time, in such a confused period, to instil into the Lombard people much of a sense of the potential of Arianism as a nationalist rallying-call.

The second point is that the coup of 626, in which Adaloald was removed, was supported by the Catholic bishops of the Lombard kingdom, as we learn from an indignant letter of Honorius I.[15] If Adaloald had rejected the Three Chapters schism, as Bognetti thought, this would not be wholly inconsistent; but there is insufficient evidence to allow us to say that. On the other hand, the fact that both the bishops (i.e. the Romans) and the Lombards concurred in Adaloald's fall, and that the pope and the exarch deplored it, shows a rejection of Adaloald that was not restricted to Lombard nationalists. Paul says he went mad; this is at least possible. Alternatively, like Amalasuntha and Theodahad a century before, he may have been planning a whole-scale reconciliation with Byzantium on the political level. But to postulate an irredentist grouping among the Lombards with a coherent religious ideology and a role as political watchdogs seems unnecessary and anachronistic. Paul only once ever gives us an insight into Lombard political awareness: when in 663 the new king Grimoald returned to his former duchy, Benevento, to fight a Byzantine invasion force, many Lombards (including his regent, Lupus, duke of Friuli) concluded that he would not return, and abandoned his cause.[16] This is not exactly the international political vision that Bognetti proposes for the nationalists of 626. I would prefer to see the alternations of religious belief among the seventh-century kings as an indicator, far from the centrality of religion for the Lombards, of the near-total irrelevance of personal religious alignment inside a resolutely secular political system. Unlike the Franks, the Lombards did not need the Church to buttress their state. They had, as we shall see, enough survivals from the secular institutions of the late Roman state that they could use instead.

On the other hand, we can detect in our sources two different currents in seventh-century Lombard kingship, which can circumstantially be linked to religious belief: on one side, the tradition of Agilulf, of a Catholic court with links to Roman and Byzantine ceremonial and culture, followed by the descendants of Theodelinda's brother Gundoald, the Bavarian dynasty, ruling on and off between 652 and 712; on the other, what might be called a 'country' tradition, the kingship of men who had begun as dukes and only linked themselves to the court by marriage, Arioald, Rothari and Grimoald. These two tendencies did not crystallise into political groupings; they merely represented a contrast in the social origins of the men who were in a position to seize supreme power in the state. Nevertheless, Rothari and Grimoald, at least, did act differently from the Bavarians. They promulgated and associated themselves with Lombard law.

Rothari's Edict of 643 is the most systematic and large-scale exposition of Germanic custom that survives from any of the Germanic kingdoms, excluding only that of the Visigoths.[17] But the Visigothic code is heavily influenced by vulgar Roman law. Rothari's Edict, by contrast, is Roman only in its language, in certain basic assumptions about the law of property (and, to a certain extent, the role and public persona of the state), and in its comprehensiveness. It runs with care through the spheres of the court and the army, compensation for wounds, land ownership and liability (not much here), inheritance and marriage, slaves, agricultural delicts, and legal procedure. Rothari was mainly content to expound custom, though occasionally he specifically acknowledged an alteration to custom, as when he increased the money-compensation for wounds to make the avoidance of feud more honourable. But he deliberately set out as much of Lombard custom as he and his advisers could, and he put his name to it. This was a very Germanic thing to do, and was certainly a different way of boosting royal prestige from that of Agilulf. It was, furthermore, done in the context of the first Lombard war of aggression for four decades, in which Rothari conquered much of Emilia and the whole Ligurian coast. But it was only possible inside Agilulf's state, inside a sub-Roman administrative system that could produce the (doubtless Roman) personnel to collect and set out 388 titles of law at all, and that could regard the Edict, once set out, as a written law book parallel to Roman law, and susceptible to change (with Grimoald's additions, and those of the eighth-century kings). Rothari was not brought up in the court, and was Arian, but he did not oppose Agilulf's tradition; he built on it. Similarly, Cunipert (679–700) improved the administration, and increased the role of the Lombard capital, Pavia; but one of the linchpins of his administration was now Rothari's and Grimoald's law. The two traditions, rather than in opposition, seem complementary.

Grimoald seized power in 662 from the two sons of Aripert I, Godepert and Perctarit, who had begun a civil war, the origins of a blood feud that was to result in a particularly savage series of coups d'etat between their (totally Catholic) descendants in 701–2. Grimoald was duke of Benevento, though son of Gisulf II of Friuli. This is interesting as an indication of the family relationship between two duchies at the opposite ends of Italy, despite Benevento's *de facto* independence. But the fact that a duke of Benevento could feel sufficiently part of the Lombard polity to take the Crown points out something else. There were a good number of coups in Lombard history – ten or eleven, to name only the successful ones. This is sometimes taken as an indication of Lombard political weakness. How strong the state was we shall see in a moment, but the tendency to take power by coup is not a sign of Lombard disintegration, but, on the contrary, of the substantial *cohesion* of the political system. Max Gluckman in one of social anthropology's classic introductory texts showed how rebellion by people who respect the confines of a political system can reinforce, rather than undermine, that system.[18] He took the example of the Zulu state, in which communications were so bad that it would have been easy for local leaders to secure their independence. But, instead, these leaders could aspire to the kingship as successful rebels, and periodic civil wars, focused on rival candidates for a unitary kingdom, reinforced that unity. Similarly, we see in the Lombard kingdom the independence of the Lombard dukes destroyed by Agilulf, and after his reign we find no duke seeking independence. Instead, they sought the throne, with Arioald of Turin in 626, Alahis of Trento in *c*.688, Rotarit of Bergamo in *c*.702, Ratchis of Friuli in 744, Desiderius of Brescia in 756, and others. That Grimoald did the same in 662 indicates that under certain circumstances even Benevento could be drawn into this, though this may be exceptional. Grimoald left his son Romoald behind as an independent duke, and it was only in the 730s that Liutprand brought the South under royal control. What we can say is that, despite the hereditary attachment to the Bavarian dynasty that showed itself on and off right up to 712, the Lombard political system allowed for the full exercise of personal ambition on the part of leaders, both Arian and, increasingly, Catholic, who felt that they could muster enough political and military force to take power. This may produce political weakness, but does not have to, and in the Lombard case did not.[19] Analogous arguments could be applied to the succession problems of the seventh-century Visigoths in Spain.

The king's court and the construction of the state were the basis for Lombard royal power. Both were centred on a capital, Pavia, where the royal *palatium* or *curtis regia* was. Pavia had not always had this role – Alboin probably preferred Verona, and Agilulf Milan – but for the most part it was by the 620s accepted as pre-eminent, and remained so for four centuries. It was filled with monumental buildings expressing this role: the palace itself, Ostrogothic in origin, a whole range of churches founded by kings and queens from the 640s at the latest onwards, and one of the few bath complexes known to have been functioning in the seventh century. If not modelled on Constantinople, it was certainly modelled on a conception of it, and, more directly, on Ravenna. Apart from Visigothic Toledo and Charlemagne's short-lived capital at Aachen, it had no parallel in Western Europe. From Cunipert onwards, we can trace a line of grammarians practising there, culminating in Paul the Deacon himself under Desiderius around 760, and it was probably already the centre for lawyers and notaries, even outside the confines of the king's court itself.[20] The central organisation of the state was clearly on sub-Roman lines. There were certainly traditional Lombard ceremonial offices, the *marpahis, scilpor, scaffard, antepor, stolesaz*, many of which cannot be fully identified, though the *stolesaz* was the treasurer (particularly important in the imitative court at Benevento), and the *marpahis* is sometimes glossed in texts as *strator* or groom. But when we begin to find documents from the court, which only become common under Liutprand, it is not so much these men we see, but officials with clearer Roman origins, the *maiordomus, vesterarius, camerarius, actionarius,* and above all the *referendarius* and a whole series of royal notaries. It is these last who wrote royal diplomas, the formal records of royal decisions and gifts, which were set out by the *referendarius*. The *maiordomus* and the others had public duties, both household and administrative, in Pavia, but also functioned at least partly as royal representatives in the rest of Italy, like Carolingian *missi*. They heard troublesome court cases in the provinces. Liutprand sent Ambrosius *maiordomus* in spring 715 and Guntheram, the king's *notarius* and *missus*, in summer of the same year to hear the opening rounds of the long-running boundary dispute between the dioceses of Siena and Arezzo.[21] All these officials, with the help of the *stratores*, heard cases in Pavia too. These judicial functions make it difficult to disentangle their separate tasks, and the palace officials, like the dukes and gastalds in the provinces, are all often just called *iudices*. But they existed in Pavia as a definable group, and one that was, potentially, available for anyone who needed royal ratification for an act, or who wished to appeal against a judicial decision. Kings or their immediate representatives had to ratify a number of remarkably straightforward actions in our eighth-century texts, such as the authentic copy of a land grant by a Tuscan notable in Aistulf's reign, or the slight alteration of the details of the will of Gisulf *strator* of Lodi in 759. In 771 the three owners of a rather small private church near Lucca appealed to the king against bishop Peredeus on a point of law, and Desiderius directed Peredeus to rehear their case and grant them rights, which he did.[22] The king kept, too, a large number of the traditional rights and duties of the late Roman state: minting, price-fixing, the upkeep of city-walls.[23] The presence of Pavia as a political force in the kingdom was without any doubt effective.

But one thing sets the Lombard kingdom on the other side of a divide from the late Empire and the Ostrogothic state: it did not exact the land tax. Kings certainly obtained the benefit of numbers of dues on commercial activity, import tolls, sales taxes and port dues, whose exact interrelationship is almost impossible to disentangle: *datio, teloneum, siliquaticum, ripaticum, portaticum* – these certainly have late Roman roots. They also could extract corvée work (*angaria, scuviae,* or *utilitates*), probably from Lombard and Roman freemen.[24] But the emperors had regarded such dues as trivia by comparison with the land tax, which was the real basis for state activity. If this tax survived in any form in the Lombard period, it only did so in inconsistent fragments. A tithe formerly owed to the state by the church of Aquileia is, for example, referred to by a diploma of Charlemagne's of 792; but if such a high burden were in any way normal, we could scarcely have failed to hear of it elsewhere.[25] The absence of a major land tax, however, changes the whole relationship between state and society. The tax was essential for the functioning of whole sectors, above all the maintenance of the army. It consisted, beyond doubt, of the largest single financial burden on any peasant or landowner, and its annual collection was certainly the point at which the state impinged most heavily on society. It is scarcely surprising that it disappeared in the Lombard invasions, given the trouble there had always been collecting it – though it survived in Byzantine Italy. Instead, the Lombard army was supported by settlement on the land (see pp. 66ff). But this meant that no matter how Roman the forms of the Lombard state were, its institutional weight was very different. Apart from exceptional sources, such as booty or judicial confiscations, the resources of the state were now almost entirely derived from its landowning. And landowning in this period became not just a way to obtain political power and influence, as under the Romans, but political power itself. The army was now locally organised, as a public obligation, under the control of the dukes. The dukes, however, also tended to be the largest private landowners in their territories, and had their own retainers; and army service itself was graded by 750 according to the extent of landownership. The patterns of society had, that is to say, become broadly 'feudal', even though they were posed in a political structure that owed all its contours to late Rome. As long as the Empire could extract its taxes it was *ipso facto* a powerful and dominant institution. But from the Lombard period onwards the state depended for its very existence, more explicitly and directly, on consent: the consent of its most powerful supporters, dukes (later, counts) and other landowners. For the moment, it had little difficulty in obtaining it, however. The kings (with the exception of Grimoald) do not seem to have had to be very generous with their estates to gain support, unlike most other early medieval kings. Only after 900, when state power was collapsing, did Italian rulers start making large land grants. In the meantime, the survival of a developed legal system that always looked towards the royal power centres, and a balance of powers in the local centres, the cities, were the most certain bases for the hegemony of the Lombard kings, as we shall see in later chapters.

Lombard local administration was also sub-Roman in most of its forms. The kingdom was built up out of local circumscriptions that were, for the most part, the Roman city-territories and ecclesiastical dioceses. These were controlled by dukes or gastalds, who lived in the cities, thus reinforcing the predominance cities had always had in their territories. There were sometimes changes, but the reasons for them are usually clear. Boundary defence is the main one, producing large duchies like Friuli, or in other areas a scatter of administrative districts based on *castra*, defensive strong-points, such as Castelseprio and Sirmione on the edges of the Alps, and a whole string of *castra* in the Emilian and Tuscan Appennines, to counter the Byzantine Appennine defences.[26] Where boundaries between cities changed, they were usually resisted by the city which was losing its territory, and the kings had to sort out the disputes, as between Parma and Piacenza (at least four times between 626 and 854), and between Siena and Arezzo. In this last case, although the administrative boundary of Arezzo had not been enlarged, in the early seventh century during a prolonged episcopal vacancy in Siena the diocese of Arezzo was expanded to include a score of Sienese churches. The Sienese bishops regarded this as an intolerable anomaly, and their gastalds supported them. Liutprand supported Arezzo, and so did a succession of kings and popes, though a contrary judgement by Pope Leo IV in 850 exacerbated the dispute sufficiently to prohibit its resolution for many centuries.[27]

Dukes were, of course, Alboin's army leaders, attached to cities right from the start, and soon with civil responsibilities as well. Gastalds were, it seems, originally the local administrators of the royal fisc (royal revenues – by now, almost entirely in land). Rothari certainly regards the two officials as coexisting in the same city, and uses them as appeal mechanisms against each other.[28] But under Agilulf, gastalds are found replacing dukes in rebel cities, and in Tuscany most cities (apart from Lucca and Chiusi) seem never to have had dukes at all. In the southern duchies, gastalds were the only local political representatives, but in this case they were totally subject to the dukes who ran the central government in Spoleto and Benevento. The dual role of gastalds seems crystallised in Siena, where in 715 there were actually two gastalds holding office. Whether such a neat separation of powers existed generally is uncertain; but in Lucca, at least, the *curtis regia* or local political-administrative centre was geographically separate from the *curtis ducalis*, the duke's court, and at Brescia in 759–60 King Desiderius distinguished in his diplomas between the property of the king (*curte nostram*), the official property of the duke (*curtis ducalis*), and the personal property that Desiderius held or was given while he was duke there under Aistulf.[29] Both dukes and gastalds enjoyed considerable local loyalty and had great local commitment, but it is significant that with a few exceptions we cannot trace hereditary lines of them. Friuli had one to start with, but lost it in the 630s–40s. Even Spoleto had several changes of dynasty, usually enforced by kings. Only Benevento continued immune (under the former Friulian dynasty), at least until Liutprand's reign.

At a lower level than the city-territory, on the other hand, we find extreme confusion. The laws refer to minor public officials, the *sculdahis*, *centenarius*, and *decanus*. There have been several attempts to organise them in credible hierarchies and with credible circumscriptions; these have generally failed. There is no good reason to think that they had the same duties in Lombard Italy as they had elsewhere. In some cases, such officials must have had local responsibilities – Liutprand clearly assumed so in his laws, and occasionally we find documentary references to *decani* and *centenari*, possibly in charge of village-territories in Tuscany. Further north, however, they are impossible to trace in the Lombard period. In Spoleto, *sculdahes* in the gastaldate of Rieti seem to have had official functions in the gastald's entourage, and not outside the city at all.[30] The comparative uniformity of the central government and of the city administration totally breaks down at the local level. Whether this was a result of the chaos of the Gothic and Lombard wars, or whether it is merely our first documentary evidence of far older contrasts, we cannot know. The basic local unit for the Lombard state was essentially the city and its territory, making a cellular structure for the kingdom, partly as a result of Alboin's choice that dukes should rule cities, but mostly as the continuation of the traditional social and geographical framework of Italy. As long as consistency was reached here, lesser units seem to have mattered less.

With the eighth century, our political picture stabilises. Grimoald fought off the last Byzantine attempt to reconquer Lombard territory, under the Emperor Constans II in 663, and thereafter there was peace for sixty years, barring some expansion by the Beneventans (Taranto and Brindisi in the 680s, the Val di Liri in *c*. 702). The Bavarian dynasty destroyed itself in a set of coups and counter-coups in 701–12, and in 712 the last king, Aripert II (701–12), was overthrown by Ansprand; Ansprand died inside the year, and his son Liutprand (712–44) succeeded. Liutprand and his three main successors, Ratchis (744–9), Aistulf (749–56) and Desiderius (757–74) have visible identities and subtly different policies. Political history becomes possible.[31]

Liutprand's father had been tutor to Liutpert (700–2), Cunipert's son, and had been set up with the military help of the duke of the Bavarians. He was clearly in a political sense Cunipert's heir. He was not, however, part of the dynastic tradition of the court of Pavia, and in terms of his actions he owed more to Rothari and Grimoald. In Liutprand the synthesis between the two strands of seventh-century Lombard kingship, which was already beginning, became complete. His first act, in 713, was to revise the inheritance dispositions of Rothari's code. The speed of this is significant: there must have been considerable popular pressure in favour of the extended inheritance rights of women and the legitimation of gifts to the Church. Liutprand says as much in a *notitia* of 733, when he laments the greed of royal officials, and wonders why they are not content with these concessions. The laws seem to have been taken up at once; almost our first surviving Church donations follow immediately on them, in 714.[32] This concern for the explicit legitimisation of acts by kings shows how great royal authority and the force of law was, as we will see in chapter 5. It also demonstrates Roman influence, for these were changes in the direction of Roman legal practice. The Romans were the vast majority of the inhabitants of Lombard Italy, but they only begin to reappear in the sources of Liutprand's reign – though in the seventh century a few can already be seen, such as Peter son of Paul, Adaloald's aide, and the Roman noblewoman Theodota, whom Cunipert fell in love with at the baths.[33] Their actual relationship with the Lombards will be discussed later (see pp. 66–72), but it can already be seen that Liutprand was beginning to draw from their law. He did not take over elements indiscriminately; Roman features fitted inside a firmly Lombard legal framework. The rest of inheritance law, for example, remained totally Lombard. Again, in 731 Liutprand made the ordeal by battle a much more carefully circumscribed exercise, explaining: 'for we are uncertain about God's judgement, and we have heard of many losing their cases in battle unjustly; but on account of the custom of our Lombard people we cannot ban the law entirely'.[34] Attractive sentiments, and typical of the rationality of Liutprand's *ad hoc* judgements; but Liutprand's feelings are here firmly subjected to the rules of Lombard law. This traditional Lombard framework around all legal innovation was the most characteristic element of Liutprand's version of the seventh-century synthesis.

Liutprand legislated throughout his reign except for its last nine years, adding 152 titles to the Edict – 158 if we include the six chapters of the *notitia de actoribus regis*, which is essentially a forerunner of the Carolingian capitulary. Otherwise, we find him keeping a firm hand on his dukes and, after 726, making confident moves against all the other powers in the peninsula. In 726–7 he invaded the Exarchate and occupied it all except Ravenna; when he retired, he kept its western portions. In 732–3, 740, and 743 he occupied the remaining portions, including Ravenna. In 733 he moved into the South, and set his own nephew, Gregory, up in Benevento. In 739 he reacted against a hostile alliance between Spoleto, Benevento and the papacy, expelling the duke of Spoleto and occupying four cities of the Roman patrimony, before returning north to help Charles Martel fight the Arabs in Francia. In 742 he marched south again and removed the dukes of both Spoleto and Benevento, returning only to occupy Ravenna in 743. Suddenly, for the first time in sixty years, the military power of the Lombard kingdom showed itself to be without rival in Italy. Spoleto, by Ratchis's reign, seems to have been absorbed into the framework of the kingdom: its notarial practice henceforth depends on Pavia, and the kings have the power to alienate ducal property. Between 751 and 756 Aistulf even dispensed with a duke.[35] Spoleto, as a result, was to be firmly incorporated into the Carolingian Empire. Benevento, too, was at least subjected to Pavia, though in this case only by the recognition of northern supremacy, underlined by the capacity of northern armies to remove its dukes at will. What Liutprand intended for the Byzantine parts of Italy is less certain. He does not seems to have had permanent territorial designs on the Roman patrimony, and in 744, at Pope Zacharias's request, he even evacuated Ravenna. He seems to have regarded the Exarchate, although not the Lombard duchies, as having a legitimate independent existence. By the time Aistulf, who thought otherwise, came to power, the international power balance had shifted.

Hildeprand succeeded his uncle Liutprand, but was overthrown by Ratchis of Friuli almost at once (744). Ratchis seems to have followed Liutprand's policies, attacking Rome and Ravenna, and withdrawing again. His fourteen laws of 746 follow Liutprand's traditions. The problem that particularly concerns him is abuse of power by *iudices* (dukes and gastalds) and illegal opposition to them. This was not a new problem for Lombard kings (or their predecessors): Rothari and Liutprand both legislated against it and Ratchis even uses late Roman terms such as *patrocinium*, patronage, in his analysis of the situation.[36] Lombard kings, like all medieval rulers, were in fact virtually powerless against abuses of power by their local representatives (favouritism, as Ratchis notes, either for followers, or kinsmen, or friends, or for money), in view of the fact that their local power rested on such representatives. The most one can say is that they at least tried, as these laws show; and Liutprand, for example, removed Pemmo (Ratchis's father) from the duchy of Friuli for mistreating the patriarch of Aquileia.[37] What these laws do not show is the insecurity Ratchis is supposed to have had in the face of growing civil disturbance; such disturbance was commonplace in early medieval society. More serious were the measures Ratchis took to protect his borders from enemies and spies coming in, and secret information and fugitives going out, for these were directed against Francia.[38]

Francia was always more powerful than the Lombard kingdom, even during the political eclipse of the Merovingians in the late seventh century, and the Lombards took care to keep on friendly terms. After Agilulf's reign, the two maintained an alliance, unbroken except for a Frankish invasion in 662 (in favour of the exiled king Perctarit), right up to the time of Liutprand. Liutprand and Charles Martel, as we have seen, co-operated against the Arabs. Pope Gregory III's request for Frankish help against Liutprand in 740 met with no response. But the papacy needed the Franks, now, for support against the Lombards, for theological differences and eastern wars meant that the Byzantine emperors were not prepared to come to its aid. After Charles Martel's death in 741, the papacy and the Franks began a *rapprochement* that resulted in the papal recognition of the Carolingian dynasty as kings of Francia in 752. Ratchis had every right to feel worried: Francia was the traditional home for Lombard exiles, too, and, if it chose, could act in their favour. In 749 Ratchis retired to the monastery of Montecassino, having been replaced (probably in a coup) by his more forceful brother Aistulf; these problems reached a head. Aistulf, as we have seen, totally absorbed Spoleto. In 751 he occupied Ravenna, this time intending to stay, as we can see from the record of his (interrupted) building works there. In 752 he demanded tribute from Rome, and control over the *castra* of the Roman Campagna. Pope Stephen II, after negotiations had failed, appealed to the Franks. In 755 (or 754) the Franks under Pippin III invaded. Aistulf met them in a pitched battle and lost. Inside besieged Pavia he made terms with the Franks, ceding to the pope all the Exarchate (against the wishes of the Ravennati, who certainly preferred Lombard to papal rule). When he broke the peace in 756, Pippin invaded again and the treaty was repeated. Inside the year Aistulf was dead.[39]

Aistulf has usually been severely judged by historians, for he is seen exclusively through the eyes of his enemies. Paul's history stops in 744, though his oversensitivity about bad relations between Lombard kings and the papacy would have made him little use for the following period. We are left with the Frankish annals and the Roman *Liber Pontificalis*, not sympathetic analysts. The latter runs out of words to express its opinion of Aistulf: most wicked, most ferocious, appalling, impious, blaspheming are only the short epithets. Aistulf was, however, just carrying Liutprand's policies to their logical conclusions. One can only say that it was his ill luck that the Franks now showed themselves prepared to intervene, for the Franks were invincible. He was not even opposed to the pope, in a religious sense. In 752, in the middle of his campaigns, he referred the third round of the Siena–Arezzo dispute to Rome on the grounds that it was not in his competence; not even Liutprand had done that. His laws are concerned with much the same problems as Ratchis's, with the perhaps significant addition of a law about the tendency of powerful men to evade army service. The Lombards were by now probably not as committed to permanent warfare as the Franks – several Lombard aristocrats are known to have made their wills before going on campaign against Pippin – and this cannot have helped Aistulf's effectiveness against the Franks.[40]

Desiderius's reign (757–74) has the air of a postscript about it. Desiderius began, with papal support, by winning a civil war against Ratchis, who temporarily reappeared from Montecassino to reclaim the throne. In his early years he lived under the shadow of a papal-Frankish alliance, though this did not interfere with his capacity to control Spoleto and Benevento, at least. After 768 the death of Pippin and a disputed succession in Rome gave him a chance to reassert himself, but by now the Lombard kings were trapped. In an age of sharper boundaries (the Lombards had even invented passports), the Lombards could not easily accept the existence of the papal state across the centre of Italy. But by the time Desiderius was strong enough to attack it (in 772–3), Hadrian I (772–94) was a forceful pope in Rome, and Pippin's son Charlemagne sole king in Francia. Charlemagne, rather unwillingly, invaded Italy in 773 and defeated a Lombard army at the edge of the Alps. Between autumn 773 and June 774 he besieged Pavia and Verona, and then, entering Pavia in triumph, crowned himself as king.

The Lombard kingdom fell for the simple reason that geographical logic forced any ambitious Lombard king to oppose the pope in a period when the strongest army in Europe was prepared to fight at papal request. Desiderius seems in his internal activities, by contrast, to have been as confident as any of his predecessors. He had internal opponents, certainly: Aistulf's brother-in-law Anselm, abbot of Nonantola, fled to Montecassino in *c.* 760 and only returned with the Frankish conquest; and a diploma of 772 lists nine noble *infideles*, one of whom, Augino, had actually fled to Francia. None of this would, however, have mattered if Francia had not been hostile; such flights were not new. In 773–4, too, people rallied to Charlemagne, and the Spoletans threw off Duke Theudicius, who was with Desiderius. Hadrian himself selected Hildeprand, his successor.[41] But this preparedness to come to terms with the Franks cannot be seen as a cause of Desiderius's fall, for it only occurred after the military defeat of the Lombard army, when the Italians knew that Desiderius was lost. The Lombard kingdom was militarily weaker than that of the Franks, but it was nonetheless a strong and well-organised state that Charlemagne inherited.

The Carolingian Kingdom

CHARLEMAGNE spent less than a year in Italy in 773–4. Pavia had fallen in June; before the end of the campaigning season he was back in the North, fighting in Saxony. This set a pattern that persisted as long as there were kings of Italy: rule from across the Alps meant an absentee monarch. Charlemagne returned only four times before his death in 814 (776, 780–1, 786–7, and in 800–1, when he was given the symbolic title of emperor by Pope Leo III), but even this was high by the standards of some of his successors, and resulted from his wish to stabilise a newly-conquered part of his Empire. The Lombards did not, however, cause him much trouble. Hadrian I wrote to warn him of a plot in 775 between several Lombard dukes and the Byzantine emperor, but when it broke in 776, only one or two dukes were actually involved, and their leader, Rodgaud of Friuli, fell in battle. Charlemagne might have used this as an excuse to remove all Lombard dukes from office, but he chose to wait until they died before replacing them with Frankish counts – and at least one old rebel, Aio, was pardoned in 799 and reinstated, his son Alboin becoming a count too, in the next reign. Lombard rebels did have their estates confiscated, but their more loyal kinsmen retained their own lands. Hostages were from time to time taken back to Francia, including the bishops of Lucca, Pisa, and Reggio Emilia, and probably Paul the Deacon's brother Arichis, but most had returned by about 780. Charlemagne's armies may have been less circumspect, however: in 776 he had to issue a capitulary to deal with the after-effects of serious famine, probably caused by his invasions.[42]

From now on, the Lombard kingdom became a sub-kingdom of the Frankish Empire, and its institutions slowly began to alter. By 814 Lombard dukes had become counts, and mostly Frankish or Aleman; Frankish *missi* (king's messengers) presided at local courts. But the influx of northerners into Italy was fairly slow, and had barely started by Charlemagne's death. Local politics and local courts did not look very different under Carolingian rule. The social structures of Italy and the rules governing political activity remained. This was partly because they were not unlike Frankish rules, in fact: Italy and Gaul had to some extent developed in the same direction. In 774, for example, Charlemagne handed over two strategic Alpine valleys, the Valtellina and Valcamonica, to the Frankish monasteries of St Denis, and St Martin of Tours, in virtually his only large grants of royal land throughout his reign. This was a classic Frankish political act. The last Lombard kings had, however, done just the same with the monasteries they patronised, as for example when the Friulian kings Ratchis and Aistulf encouraged the foundation by Friulians of the important and strategic monasteries of Sesto, Nonantola, and Monte Amiata.[43] Politics under the Carolingians remained as it had been under the Lombards: the politics of land.

The Frankish conquest made no great changes in the map of Italy. Charlemagne, had of course, only conquered the North and Centre of Italy, the Lombard kingdom and the duchy of Spoleto. Spoleto remained part of the kingdom of Italy (as it began to be called), though much of its activity was more or less fully independent. The popes held the papal state lying between these two, the old Exarchate of Ravenna and the duchy of Rome. The Carolingians, however, usually maintained *de facto* powers over all of it except the Roman hinterland, and after the end of the ninth century Ravenna became a permanent part of the kingdom. In the South, Benevento kept its independence. Duke Arichis II (758–87), Desiderius's son-in-law, declared himself *princeps*, prince, in 774, and issued seventeen laws in an addition to the Lombard law code, both acts being clear gestures of defiance to Charlemagne. Benevento kept up a legitimist Lombard tradition for three centuries more, until the Norman conquest of the late eleventh century. Charlemagne, egged on by Pope Hadrian (who had territorial claims in the South), invaded Benevento in 787. Arichis called on Byzantine help, but then died. His heir Grimoald III was a hostage in Frankish hands. In return for his liberation, Grimoald had the embarrassing task of defeating the Byzantine support army that arrived in 788, headed by his uncle Adelchis, Desiderius's son. Grimoald (787–806) recognised Frankish suzerainty, but it remained nominal. He can never be seen acting as anything other than an independent ruler; he fought several wars against the Franks, and minted his own coins.[44] From the reign of Arichis and Grimoald, in fact, there is enough documentary evidence to allow us to treat Benevento as an independent entity, and, apart from occasional Frankish interventions (particularly in 866–73), its history remained totally distinct. This was even more true of the small territories remaining to the Byzantines in southern Italy, Naples, Amalfi, and the Greek zones of Otranto and Calabria, and all these will be discussed separately in chapter 6.

The political history of the first seventy years of Carolingian Italy is quickly written. In 781 Charlemagne had his four-year-old son Pippin crowned king of Italy (781–810), and spent little time there afterwards. Pippin headed an autonomous but dependent administration under a shifting group of guardians: his cousin Adalard of Corbie at first, then the *baiuli* (tutors) Waldo of Reichenau (*c.* 783–90) and Rotchild (*c.* 800). Armies under Pippin's authority annihilated the Avars in 796 and took Chieti from Benevento in 801.[45] When Pippin died, Adalard returned to supervise his young son Bernard (812–7). In 814, however, Louis the Pious, Charlemagne's last surviving son, became sole emperor. Louis, with three sons of his own, had little interest in the rights of his nephew. In 817 Louis divided the administration of the Empire; his eldest son Lothar was given Italy with the title of emperor. Bernard, though apparently not dispossessed, was not included. He revolted against Louis, with the support of several of his father's

Frankish followers in Italy – and the support or sympathy of not a few traditionalists in the North as well. The revolt failed, and Louis had Bernard blinded; he died of his injuries.[46] In 822–4 Lothar was seen for the first time in Italy (Louis the Pious never went there). A minor like his two predecessors, he was represented by Wala, Adalard's brother.

Lothar (817–55) was the least Italian of those Carolingians who spent any time in Italy. He was there for much of the decade 831–41, but mostly because Louis the Pious had effectively banished him there. He used it principally as a political and military base for his northern adventures. Unlike Louis II his son, or even Charlemagne, Lothar did not for the most part live in cities, preferring great royal estates like Corteolona or Aureola, as did the Frankish kings in northern Europe.[47] And, again unlike his predecessor and successor, Lothar scarcely appointed a single Lombard to either ecclesiastical or secular office. His appointments do not, though, show antagonism to Lombards (one of his closest advisers, Leo, was one), merely the total subordination of Italy to his Frankish interests. When in 834 the break came with Louis, Lothar had to find estates and offices for his northern supporters, and this influx represents the largest wave of northern immigration into Italy in the whole Carolingian period. Lothar secularised a fair amount of ecclesiastical property to give them fiefs, in traditional Frankish style, in addition to the confiscated lands of Louis's men in Italy, whom Lothar expelled. Even though many of Lothar's supporters died in the plague of 836–7, at his departure from Italy after Louis died in 840 Frankish influence in Italy was at its height. Italy was, all the same, beginning to show signs of development in directions different from the rest of the Frankish Empire. The Franks who came in under Charlemagne had been there for a generation, and had begun to establish themselves. And the capitularies of Lothar's reign, particularly those of 825 and 832, were the first large-scale Italian legislation since 774 not to show the dominant influence of the laws of Francia. This was something Louis II would take up when he became emperor in Italy in 850.

The narrative of Italian politics in this period, insofar as it regards the affairs of kings, is dull and piecemeal. This is partly because of the ambiguous status of Italy, neither independent nor wholly integrated into the Frankish Empire, with absentee or youthful monarchs for much of the time. But it is principally because of the almost total dearth of native history-writing for the Carolingian period, if we except Benevento, and the episcopal histories of the Roman–Byzantine cities of Rome, Ravenna, and Naples. Between Paul the Deacon's abrupt end to his history in 744 and the beginning of Liutprand of Cremona's in 888 we have nothing but jejune fragments. The principal one is the history of Andreas of Bergamo, written as an epitome and continuation of Paul the Deacon in the 880s. It offers us a fairly detailed and well-founded picture of Louis II's last decade, and the problems of the years after his death in 875. Before this, however, it is startlingly ill-informed. Ratchis and Aistulf are known as lawgivers, with the number of their laws accurately given. Apart from this, Andreas 'cannot remember their deeds, but from what we have heard, they were both brave, and the Lombards in their time were terrorised by no one' – even Andreas's Frankish informants have forgotten Pippin III. The 773–6 wars and Bernard's revolt have become folk tales, as has Archbishop Angilbert of Milan's mediation between Louis and Lothar. Almost nothing else survives – between 833 and 863 there are no Italian events in Andreas's text whatsoever.[48] Andreas is certainly inept, but his ignorance is significant. The Frankish kings, up to Louis II (who spent his whole reign in Italy), made no real impression on the Italians as kings of their own country. Their wars in Italy, against Slavs in the east, Lombards in the South, Arabs on the coasts, are only recorded by Frankish chroniclers. The administration of Italy was omnipresent, as we shall see, but its leaders were forgotten. The only way to rule Italy properly was to live there, and only Louis II, of all the independent Carolingian rulers of Italy, did so. Only he made any real impact on the kingdom.

Underneath the colourless rule of the early Carolingians, on the other hand, the sophistication of the administrative system reached its height. Only under Lothar did the efficiency of the state begin to break down, for, except for the 830s, Lothar's rule was effectively that of an absentee monarchy. The administration was based essentially on the Lombard patterns that Charlemagne found already in 774: the public official hierarchy based on dukes and gastalds in cities, and the central administration in Pavia. These patterns were still based on landholding, the key to all post-Roman political power. The tolls, corvées, and services that the Lombard kings collected were still taken under the Carolingians and their successors, and are much better recorded, too, but still represented only a minor part of royal income and resources, except for the most important service, that of the army.[49]

The politics of landowning has already been mentioned as a problem for the Lombards, but it is in the Carolingian period that it begins to be clearly documented, and some local contrasts begin to appear in our evidence. Early medieval kings in Europe tended to have two related sets of problems in establishing their own power: that of consent, and that of control. Put crudely, a king had to get his aristocracy to agree to and help him in his own actions; but he also needed to keep some authority over the actions of his nobles in their own territories. The Carolingians in Francia (at least after Charlemagne himself) had little luck in the second of these, and even to obtain the first had to grant out much of their own property as outright or conditional gifts. In Italy it was easier. Active Lombard kingship had stabilised monarchical power at a level high enough to obtain support from the aristocracy in return for comparatively small gifts. This practice was maintained by the Carolingians. Kings seldom granted lands, and then only in small quantities. Even Lothar, when settling his supporters in Italy in 834, prudently gave them ecclesiastical land rather than his own. Our documents record outright gifts to the church more often than benefices to lay vassals ('feudal tenure'), and this certainly understates the number of benefices that there were. But 'feudal' landholding was never very significant in Italy, and, in the ninth century at least, it is clear that royal generosity in Italy, unlike France, never seriously undermined royal landowning.[50]

The effect this had on the upper classes will be described in later chapters, but one immediate result deserves discussion here. Kings who did not hand out large amounts of land were in a poor position to establish their protégés with local landed supremacy as often as they might like. It took three generations for consistent royal patronage of Franks in official positions (especially as counts) to be transformed into effective Frankish hegemony in local areas. If kings did not set up their protégés as landowners, their ability to affect power balances on the ground was somewhat limited. Kings could play with the distribution and redistribution of public offices, and did; but it was never easy, for example, to control the illegalities of a count in his county, if he was a loyal and effective supporter of the king. After about the 830s, it was not even very easy to prevent his son succeeding to his office. Carolingians coped with the problem of control in three principal ways: by direct intervention and the strengthening of the official hierarchies, particularly through legislation; by more *ad hoc* means, especially the extensive use of *missi*; and by the political use of the Church to balance the local power of the lay aristocracy.

There can be no doubt that the Carolingians regarded it as their responsibility to intervene in society more comprehensively than any other early medieval rulers. Their legislation, or 'capitularies', makes up two folio volumes of Latin text in the standard edition. Kings and emperors issued administrative decrees about a wide range of topics, which were binding, irrespective of the personal law of their subjects, Lombard, Roman, or Frankish. In 832, for example, Lothar issued two capitularies in Italy. In the first, he legislated about the provision and endowment of baptismal churches; bloodshed in church; the legal rights of Jews; contempt of court; conspiracies sealed by oaths; the oppression of the poor; the disregarding of imperial instructions; the refusal to accept good money; false coining; rules for taking evidence; and the price for writing diplomas. In the second, he instructed his *missi* to inquire about an equally wide range: monastic endowments; the organisation of mints, and local minting frauds; ancient weights and measures, usury; just judgement; anyone who had not sworn fidelity to the king; the neglect of royal property and palaces; the holders of royal benefices and fiscal land; the restoration of churches; recent depre-dations of Church property; conspiracy; and the upkeep of bridges and roads.[51] This list is a fairly representative example of the standard preoccupations of Carolingian kings in Italy. North of the Alps the picture was slightly, but not very, different. One particularly striking instance of intervention, the Carolingian attempt to preserve an entire social group of small landowners to serve in the army and participate in local courts, will be discussed in chapter 5.

How the Carolingians put such decrees into operation is a more serious problem. In Francia, they were probably promulgated orally, and how much their existence was generally known at all may be doubted. In Italy, though, we have explicit references to them in documents, and a more literate aristocratic class may have been fairly well acquainted with them. The local counts, centred on the network of Italian cities, were the men responsible for their operation. The Carolingians relied considerably on their counts, and we can see comital responsibility steadily being extended throughout the ninth century over a number of the Alpine and Appennine territories that had remained independent of city authority under the Lombards. Not wholly dependent on the counts, but also city-based, were a range of judicial officials. The most important of these were the *scabini*, usually local small landowners, whose responsibility it was to run the courts, a major instrument of Carolingian government, and in themselves a considerable financial resource.[52] But the counts exercised major political and executive responsibility, as a consequence of their position as local military leaders, and many of Lothar's 832 laws were quite likely to be themselves broken by counts or their vassals, particularly those concerning the depredation of Church property and the oppression of the poor. It is for this reason that Lothar issued parallel investigative instructions to his *missi*.

Missi, king's messengers, were not a Carolingian innovation. The Lombard kings were already sending out their representatives to check on dukes and judge major court cases. The Carolingians, however, made *missi* a basic feature of their rule. A *missus* was the organ of central government in the provinces. If he was defied by a count, the count would know that an army of reprisal was bound to follow. At least, this is how the capitularies tell us the system was supposed to work, but legal texts tend to idealise institutions. Carolingian government did not really function so neatly; it worked more as a series of *ad hoc* measures, each to counteract the effects of the one before. The 'institution of the *missi*' is a more formalised way of saying that Carolingian kings continually sent people out to correct the depredations of other people. So Charlemagne sent *baiuli* with Pippin to make sure of the just government of Italy; but we only even know of one of them, Rotchild, because of his illegalities. In about 800, for example, he expelled Abbot Ildepert from the monastery of S. Bartolomeo in Pistoia and gave it in fief to the Bavarian Nebulung, until other *missi* came and reversed his act. Wala's biography gives a dramatic account of how every level of the Italian judicial system and aristocracy conspired to prevent a widow from receiving justice from him in *c.* 822.[53] When *missi* were themselves counts, as was common, the counts they were investigating were not invariably dealt with with total disinterest. All the same, we should not use too high a standard when we judge Carolingian officials. Kings may have bemoaned the oppression of the weak, but they do not seem to have regarded it as insupportable except when the capacity of the weak to perform military service was threatened. The state did not for the most part expect great feats of honesty and justice from its servants, and within a limited framework, some *missi* served their masters as well as was necessary.

Donald Bullough in some neat documentary detective work uncovered the career of one of these, Leo, who signed charters with a characteristic formula between 801 and 841.[54] He started as a vassal in the following of the Aleman newcomer Hebroard count of the palace; in 812–4 and in the 820s he was with Adalard and Wala, the archetypal Carolingian emissaries. By this time he was often referred to as *missus*, and witnessed charters and court cases in places as far apart as Rome,

Spoleto, Pistoia, Reggio and Milan. By 823–4 he was probably count of Milan. In 837 a chronicle described him as being held 'in great esteem' (*magni loci*) by Lothar, and running some of the organisation for Lothar's cold war against his father. By 844, his son John had succeeded him as count of Milan, adding Seprio to it. Leo was a professional administrator, with forty years of service, under rather more transient leaders. One could not categorise him as part of a 'governmental system', but he and his obscurer colleagues provided the real continuity and effectiveness in Italian government. He was transparently a local man. Bullough assumed, probably correctly, that he was Lombard, though he did have Frankish kinsmen. At any rate, he was not an important landed aristocrat, unlike the major counts. Yet he was active in every sphere of Carolingian government. His career shows how much authority the Italian central government could have. Leo, with no family prestige, could do much with only the sanction of Pavia behind him. The Lombard kings had probably already used men like him; Louis II was to extend the tradition, and rely very largely on unknowns. It is significant, though, that Leo's countship was very close to Pavia. As a local public official without private lands, his powers would have been far less. The frontier countships (or 'marches'), in particular, were rarely entrusted to anyone except members of the *Reichsadel*, the imperial nobility. Only they had the private landed base and military power to maintain authority there.

The other power that the Carolingians began to exploit was that of the Church. The Lombards had never formally used the Church in government. Acting (unlike the Byzantines) in the Roman tradition, they tended to keep secular and ecclesiastical matters separate. They never rejected ecclesiastical politics altogether; we have seen them founding monasteries in political contexts, and the aristocracy did the same. Charlemagne patronised such monasteries as part of an attempt to gain acceptance of Frankish rule in Italy.[55] But Charlemagne, and still more his successors, went further than this: churchmen, particularly bishops, became an instrument of government. Frankish capitularies, too, unlike Lombard laws, dealt prominently with ecclesiastical matters. In Francia, this was normal practice, and its appearance in Italy is part of the assimilation of Italy to Frankish governmental traditions. The bishops themselves, however, were usually Lombard, except the most important ones, like Ratold of Verona under Louis the Pious and above all Angilbert II of Milan and Joseph of Ivrea under Lothar and Louis II. The importance of this Lombard predominance springs from the position of bishops in the power structures of Italian cities.[56]

As we saw in chapter 1, bishops and their churches had considerable landed power from the fifth century onwards, in some cities. The Lombard conquest at first prevented the extension of this power (except in the Roman-Byzantine cities, where it continued), but by the eighth century the bishop was the largest landowner in most of the city-territories for which we have documents. In Lucca, influential local families furnished a nearly unbroken succession of bishops from the 710s to 1023. The local power of bishops was in most places closely connected to the most important families of the area. Bishops were central to political life at all levels except that of the state. The disappearance of this exception under the Carolingians at least seems logical, and fits in not only with Frankish practice, but also the implications of the political co-operation between the Carolingians and the papacy that replaced the enmity of the Lombard period. But it countered the tendency to give all secular offices to Franks. Lombard aristocrats were increasingly excluded from the state patronage network – between 814 and 875 only two or three Lombard counts can be traced. They focused their attentions on local positions, of which the bishop was the most important. Kings had de facto powers of choosing bishops, and Lothar and Louis II often exercised them. Lothar always chose Franks, Louis usually Lombards. At other times, however, bishops were locally elected, and remained the foci of urban power structures. Franks and Alemans increasingly established themselves in different parts of Italy, and, when they were counts, began to inherit their offices and act more and more independently. But, for the most part, bishops when chosen locally were not chosen from Frankish families. It would be an error to see this as an ethnic opposition between Frank and Lombard; it is much more a sign that the Franks never made a deep impression on local society in most of Italy (see pp. 73–4). But bishops and counts by virtue of their offices were indeed in potential opposition. Both offices held large quantities of land, and, with the new Carolingian reliance on bishops, their functions began to clash. Counts often attacked episcopal property, whether out of greed or, increasingly, in self-defence. Bishops were given judicial powers and, more and more during the ninth century, legal immunities against counts. This was partly the deliberate policy of certain Carolingians, who perhaps valued the moral contribution of bishops to politics, though bishops were just as liable to oppress the weak.[57] They were, on the other hand, in non-hereditary offices; and the state also probably realised that a local balance of power was in its interests. While rivalries at a local level were balanced, the state would survive and be strong. When, however, one office (or one family) emerged as victorious in each city, as happened in very many places between *c.* 880 and *c.* 920, then the cohesion of the state was threatened.

Politics at this local level is the key to understanding Italian history, and from the ninth century it becomes possible to follow it in several places. Two examples, Brescia and Lucca, will point out some of its implications. Brescia provides a good example of the potential of having a large amount of land, particularly in the history of the Supponid family. Their first known family member was the Frank, Suppo I, count of Brescia in 817 and instrumental in putting down Bernard's revolt. Perhaps as a result, he was given Spoleto in 822, his (probable) son Mauring keeping Brescia, and briefly also becoming duke of Spoleto in 824. In these years and the decades following, the Supponids built up a landed base consisting of estates spread right across northern Italy, probably by the standard mixture of means: royal gifts and fiefs, the appropriation of comital land, acquisition, extortion. Another family member, Adelchis I, was count of Parma by the 830s, in 841 perhaps Cremona, and, once more, Brescia. This eastern Lombardy western Emilia axis remained a rough centre of Supponid interest, and when the family reached its height with the marriage of the Supponid Angilberga to Louis II, she obtained land from her husband in the same zones, as her will of 879 clearly shows.[58] Supponids henceforth were often counts of Brescia, Piacenza, and Parma. The greatest of them, Suppo II and his cousin Suppo III under Louis II, are found in other places as well: Suppo II in Parma, Asti and Turin; Suppo III (Louis's *archiminister* and *consiliarius*) in Spoleto again. They did not fully control any of these cities; they did not need to, with such a breadth of influence. In Brescia, they shared control with the bishops, and the rich monastery of S. Salvatore (later S. Giulia), Desiderius's foundation, and usually ruled by royal princesses. Bishops included the Frank Notting (844–63), another of Louis II's aides, and, earlier, the Lombard Rampert (*c.* 825–44), who built up the fame of several local churches with the help of miracles and relics, and the political backing of Archbishop Angilbert of Milan.

These institutions show a complex interweaving of links, especially through S. Salvatore, which was patronised both by bishops and counts. The dukes of Friuli, close kin to the Supponids (and to the Carolingians), can also be seen sending their daughters to the monastery; and the Supponids and the bishops of Brescia both loyally supported the German and Friulian faction in the succession disputes that broke out after Louis II's death in 875. In Brescia, we cannot trace rivalries inside the city between these forces. The reason is probably that all of them had connections across the whole of northern Italy, and operated on a wider stage than just a single city. This also explains why they refused to exploit the shifting alliances of the decades after 875. The Supponids, in particular, needed a strong state, for their landholding was extended across so much of the North that only the state could guarantee the peace that they needed to keep it all. It may not be coincidence that they disappeared as a family in the same decades of the mid-tenth century in which the Italian state broke up. Other families, though not as important as the Supponids, were similarly stretched. A complex and fragile set of landowning networks reached across most of northern Italy, in a temporary equilibrium that was both supported by the strength of the state and allowed it to be strong. Louis could trust the Supponids in a myriad of offices, because they needed him. They, in turn, did not have to base their ambitions on the territorial control of single counties, merely on the office of count, in any county. Families with interests restricted to only one county were, on the other hand, though often weaker, actually more dangerous to the inner cohesion of the kingdom.

These dangers were clearest in this period on the fringes of the Italian kingdom, the three great 'marches' of Friuli, Tuscany, and Spoleto, totalling together over a third of its land area. The term 'march' is convenient, but it is late, and makes the three look more homogeneous than they really were. Friuli and Spoleto were, of course, old Lombard units, and their rulers were generally called counts or, still, dukes, until the 880s. Tuscany was a development of the early ninth century. All three had dynasties with hereditary succession by the 840s, and *de facto* autonomy under the three families, the Unruochings, Bonifacii and Guideschi, as we now call them, though they did not. These three were each major representatives of the Frankish imperial nobility, with interests in many different areas of the Empire, but in Italy each was based exclusively on the march it controlled. There was, as a result, no structural reason why any of the families should, once established, use its local power to strengthen the Italian state. The three families used their opportunities to the full, but in different ways. The Unruochings in Friuli, with close links by marriage to the Carolingians, had a reputation for loyalty. The Bonifacii in Tuscany were co-operative until after Louis II's death, and then were principally interested in local autonomy. The Guideschi in Spoleto kept their links north of the Alps, but they ruled the most distant duchy; they were from the first chiefly concerned with their own autonomy and in the affairs of Benevento, and resisted any king who tried to control them.[59]

The building-up of this sort of power is best seen in Lucca. In 812–3 the Bavarian Boniface I appeared as count. Unlike his predecessors, he seemed to control most of the countships of the Arno valley. His son Boniface II succeeded him in this, and in 828 is described as in charge of the defence of Corsica. He took a fleet out against the Arabs, and actually raided Africa.[60] Sea-defence had been the responsibility of the counts of Lucca since the 770s, and with the increase in Arab attacks, the consolidation of comital authority in Tuscany was a rational response. Lucchese documentation shows us the count accumulating powers at the local level too. The bishop of Lucca, for at least a century the dominant figure in the city, lost control of the urban notariate in the 810s, and a succession of obscurer bishops followed (including two Franks) until the 850s, with the accession of Bishop Jeremias, from an important local family, chosen through Louis II's influence. The counts of Lucca could not directly control the bishops, for the latter had too large a landed base and network of local connections, but they limited episcopal authority to ecclesiastical affairs. If bishops of Lucca gained greater influence, it was not in Lucca, but as king's *missi* on a national level, as when Bishop Gherard I led an army into Calabria for Louis II in 870.

In 833 Boniface II came out in support of Louis the Pious and was dispossessed by Lothar. He retired to his lands in southern France. Even the most involved Italo–Frankish magnates still held property elsewhere. When, however, Everard of Friuli divided his lands (stretching from Belgium to the Veneto) between his heirs in 864, he explicitly instructed them to redivide it if civil wars caused the loss of any of it. European-scale landholding was only secure as long as the unitary Empire lasted, and after 843 the Empire was divided. By the time peace returned, Boniface was dead; but his son Adalbert I (846–86) became ruler of what was by now sometimes called the march of Tuscany, a conglomeration of the northern counties of the region, and his power was more or less viceregal. Court hearings moved from the king's court to Adalbert's own in the late 840s. Few secular powers outside his control flourished anywhere in his territories. After 875, when Louis II was succeeded by civil wars, Adalbert and his son Adalbert II (886–

915) ruled what became in effect an independent state – Adalbert II did not even bother to take sides in many of these wars, and regnal years began to disappear from his charters. Adalbert II's power was certainly based on the appropriation of the Tuscan fisc to his own family, though we cannot know when this occurred. It was not, however, just the private power of a large landowner; Adalbert kept control of the public machinery of the state, too. His personal position was strong enough for us to say that the independence of Tuscany under his rule is not a demonstration of the weakness of the state, merely its continuation on a smaller scale. As we shall see (see pp. 184–5), Tuscany's coherence actually outlasted that of the Italian state itself. But Adalbert and his successors ruled in a fairly large and homogeneous geographical area, in which the Carolingian state network could function for him as well as it did for kings. In smaller counties, or in mountainous areas like Spoleto, the establishment of similar independence led to total internal collapse, as we shall see in the last two chapters.

In 844 Louis II was sent to Italy by Lothar, and in 850 (as emperor) he began to rule without his father's control. He never left Italy thereafter, even after Lothar's death in 855, and, though emperor, had no influence or interest in northern Europe. He was, however, the first and last Carolingian to take up the opportunity to rule Italy as the Lombard kings had. The next king to try, Hugh (926–47), found it already too late. Louis enjoyed a general acceptance by his aristocracy of the power and authority he wielded, except perhaps in Spoleto. The framework for such power, the interlace of central authority, official hierarchy, and urban rivalry, we have just examined. Louis found that it had suffered from some decades of neglect, but it was still capable of acting as the basis for the power of an active and determined king, as Louis was. Louis established his control over the inner structures of the kingdom, and then, following the example of the last Lombard kings, attempted to expand his authority, intervening in the states of the South.[61]

In the late 840s Louis instructed his bishops to inquire in their dioceses about ecclesiastical and secular abuses. In 850, in an episcopal synod and two capitularies, he catalogued what they had found and enacted remedies. The synod of Pavia was his first major ceremonial occasion. Louis, Angilbert II of Milan, Theodemar patriarch of Aquileia, and the arch-chaplain Joseph bishop of Ivrea presided. But it is the capitularies that are the most striking feature of the year; they deal almost exclusively with problems of violence, neglect, and oppression.

In Capitulary 213, thieves attack pilgrims and merchants; wicked men attack villas and travellers; some property-owners conspire with them. The lay and ecclesiastical powerful billet themselves on the populace, confiscate their horses, and use their pastures; royal palaces lie in squalor, and public buildings must be restored, to be fitting abodes for foreign embassies (an interesting echo of Cassiodorus's *Variae* here – see p. 83); the Ticino bridge at Pavia needs rebuilding; *missi* are exacting too many gifts and services from the people.[62] This capitulary is the classic statement of the dismal state of Italy after Carolingian neglect, and we need not doubt that many of these problems were endemic, particularly, as we have seen, oppressions by the powerful. Louis almost openly admits defeat here: if horses are taken, they must at least be paid for at the just price; *missi* can carry on their exactions, as long as they are traditional ones. But the Pavia bridge is rebuilt; and the thieves do not appear in later capitularies. The unusually detailed list of illegalities seems to be a sign of the seriousness of Louis's intentions, and his remedies look for the most part like effective measures. What we can see of Louis's activities shows that he established a considerable level of political control. In 853 Jeremias bishop of Lucca, with the help of two recent imperial diplomas, re-established his rights over lands leased to laymen, apparently under pressure, by his predecessor. In 860 several imperial *missi* investigated and reversed the illegal takeover of imperial land by the count of Camerino, Hildepert.[63] And Louis himself began to organise a personal entourage of courtiers and administrators with which he ruled Italy directly. He used the great magnates of Lothar's reign, Joseph of Ivrea, Angilbert of Milan, Notting of Brescia, and Everard of Friuli, but after their deaths preferred to rely on relative unknowns, his personal chaplains, *consiliarii*, and vassals; almost the only magnates were Suppo II and Suppo III, his wife's kin. Under Louis, the bureaucratisation of the Pavia government even lessened somewhat. The great offices of arch-chaplain and arch-chancellor temporarily disappeared. Louis, with Angilberga as *consors regni*, royal consort, became the heads of the government themselves, and much of it moved around the kingdom with them, from city to city.

Louis may from this seem to have set himself against the influence of great lords, but he almost certainly did not. Sons continued to succeed their fathers in counties. Louis simply tried to control their activities a little more tightly, and used them less in the central government. He probably used the Church to counter some of them, and we find him appointing a whole range of (usually Lombard) bishops, largely from his own entourage, in Adalbert's Tuscany.[64] But his political basis, the fisc, was not greatly threatened by the nobility, and he seems to have left loyal aristocrats alone. He was possibly even less generous than his predecessors with royal land; only Suppo III out of all the laity is recorded as receiving an outright gift of land; and the only recipients of large gifts were Angilberga and the two royal monasteries of S. Salvatore di Brescia and S. Clemente di Casauria.[65] Louis satisfied his aristocracy in a different way: by military adventure.

In 866 Louis issued a capitulary calling people up for a campaign in Benevento, with detailed provisions for military obligation, and a list of the *missi* ordered to stay at home and organise defence and the local call-up in twelve specified areas of the kingdom.[66] Almost the whole aristocracy seem to have accompanied him. Louis had intervened in the South before: he visited Rome several times, and he led armies in 846 and 848 against the Arabs; in 848 he also helped to end the civil war in Benevento, which from then on was split between the principalities of Benevento and Salerno (with Capua as a nearly-independent third force). In 866 he came south to remove the Arabs under Sawdān (or 'the Sultan') from Bari, where they had been since 847. Exactly what was happening in the political chaos of southern Italy in this period will be discussed in chapter 6; the three Lombard states were only part of a political patchwork that included the now independent states of Naples, Amalfi, and Gaeta, renewed Byzantine influence from Calabria, the intervention of Rome and Spoleto from the Frankish orbit, and of course the Arabs. The object of Louis's expedition was to remove the latter, but it can scarcely be doubted that he intended to extend his power into the fragmented states of the South, using the force of the largest Italian army of the century. The southern states carefully welcomed him. Even the Byzantines co-operated, as they felt menaced too—the Arabs had by the 860s conquered most of Sicily. Unfortunately for Louis, Bari took nearly five years to fall, and then only to a Byzantine/Slav naval blockade in 871. Louis took the credit, at least in Frankish eyes. He did not, however, leave the South. Louis's presence there achieved the near-impossible: an alliance against him of the Beneventans, Salernitans, Neapolitans and Spoletans; later sources include Sawdān as well. In August 871 he was taken prisoner by Adelchis of Benevento while staying in the city and held for a month, only being released in return for an oath not to seek revenge.

It is hard for us to see the full force of the Benevento imprisonment, but Louis felt it wrecked his prestige. He had to have himself recrowned emperor to counteract it. And he could not, now, counteract the hostility of the southern states. Though he returned to the South in 872–3, his position there was lost. The Lombard princes went over to the Byzantines, who rewarded them by conquering nearly half their territories in the next decade, including the whole of Apulia; the Byzantines were certainly in the end the real beneficiaries of Louis's campaigns. The most Louis had to show was his power to remove Lambert of Spoleto for his part in the 871 débâcle and to replace him by Suppo III. Lambert returned in 876, after Louis's death. The last vestiges of Louis's success had by then disappeared.

Our sources are apocalyptic about Louis's last years. Andreas tells us that the wine bubbled in the barrels in the 871 harvest, to be followed in 872–3 by floods, drought, and locust plagues, and in 875 a comet, a clear symbol of the 'great tribulation' that followed Louis's death without sons, before his fiftieth year, in August 875.[67] But we cannot show that Louis's internal position in the North was weakened, except for the curious event when a group of nobles petitioned him that he should divorce his wife in favour, it seems, of the daughter of the count of Siena.[68] Louis was demoralised, though. And at his death the fatal weakness of his rule, the absence of a male heir, became clear. His two uncles, in France and Germany, had equal claims. The resultant succession dispute lasted on and off for three decades, and the state fell with it. Why this was we will see in chapter 7, but it cannot be understood merely in political terms. It was the result of structural and conjunctural changes at much deeper levels of Italian society and economy.

3. Romans, Lombards, Franks and Byzantines

THE Ostrogoths vanished without a trace; not so their successors. By 900, Italy was a complex ethnic mixture. The bulk of the population was Roman in origin, though Romans seldom appear as such in our sources. Alongside them we find the Lombards, at all levels of society, but particularly among the aristocracy; and also on the aristocratic level, newer immigrants–Franks and Alemans, and a few Burgundians and Bavarians. In the parts of Italy the Lombards never conquered we find newcomers too, this time from the eastern Mediterranean. Byzantine Italy, however, was the western fringe of an Empire that had unbroken links with its Roman past, and in the seventh – eighth-century Exarchate it is seldom easy to tell indigenous Romans from immigrants. Only in the tenth – eleventh-century Byzantine provinces of the South were the Greeks ethnically distinct, as we shall see in a later chapter (pp. 156–f.).

The mixture of peoples is the best context in which to deal with two problems about continuity in the social history of Italy. The first problem is that of the break in the sixth century: of how far the Lombard occupation destroyed the social structure of Italy, pressing the bulk of the Romans down into the lowest ranks of the peasantry, and forming a *tabula rasa* on which history, as it were, began afresh. The second question, inextricably related to the first, is that of the continuity of the patterns and personnel of the aristocracy throughout all the political changes in Italy. Both these problems have often been posed as being momentous shifts in Italian society. These do not seem to me to have occurred. All through the early medieval period, the basic social structures of Italy and the patterns of its aristocracy were so firmly related to the economy that intrusions of new peoples did not make much difference to them.

The Lombard invasion and the wars that followed, between 568 and 605, were certainly disastrous for Italy. The Italians, as we have seen, had hardly recovered from the Gothic wars before they were plunged into an experience just as violent and even more chaotic. Sixth-century observers did not feel they had to prove that the Lombards were barbaric and destructive, a *gens nefandissima*, a most abominable race, in

Gregory the Great's words; it was self-evident. A few cities in vulnerable places, like Orvieto and Civita Castellana along the Tiber, moved site onto the tops of hills to escape attack. In the bulk of the cities in what were to become the duchies of Spoleto and Benevento, the episcopate totally disappeared for at least two centuries. The early years of the Lombard invasion were years of plague and famine as well; these occurred often, alongside other natural disasters, floods, and even dragons, until the late 590s. Italy was, it seems, visited by all four horsemen at once.[1] The violent impact of the Lombards comes across to us very clearly in the works of Gregory of Tours, Marius of Avenches, and Gregory the Great, who lived in or had contact with territories repeatedly attacked by the Lombards. The fate of the luckless inhabitants of the parts of Italy the Lombards actually controlled was assumed to be even more terrible. The Romans in Lombard Italy virtually disappear from history, so much so that it could be seriously argued in the nineteenth century that every one of them was reduced to slavery. Even in the eighth century, when our documentation begins, we find scarcely a reference to them: three or four citations in the Lombard laws, two or three in charters. We tend to refer to all inhabitants of Lombard Italy as 'Lombards'; our evidence certainly allows us to. But we know that the great mass of the Italians must have been ethnically Roman. Assuming (on weak evidence) that there were far more Lombards than there had been Ostrogoths, say about 200,000, the Lombards cannot have made up more than 5–8 per cent of the population of the parts of Italy they occupied, and the percentage may have been less.

The historiography on the fate of the Romans is immense, and based on almost no evidence at all. Between the death of Alboin and the reign of Agilulf, the information that we have from contemporaries is minimal. Lombard Italy was virtually a closed country, even though many of its early dukes were prepared to negotiate with the Byzantines. The only history that was being written in early Lombard Italy was that by Secundus of Non, who seems to have been in a fairly isolated part of the Trentino, in the Alps, throughout the early years of the Lombard invasion; not until Agilulf's reign did he become part of the royal court, with greater access to reliable information. Secundus's *historiola*, or little history, does not survive, though it was used by Paul the Deacon in his *Lombard History* of the 790s. Paul is our only detailed source, but he was writing two centuries after the events of the Lombard invasion, and using material that, except for Secundus, is not particularly reliable for the internal history of late sixth-century Lombard Italy–hostile witnesses like Gregory of Tours and Gregory the Great, and some oral material about Alboin and Authari. Apart from what comes from Paul, there is no internal contemporary written evidence. Our only other material is on the one hand cemetery archaeology; on the other, the extrapolation backwards from the society shown in eighth-century texts. There are, in addition, some useful indications of conflicting attitudes to the Lombards in Roman-Byzantine Italy described by Gregory the Great in Rome.

Two passages from Paul are traditionally regarded as the key texts.

This man [King Cleph] killed many powerful men of the Romans with the sword, and expelled others [or: the others] from Italy . . . . [After his death,] in these days many Roman nobles were killed through greed. The rest were divided *per hospites* and were made tributary, so that they paid a third part of their produce to the Lombards.

The second passage is much shorter, and comes in the middle of an encomium on the happiness of Italy under Authari: 'But the oppressed people were divided between the Lombards as *hospites*'.[2] These texts are not verbally obscure: the *hospites* are certainly linked in some way with *hospitalitas*, the custom by which tribes like the Ostrogoths and Burgundians took a share of the land (either a third or two-thirds) for the upkeep of their armies. They are, however, cryptic for those who wish to take them as an accurate sociological guide. Does 'others' (*alii*) in the first text mean that all surviving Roman powerful men were expelled, or only some of them? Does 'the rest' (*reliqui*) mean other nobles, or the whole population? There are no answers here. Even if these passages are genuinely taken from Secundus, which is uncertain, and even if Secundus, secure in his remote mountain valley, actually knew much about the course of the Lombard settlement, which is equally uncertain, they are still not texts which can tell us in adequate detail what happened to the Romans; in particular, according to what protocols (if any) the Lombards organised their settlement, and how far the Roman landowning classes survived. The tendency that historians have had to take the most pessimistic line possible of the impact of the Lombards, can be countered by the more indirect evidence at our disposal.

Gregory the Great, as we have seen, regarded the Lombards as an almost abstract force of pure destruction (at least until he built up diplomatic links with the Catholics in Agilulf's court). But there are signs that not all his co-citizens thought so. In 592 the citizens of Sovana in southern Tuscany seem to have promised to surrender peacefully to Ariulf of Spoleto. In 595, Gregory complained that in Corsica the exactions of judges and tax collectors were so unreasonable that landowners were trying to flee to the Lombards. In 599 something similar seemed to be happening in Naples: 'the slaves of various nobles, the clerics of many churches, the monks of several monasteries, the men of many judges have surrendered themselves to the enemy'. The peasants of Otranto in Apulia were likely to do the same unless the local tribunes stopped oppressing them.[3] These, of course, reflect different responses. Peasants on the edge of survival were unlikely to be put off by the reputation the Lombards may have had for mistreating landowners. But the citizens of Sovana are more likely to have been trying to avoid social upheaval than court it; and the landowners of Corsica cannot have thought that the Lombards were likely to deprive them of all their property and their lives. These reactions can certainly be matched by other evidence of heroic and long-drawn-out defence by cities against Lombard attacks, and of occasional risings against Lombard rule. The Roman response to the Lombards was inconsistent; but as such, it is important. It is that of a civilian population trying to avoid trouble in a long and chaotic war. We can find similar patterns of resistance and surrender in the Gothic wars of the 540s or the Arab conquest of Syria in the 630s. The Lombards were violent and barbaric, but at least they did not tax. Being conquered by them was, to many, less serious than being fought over by them. Some Lombard leaders were, as we have seen, prepared to make individual treaties with the Byzantines and fight for them. This spirit of compromise probably extended at least some of the time to the Roman population of Italy as well. At the very least, we cannot assume that the Lombards pursued a systematic policy of the expropriation of the landowning classes, and the less systematic practice of the slaughter and enslavement of the peasantry.

Our other evidence is usually later, but it all points in one direction, that of a rapid cultural fusion between Lombard and Roman. This, as we shall see, must have involved a complex social mixture, impossible if the Lombard occupation was as radical as is often thought. It used to be said that the Lombards settled in free warrior groups away from the Roman population, and this seemed to be confirmed by archaeological finds.[4] Most 'Lombard' archaeology consists of the excavation of burials with sixth–seventh-century Lombard metalwork, which is similar to that found in early sixth-century Pannonia, where the Lombards were before 568. A set of burials (into the hundreds in some of the largest sites, such as Nocera Umbra in Umbria or Castel Trosino near Ascoli Piceno) with Lombard metalwork in most graves might well look like the cemetery for a single Lombard community. On the other hand, except in the very earliest cemetery sites in the North, a high percentage of the pottery found in such graves is much more closely related in form and fabric to late Roman coarsewares. Either it was made by the Romans, or by Lombards copying Romans: some kind of cultural mix is clear. And, indeed, a man or woman with a Lombard-style brooch is no more necessarily a Lombard than a family in Bradford with a Toyota is Japanese; artefacts are no secure guide to ethnicity.[5] A mixture of artefacts, on the other hand, is a guide to cultural contact. In one of the few full excavations of a Lombard-period settlement site, the border fortification of Invillino in the Friulian Alps, the excavators did find such a mixture, with a great predominance of 'Roman' artefacts, despite the military nature of the site. Social links between Lombards and Romans can also be assumed when 'Lombard' cemeteries are found in or just outside cities – examples are Fiesole, Brescia and Cividale.[6] The Lombards seem to have lost their language early, perhaps before 700. The loanwords they have left in Italian are mostly for notably humble (usually agricultural) objects: *greppia*, 'manger', *melma*, 'mire', *bica*, 'sheaf', *schifo*, 'boat', *gualdo*, 'wood'. By Paul's time they had also abandoned their former styles of hair and dress, which he could only recover from the wall paintings in the Palace of Monza: long hair parted in the middle, linen clothing like the Anglo-Saxons wear, with multi-coloured stripes. Instead, they adopted Roman customs of dress, leggings and trousers.[7] These developments show Roman cultural influence on the Lombards, and could not have happened if the Lombards had no social links with the Romans except as landlords with tenants, or soldiers with dependent civilians. They seem to entail a fairly broad-based fusion.

   This fusion is still more apparent in our eighth-century texts. Naming, for example, shows a completely unsystematic mixture of Lombard and Roman forms. One of our very earliest charters, for Fortonato, a Lucchese landowner in the 710s, a cleric with an obvious Roman name, also lists his five sons: Benetato is a Roman name, but Bonuald, Roduald, Raduald, and Baronte are obvious Lombard ones. Other families show a similar mixture. In extreme cases, Lombard and

Roman elements are even found in the same name, as with Daviprand in Lucca in 774, or Paulipert in Charlemagne's entourage in 788. Giovanni Tabacco showed that Lombard names have a predominance of about two to one in documents of the Lombard kingdom among landowners and soldiers; but his conclusion, that ethnic Lombards totally dominated this class, is rather undermined by the fact that a majority of slaves, too, have Lombard names.[8] The Lombards cannot have become the whole population; we must conclude that the cultural influence of their rules about naming had come to pervade Roman society as well, from top to bottom.

The mixture between Roman and Lombard can be seen clearly in the field of law. Roman law continued to exist. Lombard law seldom mentioned it, but the kings were only legislating for their Lombard subjects; Liutprand's references to it show that it survived on terms of equality. The Lombard law of persons began in the eighth century to be influenced by Roman law, but only marginally (see pp. 43-4 above). On the other hand, the few Romans who referred to themselves as such in the eighth century had all adopted customs that only properly belong to Lombard law, as with Felex of Treviso, who gave property to his daughter in 780, accepting back 'a handkerchief, as *launigild*, according to Roman law'. *Launigild* was a totally Lombard concept meaning the exchange of gifts, or the countergift that made a gift valid by Lombard law.[9] This is not very surprising. Written Roman law for the inhabitants of Lombard Italy must have been fossilised after 568, for the kings only legislated for the Lombards, and Roman legislation would have been inadequate to deal with the radically new situation of the Lombard state. The only solution was to borrow, and Lombard law would have come most readily to hand. Such borrowing must have been common. We cannot, in fact, distinguish between a Lombard and a Roman legal tradition in the actions of Italians at any social level in our sources.

This influence was not all one way, however. The laws governing personal relationships in the eighth century seem to have had a decisive Lombard stamp; the law of property, though, remained very firmly Roman. Gianpiero Bognetti at times appeared to claim that the Lombard concept of property, direct possession (*gewere*), usually by a collective group (*fara*–see below, p. 116), so completely overran Roman property-owning that any Roman absentee landowner would have been automatically dispossessed by Lombard law. This does not really make sense. Ernst Levy showed that late Roman property law was already so like the concept of *gewere* that the latter may even have been formed under its influence. As early as Rothari's code, landowning is wholly private and based, it seems, on Roman legal norms. In our eighth- and ninth-century evidence, the forms of property-owning are, with very rare exceptions, totally Roman. The best-documented forms of tenure, outright ownership and leasehold, are closely related to late Roman legal concepts, and nearly identical to those in contemporary Ravenna, where Lombard influence cannot be expected.[10] The survival of Roman concepts of possession makes more sense if some of the Roman possessors survived too.

Other aspects of Roman influence on the Lombards we have already seen: the Lombard notion of the state and its administrative role, for example, and the distinction between public and private. And, partially as a result of the survival of the Roman administrative tradition, the Lombard aristocracy moved into the cities and followed the patterns of the urban aristocracy of the Empire. We can see them doing this right from the earliest years: by 574, a large number of Roman cities had Lombard dukes; in 585, when the Franks invaded Italy, the cities were the natural strongholds for the Lombards. As we have seen, we have archaeological evidence for Lombards in cities, as well. This urban occupation may have been entirely military at the beginning. But already in Cunipert's reign, when Paul at last gives us some fairly detailed narrative, ordinary Lombard aristocrats without any obvious official status are citizens of Brescia, and probably Pavia, Vicenza and several other cities too.[11] The material attraction of city-dwelling and its economic consequences will be discussed in the next chapter; but this would be inconceivable without the survival of Roman citizens and the ideology of citizenship that they perpetuated. In the cities, too, it is impossible to tell Lombards and Romans apart by the eighth century.

The Lombard invasion of Italy was obviously violent, but this was partly precisely because it was disorganised. Every region must have had a different experience of it. The Lombard settlement varied in intensity: most heavily around Milan and Pavia, Brescia and Verona, and in Friuli; less heavily in western Emilia and around Lucca; hardly at all further south. Regional distinctions that are not directly related to the Lombards begin to appear as well. In our charter material, from 700 onwards, every zone of Italy has its own local customs and peculiarities, in social hierarchy, legal formulae, weights and measures. This may be the separate development of different localities after 568, or, quite probably, the first clear evidence of deep local differences that the Romans had never eradicated. But it shows that the systematic reorganisation of society by the Lombards is unlikely. Most of the peasantry, the bulk of society, was and remained Roman – an isolated Pistoiese charter of 767 even refers to tenants as *romani*. But the Lombards had their own slaves, half-free and small freemen, as Rothari's edict shows, and these became absorbed into the great mass of the Roman lower classes, as we shall see (pp. 100ff.). And Roman influence on the society of the eighth century implies the survival of a significant proportion of the Roman landowning classes, from owner-cultivators to large absentee city-living landlords. A clear example of the latter is the Pavese noble Senator son of Albinus, who founded a monastery in Pavia in 714 with land partly given him by the king.[12]

The Lombard settlement did not, therefore, produce a completely radical change in social structure. Doubtless many Roman landowners were dispossessed through greed, as Paul says, but enough of them must have survived to ensure the predominance of the Roman ideology of property ownership in later centuries, as well as the Roman elements in royal government discussed in the preceding chapter. The assumed equality between Lombard and Roman law in Liutprand shows that there was no necessary difference of status between Lombards and Romans, even though we need not doubt that most Romans were dependent peasants and a far higher proportion of Lombards were not. The Lombards may even, in some places, have operated the *hospitalitas* system that Paul refers to, though this is not something we can check. There were not enough of them, however, to destroy the social hierarchies of Italy, and their swift fusion with the Romans must show that they did not. When the Franks came, Lombards and Romans were much more similar to each other than either were to the new northern invaders.

The feature of Lombard society that was, and remained, totally Lombard was the ideology of the warrior people and its close links with free and aristocratic status. Tabacco has shown that in Liutprand's laws, 'soldier' (*exercitalis*, or its latinised Lombard equivalent *arimannus*) is thought of as equivalent to 'property owner' and to 'free man' (*liber homo*). This did not mean that all three were exact synonyms. There were already Lombard freemen in the eighth century who had lost their property, or never had any (see pp. 107ff.), and they were not always required to do army service (see p. 137). Not all property owners were necessarily Lombard, either. But Tabacco maintains that the great bulk of them must have been for the kings to assume (as they consistently did, even in the Carolingian period) that 'Lombard' and 'free armed property owner' meant more or less the same thing. The state, the *regnum Langobardorum*, though Roman in all its contours, was just what it said: for Lombards only.

There is no evidence of a significant juridical and military assimilation of a free Roman population on the part of the Lombards. Therefore the overturning of the conditions of property-owners at the end of the 6th century was more vast and radical than even the annihilation of the Roman aristocracy had made one suppose.[13]

At this level, the Lombard state certainly won a total ideological victory; Romans at all levels had become socially marginal. But Tabacco must be wrong to see this as showing the complete supersession of the Roman aristocracy, still less the Roman property-owning peasantry. Landownership was in the eighth century virtually the only criterion for status. But the forms that status takes are almost totally dependent on the structure and ideology of the state, in a period when the state is strong and influential. A Roman landowner would not have found it very profitable to have behaved like Boethius. Status and patronage depended on being able to fight, and probably to profess Lombard law. People could change their law fairly easily in the early Middle Ages – hence, doubtless, the disappearance of the Ostrogoths. Hence, also, the swift final victory of a modified Roman law over Lombard law in little more than two generations in the twelfth century. In sixth–seventh-century Gaul, the Francicisation of the Roman aristocracy is well known and well documented: first in customs (military service, and the increasing violence of manners that Gregory of Tours laments), then in naming; finally in law. By the eighth century, only Franks remained north of the Loire. The peaceful transformation of the aristocracy in Byzantine Italy is equally clear, as we shall see. It is easier for a dominant ideology to transform the whole shape of aristocratic society and values than Tabacco allows. By contrast, the economic realities of landowning change less easily. By Aistulf's reign, the criterion for army service had, it appears, become simply the possession of property, regardless of ethnicity.[14] And, even though the Lombard imagery of the free armed warrior persisted, in the Carolingian period military service began more and more to exclude the poor, as we shall see (see pp. 137 ff).

THE Frankish occupation after 774 did not alter this Lombard predominance, though it did bring the Lombards and Romans closer together as the indigenous population of Italy, the Italians. A formulary of the eleventh century expresses the similarity of Lombard and Roman legal practice by contrast with the northern invaders. In the ritual of the sale of land, for example, Lombards and Romans must hand over a charter of sale containing certain formulae expressing legal obligation, in return for the price. Frankish, Visigothic, Aleman, Bavarian and Burgundian vendors must additionally 'place the charter on the ground, and on the charter throw a knife [except for Bavarians or Burgundians], a notched stick, a glove, a sod of earth, the branch of a tree, and an ink-stand'. The formulary includes some fairly late developments, but we can see Franks and Alemans performing these rituals in ninth-century charters.[15] About two-thirds of these new arrivals were Franks, about a third Alemans (particularly in Verona); the other groupings were rather smaller in numbers. We have already seen the Carolingians appointing Franks to official posts in the secular hierarchy. Counts and most *missi* were fairly consistently Frankish until the mid-tenth century in northern Italy, though Lombards soon reappeared in southern Tuscany and Spoleto, where the Franks never settled. Frankish settlement by a class of small aristocrats and soldiers is well documented in the strip of land at the bottom of the major Alpine passes between Pavia and Verona, and in some strategic zones elsewhere (Asti, Piacenza, to a lesser extent Lucca), mostly as a rural aristocracy. Only occasionally do we find them in cities, except in their official capacities. It is doubtless partly for this reason that the Franks, with the exception of the greatest families, did not have sufficient impact on localities to become part of the group of families from whose ranks bishops were elected. Bishops, when not chosen by kings, tended to be Lombard.

The Lombards (and the Romans) greatly outnumbered the Franks (and the Alemans) inside the landowning classes – at lower levels, there were probably no Franks at all. But, as we have just seen, the Lombards found lack of numbers no handicap in becoming the dominant social group two centuries earlier. The Carolingians, however, as we saw in the last chapter, did not make the state Frankish – only its personnel, particularly in local government and at the heads of armies. Lombards were not dispossessed of their lands, unless they revolted. From as early as the 780s, they appear as vassals in King Pippin's entourage. They were no longer the major recipients of royal patronage, and this probably weakened their positions, especially under Lothar; but from Louis II onwards, Lombards begin to benefit again from the interest of the king. The Aldobrandeschi, for example, were a Lombard family from Lucca. In the years after 800 they began to build up property in southern Tuscany by acquisition and lease, establishing a strong local power base far from other rivals in the very years when royal patronage of Lombard aristocrats was at its nadir. The family was thus excellently placed when Louis wanted to counterbalance the power of Adalbert I in northern Tuscany: Jeremias became bishop of Lucca, his brother Eriprand an imperial *missus*, and the third brother, Ildebrand, a count. Jeremias gave or leased all the episcopal property in southern Tuscany to his brothers, allowing them to establish immense family power there that lasted for six centuries.[16] Nor were the Aldobrandeschi an isolated case. Many of the 'new' nobility of tenth-century Tuscany can be traced back to the Lombard families of the eighth century, thanks to the exceptional documentation of early medieval Lucca. The same was for the most part true of the Lombard aristocrats of the tenth-century North. The assumptions of the upper classes remained Lombard, particularly those surrounding the position of the *arimanni*, the free warrior people, even though this stratum probably now included Franks as well. The powerful Frankish comital families found themselves fitting into a framework that was still essentially unchanged from the time of the Lombard kings. The focus for social activity remained the city, unlike north of the Alps, and Carolingian administrative reforms even strengthened this. Where Franks did not become urban-dwelling families, as they mostly did not, they became socially marginal. Because the Carolingians did not attempt to alter the ideological foundations and material basis of the state, Lombard aristocratic families did not have to become Frankish to survive, as their Roman predecessors (and perhaps ancestors) had done. Even if they had had to, some of the basic elements in the structure of society, like the tendency for aristocrats to live in cities, would have persisted.

THE social development of Byzantine Italy confirms some of the points made for the Lombards and the Franks. The major portions of Italy that the Lombards never fully conquered were the Exarchate of Ravenna (more properly, the Exarchate and Pentapolis) and the duchy of Rome. Venice, Istria and Naples remained unoccupied as well, as did the more Greek areas of the South, which will be discussed in chapter 6. The exarch was the civil and military governor of Italy from the late sixth century, sent out from Constantinople and changed fairly frequently. Italy was far from the central provinces of the Empire, and local rulers, allowed too much time to establish themselves, might revolt – as indeed happened in 619 and 651. The Romans and Ravennati themselves were not quiescent subjects, either, and there were serious local disturbances over ten times between 600 and the conquest of the Exarchate by Aistulf in 751.[17]

The social structure of the best-documented Byzantine areas, Ravenna, Rome and Naples, was the direct successor of that of late Rome, with no violent break such as that of the Lombard settlement elsewhere in Italy. By 700, however, it had altered out of all recognition – indeed resembled, rather, that of the Lombard state itself. In one important respect, such a resemblance was superficial. The state still taxed in the Exarchate, and thereby maintained a complex administration and an army (though after the mid-seventh century the pay that the army in Italy received was probably low by comparison with its landed property). These taxes were high, at least at the beginning. The Sicilian estates of the church of Ravenna under Archbishop Maurus (642–73) yielded 50,000 *modia* of corn (and much other rent in kind), and 31,000 gold *solidi*. Of this last, a full 15,000 was due in tax.[18] It is likely, on the other hand, that less socially responsible landowners were (as in the fifth century) capable of tax-evasion, particularly soldiers. And Byzantine Italy was not like the late Empire in supporting an administrative-military hierarchy that was separate from the civil aristocracy. The structure of the state had simplified, and the ruling élite had become entirely military. This process had begun in the Ostrogothic period, as we saw in chapter 1; against the pressure of the Lombard invasions, it accelerated. The leaders of the *numeri*, or army units, became the dominant figures of society. Senators moved south into Sicily, where they could still be found in the seventh century, and east to Constantinople. By the end of the sixth century, the *curia*, the city council, no longer existed in any of the Byzantine cities of the North, except perhaps in Ravenna. Only in Naples, where there was no serious Lombard threat until the 590s, did the militarisation of society come rather later. Gregory the Great describes civilian factions in the city associated with and opposed to bishops, in traditional late Roman style.[19] Naples was a prosperous city, and it remained more civilian. Soldiers were in a minority, and the *curia* even survived until the tenth century, though already by the eighth century the military commander, the consul (or duke), was unchallenged ruler in Naples too.

As the leaders of Byzantine society became more and more usually soldiers, the civilian aristocracy as a whole lost status. Although it continued to exist, for the civil-military distinction was carefully maintained, its most important members found their way into the army. Conversely, soldiers of all military ranks, with their links with the rich, taxation-based, patronage network of the administration – and, as we shall see, the Church – found it easy to buy, marry, lease, or extort their way into landownership. By 700, most of the great lay landowners were military.

The army of the late sixth century came largely from the East, and its social origin is visible in our texts. By 591, Tzita, of the *numerus* of the Perso-Armenians, was already married into the landowning classes (his father-in-law Felix was *defensor* of the church of Ravenna).[20] Fashions of naming, as in Lombard Italy, followed such an influx. In the seventh century, nearly half the names recorded in Ravennate documents are of eastern origin. The complex rules of naming of the Roman Empire vanished. Apart from these eastern names (and a few surviving Gothic ones), men were simply called Stephen or John, or Sergius, the names of saints. It becomes as difficult to trace families through the seventh century as it is in Lombard Italy, although the ancestors of any of the tribunes or judges called John in eighth-century Ravenna could have been sixth-century Ravennate aristocrats, the Melminii or the Pompilii. This development in naming is certainly related in some way to the militarisation of the social hierarchy, for complex naming had never been so necessary in the army. It does not, however, show vast eastern immigration. Neither seventh-century eastern names nor seventh – eighth-century saints' names necessarily denote new families, though there certainly were some. There can never have been very many easterners in Italy; certainly they were a far smaller proportion of the population than even the Lombards in Lombard Italy. In the seventh century, in fact, though the number of eastern names was still high, immigration had already ceased. The Byzantines needed all the soldiers they could get for the Persian and Arab wars. Military recruitment in Italy became local again: new *numeri* were based on Italian cities, Rimini, or Fermo, or Nepi. But the eastern military influx had already had its effect. The whole terminology of social organisation had become militarised: inhabitants of Comacchio, on the frontier, were referred to – even by the Lombards – as *milites*, 'soldiers'; the whole citizen body of Trieste is referred to as a *numerus* in the Rižana court case of 804.

This militarisation of social imagery has remarkable parallels with Lombard Italy, where local rulers were dukes, and ordinary freemen had military titles such as *vir devotus*. The population of Siena in 730 was referred to as an army (*exercitus*).[21] The Lombard army and its hierarchy encompassed society, just like the Byzantine army did, but it does not mean in either case that everyone necessarily served in it. In Byzantine Italy, in fact, the army had even become a professional élite, and the Triestini at Rižana, though in theory a *numerus*, were actually petitioning *against* forced military service for their new Frankish masters, as we shall see. These changes in terminology simply show the transformation of the orientation, and to an extent the ideology, of upper-class society. Social leaders had different offices, different functions, and different names from their predecessors. But the basis for leadership was still land, and at least a few of the leading families of Byzantine Italy must have still been those of the fifth–sixth centuries in new guises, though there were certainly new families as well, both eastern and indigenous Italian. The fact that such a complete transformation could take place peacefully should show that something similar could have taken place among the Lombards as well. In both cases the civilian Roman aristocracy ceased to be politically influential. Some of its members went under, expropriated (at least in Lombard Italy), refugee to Constantinople or Sicily, or unable to maintain possession of widely-scattered property in too many war zones. Many others, however, survived by becoming members of the new élite, alongside Byzantine or Lombard military aristocrats, and even rank-and-file soldiers, risen in war; marrying into their families, and soon becoming indistinguishable from them.

In one respect the society of seventh-century Ravenna, Rome and Naples was different from that of Lombard Italy, though in two or three centuries' time Lombard cities would catch them up: in the role of the Church. We have seen how bishops become important adjuncts of civil administration in late Roman northern Italy. Under the Lombards they ceased to be, and even when the Lombards accepted Catholicism, they remained politically marginal, at least on the national level. In the Byzantine cities, however, they did not. The popes in Rome already had large lands, and, with the collapse of the Senate, took over effective rule of the city in the late sixth century, supporting the remaining populace with grain handouts. The archbishops of Ravenna had begun to accumulate land as well, particularly from several very large imperial concessions (in return, in some cases, for loans), from 550 onwards. In the seventh century, the archbishop was second only to the exarch as a power in Ravenna; the two usually co-operated closely, with mutual profit (unlike Carolingian counts and bishops, and unlike the stormy relationship between the exarch and the pope). The enormous lands of pope and archbishop directly represented vast economic and political power. They also, however, represented considerable opportunities for patronage. From the seventh century onwards, both in Ravenna and Rome, military aristocrats began to lease Church lands. The Church in some cases had little choice; the alternative to giving a lease (at a fixed rent, often nominal, for several generations) was often outright loss; but these leases did mean the acquisition of political support – the requirement was sometimes written into the contract.[22] A noble family could build up considerable landed power on the basis of leases, at a time when elsewhere in Italy leases were restricted to the peasantry. The Church was in this way linked firmly to the political fortunes of its new aristocratic tenants. Archbishops of Ravenna often came from their families; so a little later, after 750, did popes. In Naples, from the late eighth century onwards, only one or two families prevailed, usually providing both the bishop and the duke/consul; sometimes, as with Stephen II (754–800) and especially Athanasius II (876–898), the same man held both offices.[23] Naples had a small territory, of course, and little scope for the building of a complex network of noble families. The families of the 590s probably lost their landowning bases when the Lombards conquered the rest of Campania. The other Byzantine city-states of the eighth–ninth centuries and onward showed similar overlaps of lay and ecclesiastical offices inside their leading families – in Gaeta and Amalfi, and in Venice too, with the ninth-century hegemony of the Partecipazio family, the first great Venetian dynasty. Throughout Byzantine Italy, in fact, the importance of the Church was mirrored in its tight relationship with the social hierarchy in each city. In the eighth century, Lombard cities were beginning to show this as well; bishops from Bergamo and Lucca were already visibly aristocratic. When, in the ninth century, churches in Lombard Italy began to lease out their lands to aristocrats, the rest of the process begins to be visible too. By the tenth century, as we shall see, the tenants of Church land became the new aristocracy, and often became bishops themselves, as in Ravenna in the seventh century.

The Byzantine state in Italy remained more complex than its Lombard–Carolingian neighbour. This is very clear from the Rižana case of 804, in which the inhabitants of Istria and its nine cities, recently conquered by the Franks, complained about the exactions of their new ruler, the Frankish duke John. They listed the privileges that they had once had, and the duties they had formerly paid to the Byzantine state. John, however, had seized lands, changed the customs, and taken fiscal dues for himself. The Istrians had, among many other things, had their rights of sea-fishing taken away, and their rights to pasture in public forests; their official hierarchies, the positions of tribune, *domesticus*, *vicarius*, and *hypatus* (consul), had been taken away or filled by Franks; some of them were forced to serve in the army in person, alongside their slaves; John had begun to demand corvée-work in the Frankish manner, and still demanded taxes (344 *solidi mancusi* from the nine cities), which he kept for himself.

All these obligations we do through violence, and our ancestors never did them; our kinsmen and neighbours in Venice and Dalmatia, who are still under the power of the Greeks, as we formerly were, deride us. If the Emperor Charles helps us, we can escape; if not, it would be better for us to die than live.

John, defending himself, said that much of this was because he misunderstood the customs of Istria, and that he would of course make amends and cease to exact corvées. Whether he did or not is unknown.[24] The picture one obtains from this case, in all its complex detail, is of an unsophisticated and ruthless Frank running roughshod over a highly complex and balanced set of social conventions, at least as they were deliberately idealised in the memory of the Istrians. But some things had already changed: 344 *solidi*, if it is the remnant of the land-tax, is only a fraction of what it had been. Even the Byzantine state had here simplified itself in that respect. The offices the Istrians had lost had their close equivalents in the Lombard–Carolingian state, though the hierarchy was less complex there. The underlying structures of society, which we will look at in the next two chapters, were by 800 much the same on both sides of the border in Italy. The directions of development were similar, though the speed of development varied from place to place. And on neither side did immigration make major differences to the fabric of society. If immigrants displaced individual Romans, they did not alter the basic socio-economic structures of Italian life. Only mass settlement could have achieved that, and this, as we have seen, did not occur. The early medieval Italian economy, as we shall see in the next chapter, was in all important respects the direct successor to that of the Empire.

4. Cities and the Countryside

The City

In the kingdom of Italy, that is to say northern Italy and Tuscany, there had been during the Empire some hundred *municipia*. In 1000, over three-quarters survived as functioning cities. Of those that were abandoned, no more than a handful seem to have obtained bishops under the late Empire. They were, then, probably in a state of advanced decay before our period even begins. From 400 to 1000 we can trace an almost complete urban continuity, which continues to this day: out of fifty modern provincial capitals in the same area, thirty-five were cities under the Empire. North and north-central Italy has remained an urban society for the past two millennia without a break. For the whole of that period, cities were dominant over their territories politically, socially, and economically.

It might be, and has been, objected that this is merely a matter of definition. City-identity in both the Empire and the early Middle Ages was defined administratively: the presence of a city council, a duke, a count, a bishop; the presence of walls alone sometimes seems to have underlain the juridical definition of a city. Such cities might have been empty shells, or tiny settlements of peasants. In south and south-central Italy they often were (and sometimes still are). But there was perhaps four times the density of cities in some parts of the South as in the Po plain, in a far poorer landscape. Such a restricted territorial base often meant that such cities were only villages, with just a cathedral at their focus. They had a much weaker resistance to wars and invasions. Less than half the Roman cities of the South survived the sixth–seventh centuries, even as bishoprics (see below, p. 148). The geographical persistence of the northern cities contrasts clearly with this. This does not, however, merely indicate greater administrative or ecclesiastical continuity. In the North, we can see a true urban society functioning all through our period in the cities for which we have documents, such as Ravenna, Lucca, or Milan, and we can guess at it for most of the others. This assumes, of course, a clear economic definition of the city. I would pose the following for the sort of pre-industrial Mediterranean society we are dealing with: a comparatively large population centre, functionally distinct from other population centres around it, with three or more of the following features – craftsmen and artisans (especially), a concentration of landowners, an important administrative and religious role and an important market. These features will be discussed more fully later.

Some cities vanished, certainly. Sometimes they were destroyed in war and not reoccupied (Brescello on the Po, after being burnt in 586 and 603, was probably abandoned for several centuries), but this was uncommon. Far more typical was the slow decay and abandonment of cities in marginal areas. Luni, for example, on the Ligurian coast, though a county and a bishopric until the tenth century and later, seems already to have been in decline in the late Empire, when its forum was stripped of marble. Recent excavation has shown sixth-century wooden huts on the forum and in the monumental area around it and by the eighth century most occupation seems to have been restricted to the zone around the cathedral. This decline is all the more striking in that Luni was the Roman outlet for what is now called Carrara marble. But marble ceased to be cut in the late Empire, when so much stone was available in the disused temples of every Roman city. Luni was situated in coastal marshland backing directly onto a territory consisting of remote valleys and steep hill slopes, a hinterland too poor and underpopulated to act as an adequate basis for city life without some other economic function to back it up. When the Lombards, who did not take Luni until the 640s, occupied most of this hinterland, and changed the road network to bypass the city, they administered the coup de grâce. Some other cities declined like Luni. Others moved site, like Ventimiglia or Altino, the forerunner of Torcello and then Venice. But these were atypical. The typical Roman city survived; and still does.[1]

The physical appearance of early medieval cities is in itself a proof of their continuity. To be sure, they did not look very impressive. The size and technological sophistication of late Roman architecture had no succession after the sixth century. The temples and civic buildings of late Rome were mostly left to rot, or used as quarries. The churches that were built after 600 were small, even the great prestige ventures like S. Salvatore in Brescia or S. Maria in Cosmedin in Rome, though this may be at least partly just a change in architectural style; they were certainly rich inside. Private housing seems often to have been of wood, and set back from the road, with a courtyard in front and a garden behind, looking perhaps more like a run-down garden suburb than like

Pompeii. In many cities we find reference to agricultural land (particularly vineyards) inside the walls. Some historians have seen in this the 'ruralisation' of the city. This, however, would be very much of an exaggeration. City and country were certainly not wholly differentiated. Peasants could live in the city and issue out to farm the countryside, as in much of southern Italy they still do. But cities acted as foci for the countryside, and urban life in general was quite unlike rural life, in much the same way as in Antiquity.

The first thing that defined a city was its walls. These were Roman, though kept up by Lombard kings and later by the cities themselves. In 739 an unknown author wrote a panegyric on the city of Milan, describing its glories. The walls came first:

There are towers with high tops around the circuit, finished with great care on the outside, decorated with buildings on the inside. The walls are twelve feet wide; the immense base is made with squared blocks, elegantly completed on top with bricks. In the walls are nine marvellous gates, carefully secured with iron bars and keys, before which stand the towers of the drawbridges.

With defences like these, it is scarcely surprising that people stayed in cities during the sixth-century wars, nor that successive rulers kept them up. Walls gave a city identity in all senses. They also gave it its shape. Roman street plans were usually squared (and often aligned with the squared fields of the countryside); the square of the walls crystallised this. The two main streets of such cities ran from gate to gate, crossing at the middle, normally at the forum. The simple survival of Roman walls made this permanent. But in many Italian cities a virtually entire square plan survives to the present day – Turin, Albenga, Piacenza, Milan, Cremona, Brescia, Verona, Bologna, Florence, Lucca barely start the list. This is, it is true, sometimes possible in cities of quite low population (Aosta is one likely example), especially if streets are, as in Italy, thought of as public property; but so many instances must point to less limited conclusions. In Lucca in 890 two leases show us a row of five houses, all fronting directly onto the street, in the city centre. Here, at least, the street plan certainly shows continuity of fairly dense occupation.[2]

Milan did not just have walls: 'The building on the forum is most beautiful, and all the network of streets is solidly paved; the water for the baths runs across an aqueduct.' Here we are transported back into the world of late Rome. The aqueduct must have been an object of particular pride, for there were few left in the eighth century (in Rome, Naples, perhaps Brescia, probably Pavia; not many other places). The forum, on the other hand, remained in most cities. In Antiquity, it had been the political centre, where the city council had met, and a focus for civic building. In the early Middle Ages, it had two rivals, the royal palace and the cathedral, reflecting the two major powers in every city, the state and the bishop. The forum lost a direct political role after the city council disappeared in the sixth century, though it remained an economic centre, and the market was still held there. This, too, is still so today in many cities. The forum is rarely, however, still the city centre. The palace, or royal court, was often built on or near it, but the force of the palace waned when the Italian state collapsed in the tenth century. The cathedral was, on the other hand, seldom built nearby. As the last major late Roman civic building, it was usually placed on the edge of the Roman city. And the influence of the bishop in the city made the cathedral complex more and more important. In Milan, the cathedral was built in the fourth century, in the largely open area to the north-east of the city, enclosed by a recent enlargement of the walls. By the ninth century, it was already a political focus: the first will of Archbishop Anspert, of 879, refers to the *asemblatorio*, the assembly-place of the citizens, which was in front of the cathedral, where the modern city centre, the Piazza del Duomo, is. The old forum survived, and was also now known as the *mercatum*; it had permanent market-booths by 950 (largely the property of the major suburban monastery of S. Ambrogio). House prices around it and the nearby mint were high in the tenth century and later.[3] But Milan, as we shall see, was a great commercial centre. Elsewhere, the forum became marginal faster. In Brescia, the forum is now in a quiet residential quarter of the old town; it lost its importance before the Roman *capitolium*, which still overlooks it, could be fully cannibalised for other purposes (though it certainly remained a market). The medieval and modern city centre straddles the line of the Roman walls, beside and opposite the cathedral.

These movements of focus inside early medieval cities show clearly the close relationship between political power and status, and buildings. This was in itself a Roman tradition. Cassiodorus wrote, on the splendour of Theoderic's palaces: 'They are the pleasures of our power, the fitting face of Empire . . . they are shown for the admiration of envoys, and by their initial appearance their lord is judged.' Three hundred years later, Louis II said much the same: 'Public buildings, which in each city were long ago built to the adornment of our state, are to be rebuilt for our own use, and so that they should be fitting and decorous for the embassies of foreign nations that come to us.'[4] The builders of churches knew this best. Church-building was the direct successor to the monumental building and rebuilding of the Roman city. In the first century, Agrippa put his name on the portico of the Pantheon in Rome. So, in the late Empire, donors of mosaic pavements in churches had their names listed inside the door, with the number of feet of mosaic they had paid for. Some churches were even named after their founders, like S. Maria Theodota in Pavia and Sumuald's S. Pietro Somaldi in Lucca. Agnellus wrote much of his history of Ravenna solely from the donor inscriptions on the churches of the city. Bishop James of Lucca (d. 818) felt that his foundations and endowments were all he need record on his epitaph; not even any pious rhetoric. Bishops were the major donors, as was appropriate, not only because of their religious responsibilities, but because they were usually the richest urban landowners. The number of newly-founded churches that appear in cities in our period is one of the clearest signs of the prosperity of city-dwellers and their preparedness to spend conspicuously. In Pavia, some forty-five churches are known by name before the Hungarians sacked the city in 924. In Lucca, fifty-seven churches are recorded before 900. Anyone with claims to status clinched them by building a church. The Emperor Justinian complained in the Byzantine context that men were so keen to be known as founders of churches that they often did not even provide for their churches' furnishings or upkeep.[5] The only major differences between this and late Roman civic munificence were that a far wider social range could participate in piety and church-endowment in the early medieval period, not just civic officials, and that far more churches were built than late Roman civic buildings. It is as a result of this last point, as well as because of the lesser wealth of early medieval aristocrats, that churches were fairly small and unimpressive by comparison with the monuments of late Rome.

Lucca, the best-documented city in early medieval Italy, shows these patterns clearly. The near-perfect survival of its Roman plan, and the housefronts of the late ninth century, show that it retained at least some degree of its Roman building density. Its churches were distributed fairly evenly across the city; there were no obvious open areas. Houses are referred to as being built of wood, brick, and stone; stone is by far the most common. Two-storeyed houses are increasingly frequent between

700 and 1100; by the tenth century, even the occasional tower-house. The royal palace (*curtis regia*) and mint were close to the forum in the centre; the cathedral complex was in the south-east corner of the city. In Lucca, however, the capital of Tuscany, the duke's palace (*curtis ducalis*) outside the city walls became far more splendid, arousing the jealousy of Louis III in 905. When King Hugh overthrew the marquis in the 930s, he installed the king's palace there instead. The ducal palace was not the only extramural building in Lucca, either. Over a third of the churches and half the houses cited in Lucchese texts before 1000 are identified as being outside the walls. A string of suburbs surrounded Lucca from our earliest eighth-century documents; some had acquired the name of bourg (*burgus*) by the tenth century. A high percentage of the population of Lucca lived outside the walls from as early as we know. Lucca was a major centre, and perhaps precocious, but many other cities must have overflowed their walls well before the end of our period.[6]

Lucca's inhabitants are also illuminating. Again from our earliest texts we find a range of merchants and luxury artisans, goldsmiths, cauldron-makers, doctors, tailors, builders, moneyers. All of these are recorded either in the city itself or in its immediate vicinity. Some, indeed were landowners, as, for example, Justu the goldsmith from *porta S. Gervasi* in 739, the quarter of S. Gervasio's gate (quite a number of cities had recognised subdivisions; those of Ravenna even fought each other in ritualised battles, every Sunday afternoon). A north Italian master builder, Natalis, bought land south of Lucca in 787–8, and by 805 was sufficiently prosperous to found an urban church.[7] Not only merchants and artisans were city-dwellers, though; we find urban aristocrats as well. In the eighth century, over half of the twenty largish landowners recorded in Lucca and its territory seem to have been city-dwelling. And this excludes the lands of the city churches and, above all, the cathedral, easily the largest landowner in the territory. The lands of the state were administered from inside the city, too. The land controlled by urban inhabitants and institutions must already – or still – have formed a good proportion of the entire Lucchesia. Inside a narrower geographical range, the rural population probably used the Lucca market for their surplus exchange, as well. Lucca was clearly socially and economically dominant in its territory by any criterion, in ways that had not substantially changed from the Roman world, and would not greatly change henceforth.

I emphasise urban landowning rather than urban commerce here, and this is deliberate. Roman cities were not principally commercial centres; they were political-administrative centres based on the taxation of the countryside, and given socio-economic weight because the great landowners of the Empire nearly all lived inside them. Only then, through the buying-power of the state and the aristocracy, did commercial interests come to be present. In only a very few cities in the West, usually great ports, like Ostia, and indeed perhaps nowhere else, was commerce in any sense predominant. In the main, this was equally true in Italy even in the twelfth–thirteenth centuries. Genoa and Venice, were, of course, almost exclusively commercial centres, but they were the exceptions. Smaller inland cities, more typical of the communes, like Mantua, or Arezzo, or Parma, were always controlled by landowners. And even entrepôt cities like Milan and Cremona, with a thriving commerce, were at least as much cities based on landowning. We do not then have to identify a historical break in the economic base of our cities, now landownership, now commerce (let alone industry); now aristocratic, now bourgeois. Ancient cities were (in Weber's terms) centres of consumption, not production, parasitical on the countryside; so, inside narrower limits, were twelfth-and thirteenth-century cities. The commerce of the central Middle Ages, though it ceased to be wholly dependent on the buying-power of Italian landowners, was for the most part luxury international exchange. The bulk of the population certainly rarely bought it. There was never any great commercialisation of agriculture in medieval Italy, and the population of the countryside was only involved in commerce at all insofar as it was on the receiving end of monopolistic practices and price-fixing calculated to benefit city markets and workshops at its expense.

We have already amply seen how the political and administrative structure of the Lombard kingdom and its Carolingian successor remained urban, as part of royal claims to a Roman tradition of public administration. The Church, too, was firmly urban, with the exception of the network of rural monasteries, some of them with very wide estates, that began to appear in the eighth century. Even those, though, were mostly explicitly founded in remote areas, as an attempt to avoid a secular society that was defined as being urban. And, as we have seen for Lucca, landowners remained urban too. A good example is Taido, the king's *gasindio* (retainer), son of Teuderolf, citizen of Bergamo, who made his will in 774 (while Desiderius was being besieged in Pavia). His (or his father's) citizenship seems to have been a title, just as was the status of *gasindio*. He distributed a long list of property to thirteen churches, the largest gift being to two urban churches, and he commanded the bishop to sell the rest at his death.[8]

It may not seem inevitable that landowners should have stayed in cities. The concrete material benefits of being institutionally part of the citizen body had disappeared when the state centralised taxation in the late third century. The institutional pull of the city-based Lombard state patronage network, though strong, could not match that of the centralised tax-based state of the late Empire. And any student of early medieval Europe is well aware of the de-urbanisation of much of the West under the Germanic kingdoms. Lellia Ruggini has put a case for Italian landowners leaving cities even under the Ostrogoths. Her evidence, however, only relates to Bruttii (modern Calabria), always a marginal area.[9] The de-urbanisation of the West was mostly restricted to those regions, like Britain and northern Gaul, which were least affected by Rome. Southern Gaul, at least in its agriculturally prosperous parts, remained urban; so did much of Spain. The upper classes, Roman and Germanic, of the Mediterranean fringes of western Europe continued to find that urban life was their major social focus. We have seen (see above, p. 68) that the Lombards settled in cities as early as the sixth century, doubtless under Roman influence, which was represented best by the continuing force of the episcopate. Administrative continuity meant that all important offices remained urban, though there were now fewer of them than under the late Empire. And the attraction of civic life was itself a self-perpetuating force. The chance for aristocrats to measure themselves against their peers came best in an urban context – if someone built a church in the city, other people could actually see it. The economic reasons for staying in the city were no longer dominant, but the inertia of values allowed urban living to keep its allure. The ideological pre-eminence of urban life in Italy throughout the early Middle Ages is clear, and the survival of the institutions of the state and the church in cities contributed a definite solidity to urban economic activity, too, even if it was less firmly based than under the Empire. There were rural nobles, particularly in the Appennines, which had never been fully romanised during Antiquity. When the Italian state decayed in the North, some of the great aristocratic families ruralised themselves too, as we shall see (see pp. 183–4) – in some senses, the eleventh century, despite its active commercial revival and urban expansion, was the lowpoint for the political dominance of Italian cities. But this in itself shows the importance of the persistence of the city as an administrative centre for the state up to at least the tenth century. And even in the eleventh century, as the rise of the communes shows, the balance lay with the cities.

The administrative, ecclesiastical and aristocratic patronage network, all based on landowning, underlay all other urban activity. Even the urban poor could live by it: feeding the poor was, from Roman times, a proof of civic munificence, and this role was taken over largely by bishops. Gregory the Great and his eighth-century successors in Rome regarded it as one of the main purposes for the produce they received from their estates.[10] The packets of pasta distributed by Monarchists and Christian Democrats at recent elections in Naples are in many ways the direct successors of these handouts. But commerce and artisanal work, based on aristocratic demand, was a more vital process than this, and, in its commercial development, early medieval Italy was well ahead of any other part of the Christian West except Arab southern Spain.

Early commerce was undertaken very largely under the protection and through the mediation of the state – another Roman tradition. Rothari put foreign merchants under his protection. Liutprand (or Grimoald) issued a detailed code, fixing prices for the builders' federation, the *magistri commacini*, for specific tasks: tiling roofs, building walls, whitewashing, putting in partitions and windows, digging wells. Ratchis and Aistulf required licencing for all merchants – merchants were unreliable and rootless; they might trade with enemies, and their merchandise might be stolen. The kings clearly regarded the values of goods as fixed, although men were too often inclined to raise prices, especially in times of famine, or when armies passed. The Carolingians issued laws to safeguard the 'just price' of commodities, particularly foodstuffs. These were attitudes firmly ingrained into medieval society; even the communes maintained such laws. Prices certainly changed, and even land prices rose dramatically after the late tenth century, but the concept of a 'freely determined' market price was not an acceptable one to most Italians. Prices were in principle related to social needs.[11]

The state was not only interested in commerce as a problem of social disturbance. Merchants could fight; in 750 Aistulf issued a law to determine what sorts of arms greater and lesser merchants should carry when called for army service. And merchants paid tolls to the government, which could provide a considerable income. A succession of kings from Liutprand onwards made treaties with the men of the Byzantine territories along the Adriatic, first from Comacchio, then later from Venice, determining how much money they should pay at each port along the Po and its tributaries: at Mantua, the mouth of the Mincio, the ports of Brescia, Parma, Cremona, the mouth of the Adda, Piacenza, and the mouth of the Lambro.[12] Markets owed tolls too. In fact, almost all we know about markets in our period derives from grants of market tolls to churches under the later Carolingians and their successors. Before these, we have to assume their existence. The most detailed account of such renders is the early eleventh-century text generally known as the *Honorantiae Civitatis Papiae*, which claims to describe an early tenth-century situation, though some of the details must be later. It lists dues owed by merchants coming into Italy over the Alps; the special gifts owed to officials and the palace of Pavia by the king of England and the duke of Venice to commute these dues for their merchants; the percentage payable to Pavese and Milanese moneyers in return for striking coin, and the tolls owed by them to the palace; the taxes due from the gold-panners of the rivers of northern Italy, the fishermen, leatherworkers and soapmakers of Pavia, and so on.[13] These professions are all organised into *ministeria*, which have seemed to many historians to be the descendents of the corporations of the Empire (or the *scholae* of Byzantine Italy). This has never been proved, and there is no continuity in the social context of such organisations: the state controlled the whole administrative structure of corporations under the Empire, and it is very unlikely to have done so after 568. But there must have been at least a continuity of systematic training and qualification in the artisanate throughout our period, and already in the eighth century we find evidence of *magistri*, master craftsmen, in a variety of occupations – building, the notariate, ironworking. Our knowledge of the artisanate is always indirect, and comes from chance references: grants of rights by the state, the land acquisitions of successful craftsmen, witness lists. Nevertheless, we have evidence of a wide range of trades already in the eighth–ninth centuries: workers of gold, silver, copper, iron; makers of leather, cloth, soap; builders of houses and ships. There was even mineral extraction: salt-working, gold-panning (as we have seen), and silver mining – the bishop of Volterra was granted the tolls due from the mines of Montieri by the marquis of Tuscany in 896.[14]

The basic lines of Italian commercial activity were probably laid down by the salt trade, for salt is the oldest commodity. It has always been a necessity, especially in hot climates. Italian salt came from the coast: the Adriatic lagoons, the Vada flats south of Pisa, the Tiber mouth. The traffic from Vada to Lucca and Pisa is traceable from the

760s (there is fifth-century evidence, too), and was one of the origins of Pisan maritime activity. But the Adriatic salt trade was, far more visibly, the basis of all early medieval commerce in the North. The men of Comacchio at the mouth of the Po brought salt into the North in the eighth century. In the early ninth century the Cremonesi began to participate in this, and eventually bought their own ships. We know this, because in 852 they unsuccessfully claimed exemption from the tolls due to the bishop from the port of Cremona, the first round in two centuries of increasingly bitter disputes between the bishop and the citizens of Cremona.[15] Other cities may have begun to do the same. Comacchio, a small city dependent on its monopoly, probably suffered. The centre to benefit was Venice, the Rialto island, where the Byzantine duke of the Adriatic coast had recently taken up residence. In the early ninth century the Venetians began to take over the Byzantine end of the trade route, clinching it in 889 when they besieged and burnt Comacchio. But Venice, the last north Italian link with Byzantium, was well placed to bring more goods into Italy than just salt. These quickly increased in importance and volume. The Venetian merchants in Pavia at the time of the *Honorantiae* each gave formalised gifts to the king's chamberlain that must reflect their range of wares: a pound of pepper, cinnamon, galanga (an aromatic root) and ginger; and an ivory comb, a mirror, and make-up accessories for his wife. They also imported Byzantine cloth and artwork; in return, they bought slaves, grain, and Italian cloth. Much of this exchange was based in Pavia. Half the bishops in the kingdom kept up houses there, as outlets for surplus goods as much as bases to attend court.

The Venetians, devoid of any agricultural hinterland, were virtually forced into commerce, even their greatest aristocrats. Already in 829 the duke of Venice, Justinianus (Giustiniano Partecipazio), though, indeed, a mainland landowner in the Italian kingdom proper, made reference in his will to 1200 pounds of 'working *solidi*, if they come back safely from sea', our first reference in medieval history to monetary investment. The Venetians slowly built on this across the next centuries. By 992 they had occupied most of the coast of the Adriatic and obtained immense commercial privileges from the eastern emperor. By 995 they were in a position to blockade the Adriatic outlets of the other cities of Italy. Their future was firmly set.[16]

The major ports of the Italian kingdom, Pisa and Genoa, only came into their own in the eleventh century, though Pisa at least had a continuous maritime tradition from the seventh century and before.

The inland cities are better indices of the commercial and urban development of the ninth and tenth centuries, particularly Milan. Milan is not very well documented before 800, but from then on, largely through the archives of the monastery of S. Ambrogio, evidence begins to increase quickly. In the ninth century we see the same patterns as in Lucca, with prosperous artisans and merchants buying land. Some merchants were protégés of S. Ambrogio, and regularly witnessed its charters (S. Giulia in Brescia had such protégés too, and even obtained toll-exemptions from Louis II for one of them, Januarius, in 861). From the late ninth century onwards, such references increase. By 900, commerce was thriving in Milan; after the mid-tenth century, house prices soared. We can now see rural families moving into the city: two families from Cologno, to the east of the city, in the early to mid-tenth century; one from Trivulzio, to the south, the descendents of Ingo, from the 970s onward. The 'Ingonids' lost control of much of their land to merchants and moneyers from the city as they moved in. As they did so, they married into the same social groups – merchants again, and judges, the professional classes.[17] This mix of commercial and professional – one can add ecclesiastical – activities was characteristic of a whole middle stratum in the city population, that became capable of independent action in the next century in association with the far more powerful stratum of the landed aristocracy. Commerce was not the main basis for social change in Milan, but it was certainly more important than in Lucca. It was at least an element in the growing status of the city, which underlay a fairly rapid expansion in Milan's population. The new social importance of merchants was, however, less an indication of the recognition of commercial wealth as a key to status, than of the ability and desire of successful merchants to buy land. Land was still the basis of political power.

In this discussion, we have run ahead of ourselves to some extent. Late tenth-century Milan was in a very different world from a century before: the whole political structure had changed. The interests of the new merchant stratum (one could not yet say class) could in some cities, notably Cremona, affect the balance set between bishops and lay aristocrats in the Carolingian and post-Carolingian world, but this is best seen in the last chapter, when it can be put into political context. This is important, for there is a strong tendency among historians to isolate commercial growth and the activities of merchants from the society that surrounds them; to study, as it were, the grit rather than the carpet-fibre. But the activities of the members of a marginal group, no matter how firmly they may have the future grasped in their hands, is incomprehensible outside their overall social framework. Artisans and merchants were firmly enmeshed in and under the control of the society that bought their commodities. And, as late as the tenth century, they still had close links with the state. Moneyers, for example, one of the *ministeria* of the *Honorantiae*, were not independent artisans: they were the representatives of the state, minting money for it under licence, subject to strict regulations as to the weight and authenticity of their coinage. The concentration of commercial activity in Pavia, particularly in the half-century on either side of 900, was purely the result of the interests and needs of the state administrative apparatus, and after the palace was burnt in 1024 the city lost ground fast to Milan, which had probably remained the largest city in the North ever since Antiquity, and was thus a more profitable commercial focus. Commerce could probably have existed fairly happily without the involvement of the state, especially in the upturn of international trade that began in the early tenth century as Arab raiding slackened off; but it was still, for the most part, dependent on the buying-power and thus the social alignments of the aristocracy. No advantage is gained in treating tenth-century Italy as the forerunner of a 'commercial revolution'shorn of all economic and social context. It is even doubtful whether it helps our understanding of Italy to call it a 'money economy', even though money was, from at least 700, freely available, and used for most recorded transactions. Outside the urban market, most exchange took place in social contexts where it was unimportant whether money was used as a medium or not, in local markets, and outside markets altogether (cf. below, pp. 112–14). The great majority of the population saw nothing of this international commerce. They, like their landlords, lived exclusively off the land.

Agriculture and Social Change in the Countryside

THE countryside was as primitive as the city was sophisticated. Ploughs do occasionally appear in our sources, but the spade, hoe, and weeding hook seem to have been the only tools available to most peasants. Much of Italy was still covered by forest or marsh, and, though the eighth–eleventh centuries were the great age of medieval land clearance in Italy, this did not result in changes in techniques. There were no great technological developments in early medieval Italian agriculture, apart from the rapid introduction of the watermill, a standard feature of every village by 1100. The only major exception to this was Arab Sicily, outside the range of this book, where a whole array of new crops and a sophisticated irrigation network were introduced between the ninth and the twelfth century.

In the first chapter, I emphasised the geographical diversity of Roman Italy. Early medieval Italy was no less differentiated, and, from the eighth century onwards, the relative precision of our charter evidence makes its contrasts leap to the eye. Land use, diet, settlement, the survival of the free peasantry, the condition of tenants, the changes in the structure of great estates can vary totally between the territories of each city, between upland and lowland zones, between one mountain valley and the next. Even inside one territory, the differences are striking – between the cultivated upper plain and hills of the province of Parma, and the oak forests on the Po marshes to its north, or the eroded clay pastures and beech forests on the high Appennines to its south. Sometimes we already have enough evidence to tie differences in social structure to such contrasts. Much work has been done by Italian historians – and, increasingly, archaeologists – on these differences in recent years, particularly in the last decade or so. A brief survey such as this will not do full justice to them. I intend here merely to set out a few broad lines of pattern and development, rather than lose sight of them in a mass of exceptions. But exceptions there are, to every point. Some of these broad analyses apply to southern Italy as well, but more characteristically southern patterns will be discussed in chapter 6.

It is quite possible that the peasantry was the class least affected by the end of the Empire and the wars of the sixth century. The Roman landowning aristocracy was partially replaced by a Lombard one; Lombards of lesser status (including slaves) settled on the land beside Roman slaves and *coloni*. There were rather few of these, however, by comparison with the Roman agrarian classes; and, before the realities of economic life in Italy, Lombard agriculturalists lost their separate identity. We have seen that Roman property law was adopted by the Lombards; by the eighth century there is no way that Lombards and Romans can be distinguished by their actions. These economic realities were, in their essentials, simply the traditional reactions of the Roman peasantry to their environment. Peasants are not fond of agricultural experiment – they have too much to lose. And even the devastation of war is unlikely to make much difference to the way survivors cultivate the land, once they have replenished their stocks of seed corn, or replanted destroyed vineyards. War and catastrophe may make the independent status of peasants tenuous, as they put themselves under the protection of lords (willingly or unwillingly) in return for the means to survive; but they will still farm the land in the same way. And in the sixth century, landowners were, as we have seen, highly vulnerable themselves. It is indeed possible that some peasants escaped from their control. Our eighth-century evidence certainly shows us more small proprietors than are generally thought to have existed under the late Empire. Some things changed, of course. The land tax, that had driven many peasants off the land, ceased in most of Italy. And those few large-scale economic projects that the state had a hand in certainly ended. The drainage systems of the Po and Arno valleys decayed; the African pottery that dominates late Roman archaeological sites, including peasant farmsteads and villages, ceased to be available in Italy soon after the end of the sixth century (with great detriment to our understanding of early medieval settlement; we have, so far, little diagnostic pottery for the following two centuries). But without a massive and sudden collapse in the population, for which there is no evidence or conceivable explanation, we cannot expect great changes in peasant agriculture in the early medieval period.[18]

Peasant agriculture consisted, in lowland Italy at least, of the fundamental Mediterranean triad of corn, wine, and oil, eked out with beans and fruits, which were mostly grown in the small fenced gardens that every early medieval peasant had. This pattern had not greatly changed from Roman times; not until Caesar's troops were starving in central Gaul in 52 BC did he attempt to give them meat. It has not changed much since, either; only since the Second World War has meat-eating become normal for most Italians. That early medieval Italians lived like this is best seen from some eighth-century texts from several points in Lazio, Tuscany and the Po plain, which list the daily rations due to the poor in poor-relief associated with privately-founded churches. These can be regarded as examples of some sort of 'norm' in peasant diets, at least as idealised by landowners; the range of foods is probably accurate, though real diets will have varied greatly in quantity. In 764 in Lucca Rixsolf laid down a daily regimen per person of a loaf of wheaten bread, a quarter-amphora of wine, and the same amount of a mess of beans and flour made from panic-grass 'well-pressed and seasoned with fat or oil'. Others were very similar, though lard was sometimes preferred to oil, and the mess (or 'relish') sometimes included a little meat. These diets must have been numbingly dull eaten for years on end. Among the poor, meat was restricted to special occasions, and to this end every peasant household kept a small number of animals, perhaps a pig, a cow, and a hen; this was enough, too, to provide the annual gifts of yearlings that are common alongside rents in produce or money in our eighth–ninth-century leases.[19]

These diets are our only direct evidence for what people ate; but we have much more evidence about the balance of land use across Italy, and this balance was, as we shall see (pp. 105–7), directed principally towards the needs of a peasant economy. The pattern remains the same: an overwhelming preponderance of arable land (especially on flatter land) and vineyards (especially on the hills). The products of arable land, as we can see in rentals, were principally different types of corn. In Tuscany, wheat was predominant; in the Po plain, rye was commoner. Inferior corns were much less common, though it is possible that lords took the best corn-types, leaving their tenants with higher proportions of oats and millet. The Italians usually kept to a two-field system, with one year in two fallow, but may sometimes have grown legumes (beans and peas) in the fallow year. This is, if so, quite a sophisticated use of the land, but contrasts with the wretched yields that can be calculated from some of the northern Italian estate records of the tenth century, especially from those of S. Tommaso di Reggio, which did not always reach as much as 3:1.[20]

Olive groves and specialised olive cultivation were comparatively rare, though several north Italian monasteries had estates in the Italian lakes, where olives may even have been cultivated as a cash crop on south-facing slopes (to a greater extent, probably, than today). More common, particularly in Tuscany, was 'promiscuous cultivation', the cultivation of olives and corn on the same land, a practice which has until recently, for a variety of reasons, often been regarded as a hallmark of agricultural sophistication. Vines must often have been grown promiscuously too. The phrase *terra vitata*, or *terra cum vineis superposita*, arable land with vines on it, is a common one, especially in Tuscany and southwards. They were also, however, grown in specialised vineyards all across Italy, and from the tenth century onwards, especially in central Italy, we find *pastinatio* contracts with tenants, most of which provide for a change in agricultural exploitation from cornland (or wasteland) to vineyards. Landlords in these cases must have regarded vines as cash crops. They make up only a small proportion of leases, however. For the most part, lords seem to have been satisfied with taking proportions of the types of produce that peasants grew for their own purposes, the bases for their subsistence, and that meant that corn and wine were taken in comparable quantities.

The Lombards, with the experience of life in the forests of central

Europe, valued stock-raising more than most Roman peasants. Rothari's law code, while giving some attention to agricultural misdemeanours (stealing fruit, spoiling or cutting vines, ploughing someone else's field), discusses at inordinate length the legal problems of mixed and purely pastoral farming. We discover the penalties for injuries to animals from the projecting branches of hedges, the theft of a halter, death from a horse's hoof, the killing of a pregnant cow, damage by an animal in another's field or on the village street, the theft of a boar (with special provision for a *sonorpair*, the head pig of a herd of more than thirty), and so on.[21] It has often been concluded from this that the Lombard period was the great age of stock-raising and the silvo-pastoral economy, with a return to agriculture only with the great land clearances of the ninth century. This is unlikely. Rothari was legislating for his own people; but there were few Lombard peasants, and this part of the code probably had little general relevance. Most of lowland Italy continued to be cultivated in the same way as it had been, and this meant a primarily vegetarian diet for its inhabitants.

Outside Italy's cultivated zones, however, in the Po marshes or in the high Appennines, a more pastoral regime did prevail. In Roman times the mountains and the marsh were connected by systematic trans-humance between high summer pastures and low winter pastures. This is barely evident in our period (cf above, p. 12), but the contrast between agricultural and pastoral certainly still existed. Desiderius gave to S. Salvatore in Brescia, in 772, 4000 *iugera* (2600 acres) of forest in the lower Emilian plain, carefully bounded with marked trees; this cannot have been of any value in its wild state except as a pig run. S. Salvatore, under its new name of S. Giulia, left a systematic record of returns from its property, a 'polyptych', dating from *c.* 900. Recent calculations of the agricultural resources of S. Giulia's tenants, alongside those of the Appennine monastery of Bobbio (whose polyptychs date from 862 and 883), give results so low that the possibility of a back-up from pastoral farming seems highly likely. Most tenants seem to have been living off an average of about 100 kilograms (220 pounds) of corn each year – in some instances, less than 64 kilograms (140 pounds), a long way below the minimum necessary to live. These figures can be often seen as indicating the reduced importance of corn in marginal areas, in the mountains and in the lower plain, where much monastic land was; but this cannot explain all the returns, and they still represent a problem. S. Giulia's own household slaves, however, apparently more often based on the central cultivated areas of Lombardy, were fed exclusively on corn – up to six times as much as tenants, if the polyptych's figures are accurate.[22]

Exactly how much of Italy was pasture or just uncultivated forest, scrub and marsh, in, say, 800 could not be guessed at: most of the land above the 500 metre contour on our maps, excepting most mountain valleys, perhaps; below that contour only the vicinity of the great rivers, and some of the more barren uplands, such as central Tuscany, or the Murge in Apulia, though there were certainly patches of woodland on the heavily-settled parts of the plain, too, particularly in the North. In the ninth century, however, perhaps already in the eighth, we begin to get signs of systematic land clearance, mostly by monasteries, though this is probably because monastic archives are better preserved. Nonantola cleared the Ostiglia forest on the Po from the early ninth century onwards, for example; by the middle of the century men were returning to the neighbourhood of the city of Brescello, and from the end of the tenth century we even find record of a lay landowning family organising clearance in the same area, the house of Canossa (see p. 183). In the central Appennines, north of Rome, we find Farfa involved in land clearance, too, probably in large part based on the work of independent peasant pioneers of the eighth–ninth centuries.[23] It is this activity, whether directed outwards to the great forests, or inwards to the woods of the long-settled areas (where its record is left mostly in casual references and occasional placenames), that marks the true economic dynamism of early medieval Italy, far more than the rise in international luxury commerce. It seems to have been associated with a rise in population; at least, the divided tenant holdings and rising land prices that were common by the late tenth century have led historians to conclude that the population was rising. Whether the favourable leases granted to pioneer tenants by monasteries – coupled with a slight lessening of the economic burdens on servile tenants across most of Italy (cf. below, pp. 111f.) – were the cause of greater prosperity and therefore larger families, or whether population pressure was itself the motor of land clearance, becoming visible only when clearance began to slow down (if it did) after 950, is a problem that cannot yet be answered. Archaeology may in the future be able to give us clues about the pressure on resources, but at present far too little material has been collected to give us answers here.

Archaeology may be in a far better position, however, to tell us something about early medieval settlement, before the changes in pattern that began in the early tenth century, known generically as *incastellamento*, which led to the dominance of totally nucleated settlement in some parts of Italy, and a partial concentration of settlement in and around fortified centres in others (see below, pp. 164–7, 173–4). The pattern in Roman Italy is generally thought to have been dispersed, and this is supported both by archaeological surveys, which tend to find villa centres and scattered farms, and by historical records, which describe the Roman countryside as consisting, not of villages, but of estate units, *massae* and *fundi*, fragmented collections of properties usually named after some past owner, the *massa Firmidiana*, or the *fundus Domitianus*. Exactly how this worked in the sociological sense is unclear – we cannot easily say how peasant owners fitted their properties into this framework, for example, unless *fundi* could be very small. Classical Latin does have a word for village, *vicus*, and *vici* can be found in our texts, set slightly uneasily into the pattern, but whether they were alternative ways of organising territory, or just isolated nuclei of settlement (one or two of these have been found by archaeologists), is uncertain.

Under the Lombards, we find a firm pattern of villages right across Italy, called variously *vici*, *loci*, *casalia*, *villae*, and other more local names. These replaced *massae* and *fundi* as the units for territorial organisation (though the latter continued to be used up to the tenth–eleventh century in the formerly Byzantine parts of the North and Centre); village-territories, being defined geographically, were certainly more flexible and permanent than estate units. What this change meant to peasants is, however, extremely unclear. These villages could certainly be at either end of the fullest spectrum of settlement pattern, from concentrated, even fortified, nuclei to scatters of houses so widely dispersed that distinctions between village territories were difficult to maintain – even their inhabitants sometimes seem to have been confused. Mediterranean agriculture does not require much collective co-operation, for there are fairly few animals to graze on communal pastures, the normal basis for such co-operation, but informal *ad hoc* help was doubtless given to co-villagers. Caesarius of Arles in the 510s described the help given by neighbours and kinsmen to a man restoring his neglected vineyard in this way, in a part of Gaul very similar to Italy. In more pastoral areas, communal action was more important, however, and in the ninth century we see a number of villages from such areas acting collectively in courts (see pp. 109–11). How these villages developed from the Roman period, or, indeed, whether they had in reality always existed, is a problem that only archaeological excavation will be able to help us with in the immediate future.²⁴

We can be more certain about the changing fortunes of different strata of the peasantry, and their relationships with landlords, for on those subjects our evidence is considerable. Its outlines are fairly well known. In the late Empire, the slave production of the first–second centuries had already vanished, and we already find the relationship between landlord and tenant that is a feature of later centuries, alongside surviving owner-cultivators. Exactly how these two balanced out is irrecoverable. It is often thought that the owner-cultivators were absorbed by great estates, but some certainly survived, especially in the mountains. The late Roman term *colonus* could mean either free tenant or owner-cultivator, and we can rarely determine which is meant at any instance – the state taxed them both, and required even independent owners to stay on the land, so did not trouble to distinguish. *Coloni* by no means always did stay on the land, however. Late Roman legislation is full of laments about the flight of *coloni* (but where to?) and the resultant abandoned land (*agri deserti*) which formed a large percentage of the land lost to agriculture at the end of the Empire. Slaves were still sometimes used to cultivate their owner's land directly, but were by now usually *casati*, put into tenant houses as servile tenants.

It would be impossible to generalise about how late Roman estates were cultivated. In the territory of Padua in about the 550s the tenants (*coloni*) of the church of Ravenna were already obliged to do heavy labour service on their lord's demesnes of one to three days a week (and pay a money rent, and gifts of honey, lard, and poultry). This is the first known reference anywhere, and the last for two centuries, to the bipartite estate, known to the English as the 'manorial system' and to the Italians as the *sistema curtense*, with a demesne worked by the direct labour of tenants, and a set of tenant holdings owing labour and rent. It was certainly not universal in sixth-century Italy. The papal estate-administrators in Sicily at the time of Gregory the Great (590–604) did not extract labour service from their *rustici*, though they required many other things. Gregory in his first years as pope sent several letters to his representatives there to correct their abuses. Peasants in Sicily were, it seems, normally required to pay as rent the equivalent in corn of a fixed sum of money, varying as the price of corn varied. Administrators were apparently prone to keep these prices artificially low, and to demand extra large measures for their money, as well as extra dues, and gifts at marriage. They did not stop short of the expropriation of their neighbours. Labour service, however, is conspicuous by its absence;

tenants only paid rent. Across the next few centuries, this would remain a feature of the South. Another point about Gregory's estates needs making here, finally: Gregory's tenants included both freemen and slaves, but they all seem to have been tied to their tenures, and all seem to have rents that were fixed by custom. Already in the 590s, then, even outside the 'manorial' areas of Italy, we are finding the fusion between free and unfree that is generally taken as being the basis for the tenant stratum of medieval peasant society.[25]

The Lombards had a threefold classification of society, as shown in Rothari's edict: the freeman, the *aldius*, and the slave. The *aldius*, generally vaguely translated as 'half-free', was perpetually under the protection of, and tied to the service of, his lord; the slave was, at least initially, just a chattel. This classification, like the Roman one, began to weaken in the face of the economic relationship between landlord and tenant. *Aldii*, in particular, began to disappear. They are occasionally cited in ninth-century texts as privileged dependents, especially couriers. Tenants sometimes claimed to be *aldii* in court cases (usually as second best to being free) to safeguard the customary nature of their tenure. Lombard freemen and slaves became much like Roman ones, though the Lombard freeman was considerably more independent than the Roman *colonus*: he was not tied to the land, he had a responsibility to perform army service and appear at court, and at least in Rothari's time he was still, in theory, on a par in legal terms with the aristocracy (see pp. 131f.).

In 727, the beginnings of future developments become visible in a law of Liutprand, which starts:

> If any free man, living as a *libellarius* [a charter-holding tenant] on another's land, commits homicide and flees, then he on whose land the killer lived has a month in which to find him; [if he does not, he must pay half the killer's own movable property].[26]

Lombard freemen were already becoming tenants, and this was not only an economic contract; it meant a fall in status. Leases of the eighth century often contained clauses stating that tenants were tied to the land, and, in this law, their lords already had considerable responsibility for them. Their status was beginning to approach that of unfree tenants. This decline in the position of many freemen was, as we shall see, one of the crucial aspects of the development of Italian society from the eighth century onwards. Outside the context of the Lombard laws it is, once again, impossible to tell whether such people were Lombard or Roman, nor does it seem to matter. Lombard social divisions entirely folded into Roman ones.

In the eighth century, therefore, we again find the patterns that existed in the late Empire, though they are now rather better documented. We find free owner-cultivators, in large numbers. Above them, we have landowners of varying size, from the cultivator with some extra plots of land rented out to tenants, up to the large landowner. Even the largest, though, like Gisulf *strator* of Lodi with an estate at Alfiano (province of Cremona) worth some 9000 *solidi*, were in no sense as large as the great senatorial families of the late Empire.[27] Below them, were free tenants at various levels of subjection: some with land they owned as well as land they rented; some owing labour service, some not; some (at least after 800) subject to the private justice of their lords. Below them were unfree tenants with (in most cases) much heavier obligations, though fixed by custom. At the base of society there were still some chattel slaves (*servi praebendarii*), working on a lord's demesne or in his household, though the numbers of these were lessening. Tenants and slaves formed the great majority of Italian society throughout our period. They are comparatively ill recorded, however, and are most often seen through the eyes of their lords, an inevitable but unfortunate result of the gaps in early medieval documentation.

By the eighth–ninth centuries, the bipartite estate had become common throughout most of north and central Italy (it was never, as I have noted, characteristic of the South, where tenants just paid rent). Some of these estates, particularly monastic ones, had become quite highly organised. The internal structure of tenant cultivation (whether with labour service or not) was the basis for all the socio-economic relations of what can be termed 'feudal' society. These structures had become dominant in all society, except in some parts of the Appennines, where lordship was not yet fully established at all, and except in Byzantine Italy, where the tax network of the Byzantine state provided alternative ways of removing peasant surpluses to the benefit of the rich. How they actually worked, however, is best seen through some concrete examples. It is through local differences that the real complexity of these patterns can best be seen. This is also a good way of showing what sort of evidence we have to go on.

To begin with, we shall look at the village of Varsi in the Parmense Appennines, not too remote (about forty kilometres from Parma), but securely placed in the hills. It is the focus of a series of connected mid-eighth-century charters, which survive because they are all transactions connected with the church of Varsi, S. Pietro, and its rectors. In 735, seven people gave or sold tiny pieces of land to S. Pietro in *casale Cavalloniano*. The largest piece was about half an acre, the smallest as little as eighty square yards. Two years later, one of these seven, Munari son of Gemmolo, with two of his brothers, sold two more fields in the same place to the church. In a similar way, the church accumulated land in Varsi itself. In 736 Ansoald and his wife Theotconda sold three pieces of arable land beside the Varsi lake, bordering on the lands of four other groups of people. In 737 the two sons of Godilani sold four pieces of land 'with trees on' along the road adjoining the lake, again bordering on the lands of five other people, some of them kinsmen. Similar charters survive from 742, 758 and 774; each time, S. Pietro or local laymen received or bought tiny fragments of land. In 753, Ambrosius son of Marioni confirmed by charter the freedom of a former slave, Domoald, who had been received into S. Pietro. In 762, Ansoald, uncle of S. Pietro's rector Lopoald, conceded that he had illegally occupied some of Lopoald's land, but Lopoald, 'having considered the charity due to kinsmen', let him off the twenty *solidi* fine. Ansoald gave him two *tremisses*, and a piece of land with vines in gratitude.[28]

Varsi was not a large-scale society. The scale of its transactions was, as we can see, tiny. Many of the men in the charters were *exercitales*, Lombard freemen, but they all seem to have been owner-cultivators; no tenants are mentioned, even casually. Men appear as witnesses from neighbouring villages, but none from as far away as the plain. A smith, a builder, and a notary were among these witnesses, and most of the charters were written by a local cleric, Maurace. It was a stable society. Many villages that are lit up in a similar way by a group of charters came much more fully into the hands of a church in the space of a generation or so, but S. Pietro di Varsi, though consistently acquiring land, only obtained one or two fields at a time. Sometimes such fields adjoined its own land, a good indication of some sort of accumulation, but often not. No family surrendered all its land to the church. Many families appear fleetingly in these texts; there is no sign of any of them going under.

Varsi was a society of the Appennines; a contrast to it is provided by Gnignano in the Lombard plain, about half-way between Milan and Pavia. Here we have an interesting run of charters stretching between 798 and 856, preserved in the archive of S. Ambrogio in Milan. In the earliest charters of 798 and 824, Walpert of Gnignano and his son Leo of Siziano (a nearby village) gave several pieces of land there to their friend (or creditor), the goldsmith Arifus of Pavia. In 833 these properties, having passed to Arifus's wife Vigilinda in a marriage gift, were sold for forty *denarii* to an important Milanese cleric, Guntzo, who gave them to his friend, the Aleman urban aristocrat Hunger son of Hunoarch. Guntzo and Hunger were both engaged in collecting land in Gnignano. Hunger in a document of 836 listed tenant houses in Gnignano that had come to him from several different people, and a large property there that Paul, a notary from Pavia, had sold him the previous year for seventeen pounds of coined silver. Most of this land was destined, after the death of Hunger's close relatives, to come into the possession of the monastery of S. Ambrogio. In 840 this had already largely occurred, despite the protests of a local inhabitant, Rodepert, possibly a protégé of Hunger, who in that year conceded the rights of the monastery to its land there. In the 850s Guntzo was still in possession of land in Gnignano, but in 856, after his death, S. Ambrogio (for whom Guntzo had acted as advocate) had accumulated most of this, too.

S. Ambrogio by the mid-850s had beyond doubt become the dominant owner in Gnignano. The early charters not connected with Guntzo and Hunger must concern lands that S. Ambrogio obtained from other people, such as those which Rachinfrit of Gnignano and his brother rented out to a cleric in 832, and those that the childless Teutpald of Gnignano sold off in 839. S. Ambrogio's land first appeared on the boundary of the property of other people in 832; previously, boundaries only gave the names of the small lay owners of the early charters. By the 850s, though, S. Ambrogio's land seems to have been omnipresent in the village, along with the land of two other churches, S. Vittore in Meda and S. Stefano in Decimo. The only known lay owner surviving by the 850s was a certain Bavo, son of Rotari, a tenant of S. Vittore in 856, but also an independent landowner (with his own tenants) in three charters of 851–6, possibly the last one to live in Gnignano itself.[29]

The social patterns of Gnignano were obviously as fast-moving in this half-century as those of Varsi had been fixed. The four or five known local landowning families were from the first interspersed with the lands of urban artisans from Pavia, and inside a generation, through the mediation of two important Milanese aristocrats, these four or five local families were reduced to one; churches held the rest. This may not be typical of other villages around Milan, for the extent of Gnignano's documentation is unusual, and S. Ambrogio may not have obtained so much in undocumented villages. Clearly, though, there was a drift towards large and ecclesiastical landownership in the early ninth century. The other clear contrast with Varsi is the existence of tenants. How large and socially significant local Gnignano landowners were is unclear, though some, at least, were linked to important artisans. Bavo, the last survivor, appears in a distinctly lowly role as a tenant-cultivator for some of his land. But these local owners, even Bavo, had their own tenants, both free tenants, leasing single pieces of land, and (probably) servile tenants in their own tenant houses (*casae massariciae*). Most of the population of the village probably always consisted of tenants, mixed in with the local owners. Some of them were dependent on these owners, and others, increasing in number, on outside churches. It is thus as real to say that the developments of the early ninth century in Gnignano meant that tenants, instead of paying rent locally, had to pay it to outside owners, as to say that local landowners lost their land to the Church.

What we lack in the case of Gnignano are leases made by these tenants; few survive from Lombardy at all in this period. The sort of rents payable by tenants in this part of Italy are best seen in the polyptychs. As an example, I quote here part of that of 862–883 for Bobbio, the entry for the estate based on Travo, thirty kilometres south-west of Piacenza.

> [In demesne] 60 *modia* of corn can be sown each year, 18 *anforas* of wine collected in a good year, and 11 carts of hay. There is a wood for 40 pigs, and a mill . . . . There are 11 *libellarii* [tenants by charter] and 19 *massarii* [customary tenants]; they render a third part of their corn, totalling 223 *modia*, a third of their wine (80 *anforas*), 7 *solidi*, 74 hens, and eggs. The *libellarii* do 24 days labour-service a year; the *massarii* as much as they are ordered.

We do not know of any inhabitants of Travo that were not tenants of Bobbio, and the village was therefore perhaps more homogeneous than Gnignano, but not all these tenants lived in Travo itself, for in 835 the estate was described as 'Travo with its dependencies'. Tenant houses were probably scattered around nearby villages. The rents are certainly typical enough to serve as indications of what was normal in Lombardy.

These three examples show the range of evidence that charters can give us, and they point up the contrasts that can be found in different –

and often the same – areas of Italy. There is one important similarity, though, and it is a norm over almost every part of Italy: the fragmentation of property. In both Varsi and Gnignano, property was dispersed across wide areas. Even in Travo, an apparently coherent estate, tenants were dispersed around other villages. Landowners did not have, for the most part, estates in a single bloc of land, constituting a single village or even part of one. Instead, they tended to have, at best, an estate centre in one village and tenant houses stretched across several others. The tenants themselves, like the owner-cultivators of Varsi, would have holdings consisting of numerous fields scattered across one village, or often more than one, and many of these fields would be very small. Teuprand and his wife Gumpranda founded an urban church in Lucca in 764 and handed over to it a set of properties that were intended to be a landed base sufficient for its functioning. These consisted of a tenant house with its lands in Sesto, ten kilometres north of Lucca, another on the coast, twenty kilometres to the north-west, another about seventy kilometres further down the coast with a quarter of its lands (one guesses that Teuprand's three brothers kept the rest), a quarter of an estate about five kilometres north-west of Lucca, a quarter olive grove in the hills near Sesto, and three other fields scattered across the plain to the north and east of the city. It is ownership of this kind that the apparently random fields of Varsi and Gnignano denote; and this randomness is the product of many generations of partible inheritance.[30]

This fragmentation had many consequences, apart from the most obvious, that peasants had to travel around more to cultivate their land. Land was carefully divided between co-heirs, down to the smallest field. This had implications for economic co-operation inside the family, as we shall see (pp. 119–20). The weakening of one's control over one's tenants if they lived in single houses many kilometres away is a point that will also recur (see pp. 111f.). The consequence that I want to point out here is the great difficulty involved in any economic planning. Lay landowners could not keep their estates together for more than two generations at the most, as all inheritance was partible. Churches and monasteries saw their estates build up as the product of random gifts and sales, and even at Gnignano, where S. Ambrogio acquired a certain dominance, its lands were intermingled with those of other landowners. Consolidation was a vain hope, except in the unusual cases where a church had acquired the great bulk of an area. Landowners could not, for the most part, control what their tenants grew on their plots of land, for these could not always be easily separated from the lands of other landowners. And in a society like that of Gnignano, where single fields and tenant holdings moved from owner to owner like counters, the tight structure of the bipartite estate must have been very difficult to maintain. Labour service cannot ever have been easy to extract from tenants living as much as twenty kilometres from an estate centre. A small landowner with only a few tenants is likely to have cultivated his demesne himself (or with slaves), or to have had no demesne at all, relying entirely on rents.

Travo was clearly more organised than this; and indeed the excep-'scale, and they are the products of organised estates like Travo, with a the polyptychs of Bobbio and S. Giulia, and of the other monasteries for which polyptychs have only survived in fragments, or not at all.[31] Here, at least, we have systematic indications of volumes of rent, heavy labour services, and some cash-cropping, even; at the very least, the systematic sale of surplus. Bobbio took, from fifty-six estates, 5679 *modia* (perhaps 9600 bushels) of corn, 1640 amphorae of wine, 2886 pounds of oil, 1590 cart-loads of hay, 5500 pigs, a variety of assorted products such as iron, chestnuts, and poultry, and rents in money. These are returns on some scale, and they are the products of organised estates like Travo, with a *curtis*, an estate centre (in monastic parlance, a *cella*), the focus for demesne land on which tenants did service, varying from several days a week to a few weeks a year. The only instances we can identify of whole villages coming under one lord are from such monastic (and, more rarely, episcopal) properties. These villages were almost certainly, for the most part, fiscal land given to the church by kings, sometimes in under-settled or afforested areas, which monasteries by the ninth century were beginning to clear. Nevertheless, it would be difficult to claim that these monasteries had any overall conception of the organisation of their property. Bobbio's rents varied from village to village in type and volume; so did labour service. It had two different types of tenant, *libellarii* and *massarii*, each with varying burdens inside the same estate or village. The types of rent delivered, though resulting in impressive totals of every kind of produce, are clearly in each case those typical of the subsistence agriculture of the area from which they came. Even the great monasteries were faced with a near-impossible task if they wished to systematise their properties, except when they had themselves organised the clearance of the land, a situation that always tends towards greater uniformity (cf below, pp. 166f.). And the great monasteries were in a minority. Most land was owned by far smaller institutions, or by lay nobles, whose world was one of extremely fragmented landowning. As a result of this, it is more useful to see the basic economic structures of society as being built up, not out of estates, but out of the units of peasant cultivation, tenant holdings or *casae massariciae*, and the small properties of peasant landowners. The rents and obligations of tenants, though often heavy, were far more external to the life of the tenant than they would have been in some parts of northern Europe, where entire village collectivities owing obligations to a single manor were more common. In Italy, the administrative centre of an estate could be miles away. Even if demesne work was owed inside the village, it was often on fields just as fractioned as those of the tenant himself, and often such tenants were the only ones in their village to be dependent on their landlords. Most villages, like Gnignano at the start of its run of charters, consisted of mixtures of peasant proprietors, small landlords, and tenants of a variety of lords. The village itself, and still more the family, were far more important foci than the great majority of estates. Landlords were seldom capable of influencing the processes of production; rents were in general customary, and cash crops were rare. With some important exceptions, such as the organisation of land clearance, agriculture was the concern of the peasant alone.

The period between the late eighth and the late tenth centuries saw two contradictory processes: the weakening of the political and social position of the free peasantry, and the weakening of the economic structure of estates, and thus the economic base of the landowning classes. To conclude this chapter, we shall look at each in turn.

We have seen that eighth and ninth-century kings were prone to issue laws bewailing the oppression of the poor. The state was chiefly interested in the survival of the public position of the free, their access to justice, and (particularly) their service in the army. These rights were already becoming tenuous for free tenants, who were increasingly becoming subject to their lords. We saw the beginning of this development in Liutprand's law on *libellarii*. By 813 a capitulary gave to landowners the responsibility for making their dependents perform state services – slaves, *aldii*, and *libellarii*, 'whether they had always been, or had newly become, tenants', alike (see p. 137). Not every *libellarius* was an ex-proprietor; the word simply means 'tenant, holding by right of a charter', and it is only after 800 that it becomes common. There were always free tenants in early medieval Italy, but it was only in the ninth century that it became normal to confirm their contracts with their lords by means of a written agreement. The traditional term in Lombard Italy for a tenant, whether free or unfree, was *massarius*, and this term continued to be used throughout our period (alongside, after 774, the Frankish term *manens*). *Libellarii* had to be free, for the unfree could not make contracts; they were sometimes, as at Bobbio, counterposed to *massarii*, who owed more labour service, and in some estates, less rent. In other areas, one cannot distinguish between the two: *massarii* often appear making contracts, and *libellarii* often owed dues and service as heavy as any *massarius*. Having a written lease perhaps gave tenants greater security than customary rights, but it did not necessarily convey higher status.[32]

But if not all *libellarii* were free owners come down in the world, many certainly were. Even the polyptychs, which are not normally concerned with the origins of tenants, make occasional references to them; so in Porzano south of Brescia, on S. Giulia's estates, there were fourteen freemen who had surrendered their property to the *curtis* and now held it again in return for a day's labour service per week each. Leases, too, sometimes make this explicit. In 765 in the territory of Chiusi, Bonulus sold to Guntefrid all his property; he then rented it back for twelve days per year labour service, as a tied tenant. The leases of the south Tuscan monastery of Monte Amiata were nearly all of this type, from about 804 onwards. Why free owners did this is never clear; sometimes, certainly, through economic catastrophe, when food and protection from a lord seemed worth the surrender of their land; often, one need not doubt, as a result of the violence or coercion of the lord concerned – Monte Amiata was by far the most powerful owner for miles around, in a remote area.[33]

The Church also obtained land for less directly economic reasons, through pious gifts. We have seen kings and aristocrats founding churches and monasteries, or endowing established ones with land, through genuine piety and through a desire to obtain status. The less rich and the poor were equally prone to do this. It is not easy to disentangle motives of piety and status from those of desperation and coercion, but one can do so when, as is common, donors gave to the Church one portion of their land, equivalent, it seems, to the portion of an extra son. When donors gave all their land it is often possible to see from the text that they had no direct heirs, as in the case of Guinifred of Pistoia and his sons in 767, who gave all their property to the church they had founded 'since we do not have sons or daughters or kin to whom we can give our property or our cause'. Sometimes they miscalculated, as with Goderisius of Rieti, who was taken to court in 791 for occupying land of the monks of Farfa that he had himself given them. He explained: 'it is true that I gave this property to the monastery; but afterwards I had sons, and now neither I nor my sons can live, for need oppresses me.' The eighth century was the great age of these gifts, apparently, as we have seen (pp. 43), unleashed by Liutprand's law legalising Church donations in 713.[34] After the first decades of the ninth century (varying from place to place) they became much less common. The reasons for this are unclear, and some historians conclude that it is because there were no small or medium landowners left; they had all become tenants. This is a little apocalyptic, especially as the most generous donors were childless, and it is difficult to see how their heirs could have become *libellarii*. More likely is the fact that the churches of Italy had become so rich, swollen with these donations, that they had lost their attraction to the pious. The compulsory payment of tithe to the Church, instituted by Charlemagne, may also have lessened the popularity of the Church among the poor. Only in some rather remote areas, such as Monte Amiata and the area around Farfa, did gifts continue. Here, as I said, one can certainly guess at coercion, and by 900 these two monasteries were virtually sole owners in large tracts of the countryside around them

The Church extended its property as the chance result of pious gifts and through deliberate aggrandisement; it could also from the ninth century use its hold on tithes to weaken peasant independence. Lay aristocrats, too, extorted land from the weak or accepted it from the starving in return for protection. Small owners became more and more vulnerable to their wealthy neighbours across the ninth century, and even more in the tenth, when lords took over some of the judicial prerogatives of the state. Not all of them, however, were absorbed as apparently passively as the peasants of the Amiata; some defended themselves, and a few even fought back. Peasant resistance was in fact as old as Rothari's edict, where the conspiracy and sedition of 'rustic men' and slaves is punished with heavy penalties.[35] In the Carolingian period, however, we find a number of court cases in which peasants proclaim their rights, usually without success.

These cases were very various. In Milan in 900, eleven men of Cusago (ten kilometres west of the city) claimed that they were free *arimanni*, and not *aldii*, even though they did labour service for the *curtis* of Palazzolo, the property of the count of Milan; for they owned small amounts of property in Bestazzo as well as that for which they did service. The count's advocate called thirteen 'noble and godfearing men' to prove that the men of Cusago were *aldii*, but unfortunately they all swore that the men of Cusago were in the right. This case shows very clearly how vulnerable small owners were to the claims of their influential neighbours and landlords; it is one of the very few they won. In 845, the Veronese monastery S. Maria in Organo brought a case against its alleged slaves in the county of Trento, where the slaves were refusing rent and labour, and claiming their freedom. When Lupus Suplainpunio and seven others claimed that they were legally free owners and just doing services through a commendation (protection) agreement, S. Maria conceded their freedom but successfully claimed their land on the ground that their services were rent for the land itself. S. Maria in this case had moved from obtaining labour in return for protection, to outright ownership of the land of her protégés, and a claim (so far rejected) that they were her slaves. In Pavia in 880, two men of Oulx in the Piedmontese Alps tried to reopen a case they had previously conceded, concerning their personal freedom, on the ground that 'the whole thing was perpetrated on us by force'; not surprisingly, they lost as well. The men of Oulx were probably already tenants of the monastery of Novalesa, who were trying to establish the boundary between free and servile tenancy, an important boundary for those tenants who wished to avoid arbitrary exactions and punishments. There are several similar court cases from Milan and Pisa.[36] These represent, of course, a different stratum of resistance from those of the free proprietors of Cusago, or even Trento, but the two groups have obvious parallels. It is interesting that many of these cases were from mountain areas, and several were from areas where monasteries had recently obtained land from other owners, especially the fisc, and were (it seems) trying to bring their lands more firmly under central control.

This last point is clearest in the case of the men of the Valle Trita, a very remote area in the Abruzzese Appennines, who were claimed as slaves by the monastery of S. Vincenzo al Volturno after a cession of fiscal land to it by King Desiderius. The men contested their status, claiming their lands to be their own property, in five court cases between 779 and 872, it sometimes required the whole force of the Carolingian state to get them to come to court at all.[37] We cannot say the monastery ever won; these court decisions were clearly systematically disobeyed, and the end of the run of cases coincides with a century of weakness of control over any of its lands by the monastery. Here, then, an attempt by S. Vincenzo to subject remote peasants, who had probably only owed a very formal dependence to the king, to the estate structure of monastic landowning, failed. In the North, such monasteries were more successful: S. Maria in Organo in Trento; S. Ambrogio in the Valtellina and in the Limonta cases on Lake Como; Novalesa in the Val di Susa. These cases are parallel to that of Cusago in that they show concerted opposition to the spread of the power of great landowners and the organisation of the estate. It may be that they are mostly from mountain areas because peasants in marginal areas have closer economic relationships and are thus better able to resist (cf. above, p. 98). But, with the exception of Cusago and probably the Valle Trita, they failed: monasteries did extend their lands, free owners became tenants, free tenants became unfree. And in the tenth century, even those free proprietors who survived often became subject to the justice of their rich neighbours, as we shall see.

While these processes were slowly whittling away the rights of the free, the internal structure of the expanding great estates was itself changing. As elsewhere in Europe, the weakening position of the free was matched by an improvement in the position of the servile. In the Limonta cases of 882–957, slaves claimed from S. Ambrogio their freedom, or at least the status of *aldii*, like the men of Oulx just discussed. When they conceded their status, they still pressed a claim that S. Ambrogio had increased their customary obligations, adding, in particular, obligations to pick and press olives. S. Ambrogio, significantly, did not claim that it had a right to increase the burdens due from slaves; instead, it brought local notables forward as witnesses to show that the obligations had always been exacted. Custom, at least in theory, was fixed, even for slaves. And slavery itself was on the wane. The fusion of free and servile in the broad spectrum of the tenant class eventually took place on the free side of the borderline, unlike elsewhere in Europe, where tenants lost their freedom. Many of our ninth-century leases already seem to be with servile tenants who had been freed. Manumissions became more and more frequent; slaves bought their liberty more and more often. In the late 990s, Otto III attempted to restrict these changes in a special capitulary 'on slaves gasping for freedom', but this can have had little effect. After the early eleventh century slavery became less and less common.[38]

The reason why tenants as a class ended up free, not servile, was beyond doubt because landlords began to rent out their demesnes and ceased to demand labour service; the direct personal links that reinforced unfreedom were lost. This development is already visible in the later ninth century in Tuscany, and even some of the estates of

Bobbio and S. Giulia. By the tenth century, labour service was rare everywhere. In the great monastic estates, this may have been through the desire of monasteries to attract tenants to clear land. Elsewhere, it was the logical conclusion of the incoherence of organisation of the great fragmented territories of lay lords and bishops. When what patterns that existed were perpetually disturbed by partible inheritance among the lay aristocracy and the random gifts still given to the church, as well as the beginnings of large-scale leases of church land to small nobles (see pp. 140ff.), the organic links necessary for demesne labour became impossible to maintain. Estates now became groupings of tenant houses, and nothing more. Leases with free tenants now became less commonly for life, three generations, or perpetual, as was common in the eighth century, and more and more for fixed terms, especially twenty-nine years. This too underlined and aided the growing independence of tenants. And, increasingly, landowners required rents in money. In the eighth century, many rents were already in money, alongside rents in kind (cereals, wine, oil, eggs, animals), and labour – though money rents, representing a higher status for tenants, were less often required alongside labour. In the ninth century, and still more the tenth, more and more rents were in money, often alongside a partiary rent in wine or oil, but little else.[39]

Money rents were, of course, the product of the specific needs of landlords, as long-distance commerce became more common. But they show two other things, too: the ability of subsistence peasants to obtain coins in surplus exchange; and the total separation of the landlord from any control over what was being done on the land. As long as he produced his three, or eight, or twelve *denarii* per year, a peasant, whether free or unfree, could henceforth exploit his land without further reference to the lord at all. By the end of the tenth century, there is even some evidence that he could sell leased land to other tenants. At this point, the 'manorial system' had clearly broken up. Even though free owners were still being forced and absorbed into large estates, the estates themselves had merely become territorially scattered umbrella organisations for the extraction of rent. Any real economic control by landowners over the countryside at ground level seems to have been lost by the late tenth century in north and central Italy.

The activity of peasants in surplus exchange is difficult to document, but must have long existed in some form. We have seen that the basic economic unit in Italy was the smallholding. Each peasant family grew, as far as it could, as wide a range of staple crops as it could manage. But

Italy is not geographically homogeneous, and different crops grow better in different areas, particularly vines on hills and cereals on the plain. Despite the existence of promiscuous agriculture, we can already see these differences in the early medieval period. The imbalances must have been corrected by exchange. Some craft products, such as pottery and leather, were also almost certainly bought, though our evidence for them is exiguous; so, also, of course, was salt. It is for these reasons that landowners found it worthwhile in the tenth century to appropriate the tolls from quite small local markets, where luxury commerce would certainly scarcely reach. Money would not always have been used in such exchanges. The Lombards for the most part only minted a single gold coin, the *tremissis* (a third of a *solidus*), which was certainly too large for most local exchange. At the end of the eighth century, the Carolingians replaced it with a silver *denarius* (a twelfth of a *solidus*), in theory more easily usable for small-scale exchange (in the Lucchesia in the ninth century, a pig was apparently worth twelve *denarii*, and a wether six *denarii*; in Francia in 794, if the parallel is at all useful, bread prices were fixed at one *denarius* for twelve two-pound loaves of wheat, or fifteen of rye, twenty of barley, or twenty-five of oats). Even so, a single coin of this size is far too unwieldy for easy money transactions as we understand them. Economic transactions must have been largely carried out using money as a standard of comparison, rather than a medium of exchange. In a traditional society, where social relationships and economic relationships are very closely linked, where one makes exchanges with people one knows, this is not as difficult as it sounds.[40] Money was certainly easily available to Italians at all levels of society; it was just not very useful. Peasants probably regarded coins as objects to be obtained by selling produce, which would eventually end up in urban markets; the coins would then be used to pay rents. Landowners, on the other hand, operating in urban markets on a far larger scale, would doubtless have used coins in a more recognisable 'commercial' way.

This is certainly all very speculative. But the customary society in which local exchange was embedded can be seen exercising its control over values. We have seen that kings desired 'just prices' to be maintained. In some cases they were even prepared to intervene and void 'unjust' sales, as after the Italian famine of 776. Values could become very fixed, with considerable regional variability. We see this, for example, in 813, in the embarrassment of the estimators who were moderating an exchange of land between the monasteries of Nonantola and S. Salvatore in Brescia; Brescia custom valued land at less than eight *denarii* per *iugum*, but Nonantola custom at well over three *solidi* per *iugum*. Adalard of Corbie had to be called in to arrange a compromise. It did not occur to anyone that market forces could be employed to do so, or indeed that market forces, at least in land, even existed, despite the frequency of land sales.[41] Exchange in Italy was very tightly linked to the social nexus in which it was found. Such socio-economic links between peasants at the level of exchange are, too, another element in the separation of landowners from peasant society.

This separation reached its height around the year 1000, when labour services had virtually disappeared, leaving a class of tenants owing, in most places, only rents in money, with some kind rent. The bipartite estate had more or less ceased to exist. Great landlords were not able to stabilise and concentrate, still less rationalise, their properties. In fact, with the rise of a new small noble class based on large-scale leases of land, often at nominal rents, greater lords (especially churches) had less control over their lands than ever before. Violence in the countryside rose, as these smaller lords tried to establish their own powers over the peasantry. Peasants as well as lords sometimes found themselves able to use the localisation of petty judicial rights and the new tenth–eleventh-century fortified territorial units, the *castelli*, to reinforce their own power and found 'rural communes' alongside the urban ones. But we are getting ahead of ourselves again; these are developments which could only occur when the state had fallen, as we shall see in chapter 7. Only in the mid-eleventh century, in the context of the reform movement, would churches succeed in re-establishing control over their rural properties again, and with the rise of the city communes they and other urban landowners began to buy their way systematically into the countryside, acting as middlemen between the peasantry and the urban market, and using that position to regain their control over the peasantry. By the twelfth–thirteenth centuries, peasants were paying rents in kind again, so that all the profit on the expanding city market could go to their landlords. Cities did not need a commercial relationship with the countryside; just its food. The development of the commercial breakthrough of the twelfth–thirteenth centuries meant, in fact, a reversal of even the modest penetration of commercial exchange into rural society.[42]

5. Solidarity, Hierarchy, and Law

Kinship and the Courts

WE have seen the survival for many centuries in Italy of a free peasantry, sometimes landowning and sometimes tenant, alongside complex hierarchies of landowners, some local, some absentee and in large part city-dwelling. The power of landowners was considerable, but insufficient to control the economic life of localities. It was equally insufficient to dominate their social life. It is easy to see that the free inhabitants of villages such as Varsi (see above, pp. 101–2) would have been effectively independent from outside pressures, except for the public demands of the state, such as army service. But even the inhabitants of villages such as Gnignano (see above, pp. 102–4), where large owners became dominant, would not have found their lords very relevant to their ordinary lives, particularly as they no longer lived inside the village. The increase in economic power of large owners across the eighth and ninth centuries certainly increased the social importance of hierarchies and lordship, as we shall see in the second section of this chapter. But the day-to-day problems of peasant communitites, small-scale co-operation, tensions, the resolution of differences were solved in different ways, through social links between equals or near-equals, particularly those based on kinship and family relationships.

The whole imagery of the Lombard and Carolingian state rested on the importance of the free, especially as soldiers, but also as participants in various public obligations and occasions such as courts. This did not save their weaker strata from being oppressed by the strong, but it did mean that their public activities were quite well documented, and that kings took an interest in their fate. It also meant that, at least in theory, the free members of society all had broadly the same status, rich and poor alike. Though this was never true in reality, it does at least mean that we cannot draw a line between aristocratic and non-aristocratic members of eighth–ninth century society (cf. below, pp. 131ff.); and the kinship patterns that we find in Italy in this period seem to have been characteristic of all levels of free society. Only in the eleventh century would aristocratic families begin to take on superficially different traits, as we shall see in the last chapter (pp. 185–7). Whether the unfree had similar patterns of social life is impossible to be sure. Our documents seldom concern themselves with this section of society; its existence, and uncertain size, must serve as a silent corrective to anything said in this chapter. There are hints, however, that in the unfree strata at least tenants, and perhaps even household slaves, had social ties not unlike those in the lower sections of free society.

This section will discuss the most important of these social ties, kinship, as well as less highly organised patterns of solidarity, the *consortium* and the village itself. Kinship is important in all traditional societies, and it is customary to contrast them in this respect with modern societies, where the public activities of citizens are regulated by law and the courts. Early medieval Italy was, however, socially very precocious, and the impact of legislation and judicial activity was also considerable. We will look at this impact at the end of this section, and at some of the contrasts between law and kinship-solidarity, as they appear to the modern observer – early medieval Italians themselves do not seem to have been so disturbed by them.

One of the first things that we are told about the Lombards is that they had large lineage groups or *farae*. Alboin invaded Italy *in fara*, and when he made his nephew Gisulf duke in Friuli gave him his choice of *farae* to keep with him. Paul glosses the word 'that is, generation or lineage', and the term 'lineage' is probably the best translation. Place names using the word seem to indicate the earliest stratum of Lombard settlement, as the word drops out of use after a single reference in Rothari's code. One of these, in the Abruzzese Appennines, is the suggestive 'Fara filiorum Petri', an already latinised lineage name, surviving in this form to the present day. Gregory the Great referred to Lombard army groups (Byzantine mercenaries, in fact) called *Grusingi* and *Gaugingi*, and these may also be *fara* names, less wholly latinised in this case; -*ing* is a common west Germanic suffix, which is often used as the identification marker for a lineage. Exactly what *farae* were for, or even what size they were, unfortunately remains obscure. What happened to *farae* is unclear too. Rothari, as I said, only used the word once, when referring to the right of a man to 'migrate' to another part of the kingdom with his *fara*. Otherwise, he referred to the 'lineage' (*parentilla*) only as the group of people from which a Lombard could claim inheritance rights, as long as he was the nearest heir and could name all his intervening relatives.[1] The *parentilla* was large, seven generations deep, but it does not seem to have had any real function. As functioning bodies, Rothari referred to smaller groups of kinsmen (*parentes*), who assembled for legal or quasi-legal activities, pledging, oath-helping (the formal swearing to the good name and innocence of an accused man), and feud.

Feud was not regarded by the inhabitants of early medieval Europe, even by kings, as the disruptive process that has at times been castigated by modern historians. It has rules, and a built-in tendency towards the re-establishment of peace, in that people who are willy-nilly involved in a feud, often with links to both sides, do not usually wish to spend most of their time fighting. In all societies, the famous long-lasting feuds are by definition atypical, for they attract people's attention precisely because they are unsolved. This is usually only possible in cases of exceptional antagonism and gravity, and usually also where the participants live far enough away from each other to be able to avoid social contact, or in places of some social complexity such as cities; the great Italian feuds have nearly all been urban (one thinks of the Montagues and the Capulets). Feud is a possibility in many traditional and small-scale communities, and the Mediterranean has always been one of its strongholds. The potential outbreak of feud underlies all the traditional peasant concern for family solidarity and peace.[2]

The Lombard kings valued peace, too. They did not, however, regard violence, except inside the king's court, as offensive to the principles of civil society. They tried to limit the occurrence of feud, to prevent it breaking out over trivia. Rothari made feud compensation greater, to make its acceptance more honourable, thus increasing the chances for the settlement of feud. But feud was part of Lombard custom, and the basic rights of any Lombard to engage in it could not be undermined. We have seen that Liutprand retained the duel (which is itself, very largely, a ritualised and restricted variant of feud), despite his suspicions of its justice (see above, p. 44), and the Carolingians even slightly extended its scope. It is, however, an ironic fact that it is from royal legislation guiding and limiting the procedures of feud that we learn almost all we know about it. Our narrative texts are sparse, and apart from the occasional tale of revenge in Paul the Deacon, Liutprand of Cremona, or especially the *Chronicon Salernitanum*, we have no accounts of major feuds until the chronicles of the communal period and beyond. Its presence and legitimacy is assumed by all the sources that mention it, however.

The structure of the kin group in Lombard society was made up almost exclusively through male-line, so-called 'agnatic' or 'patrilineal' links. When a man's daughter married, she married into a different family (Liutprand warned against marriage into a family one is feuding with) and elaborate safeguards had to be worked out to avoid her exploitation. If she sold land after her marriage, her own kin had to testify that she did this of her own free will, and was not coerced by her husband and his kin; charters showing this requirement are common into the twelfth century. This male-line kin system helped the definition of families, for a man or woman could only be a member of one family group. It was closely linked to inheritance. When a man needed his kin to swear for him in an oath-helping ceremony, he had to present them in order of inheritance, fetching them from all over the kingdom if necessary. In feud, too, the only man entitled to avenge a dead man was his son, though if he had no children or only daughters the obligation fell to a less closely-defined group of *propinqui* or *proximi parentes*, close relatives. Feud, being by its nature a more spontaneous business, could not be controlled as strictly as the ritual of oath-helping.[3]

These were Lombard rules, for they were part of Lombard law. The Romans had patrilineal lineages, too, but the law of the Empire did not recognise such private remedies as feud. There are hints, however, that Romans at least felt the need to exact revenge for the death of kinsmen. The seventh-century Italian legal handbook, the *Summa Perusina*, states baldly 'if you have avenged the death of a kinsman, you will become his heir'. This text probably reflects the practice in Rome under the Exarchate.[4] In Lombard Italy, all we can do is guess. We have, though, seen that the Romans in Lombard Italy borrowed elements out of Lombard group solidarity such as *launigild*, which by the eleventh century became part of the territorial law of the Lombard kingdom (cf. above, p. 69). It is not unlikely that they adopted feud, too, even though we cannot prove it.

Women in this world had little formal place. The Lombards (though not the Romans) regarded them as perpetually subject to men from birth to death; to father, brother, husband, and son in turn. They could rarely become the holders of land, except as heiresses or widows, and even then their control of it was legally circumscribed. The only legally independent Lombard women were the abbesses of nunneries, probably because they had taken on some parts of Roman law in their religious vows. Early medieval Italy was never, probably, a very pleasant place for women to be. Only occasionally in the higher nobility did some women of exceptionally strong character achieve some political weight, especially in periods of instability. These were usually widows of important men without adult heirs, like Theodelinda among the Lombards, and more occasionally the influential wives of living men, like Angilberga, Louis II's wife. The tenth century saw a large number of these figures: Berta, widow of Adalbert II of Tuscany, Ermengarda, widow of Adalbert of Ivrea, Willa, wife of Berengar of Ivrea, and, most remarkable of all, Marozia, who made herself ruler of Rome in 928–32. Significantly, Liutprand of Cremona, their chronicler, had no wish to find any explanation for their importance other than gross sexual licence, the only reason he could think of for their incomprehensible control over men; their power offended against all his assumptions about the world.[5] It may be better to see them as focal points of dynastic continuity (as heiresses, or the guardians of infant sons) in a century when lineage-consciousness among the aristocracy was becoming more important (cf. below, pp. 186–7). They were scarcely typical, however. Most women are only names to us, the nominal rulers of land alienated by their menfolk, or the counters with which kin groups made alliances through marriages. What they really did or thought is unknown.

The basis of kin solidarity was beyond doubt co-operation in economic activities. One is far more likely to wish to avenge one's cousin's death if one helps him prune his vines and he helps one gather one's olives. We have so far looked at the theory of feud in kinship; but feud is rare. Far more common is economic co-operation, and this is better recorded in our evidence. When Paul the Deacon's great-grandfather Lopichis, alone out of all his brothers, escaped from captivity after an Avar raid and returned (with the aid of a friendly wolf) to his ruined home, he rebuilt it with gifts from his kinsfolk (*consanguineorum et amicorum*). This is what kinsmen were for.[6] We have already seen the fragmentation of land in Italy caused by partible inheritance. It was and is typical of owners to divide up every plot of their land between their sons (daughters only inherited land if there were no sons). But the other side of this coin is that such heirs were not expected to farm the land separately, at least for one generation, and sometimes more. It was, indeed, not always necessary to divide the land immediately on a father's death; several Lombard laws discuss the rules governing communal ownership between brothers. In the Lombard period, such indivision only lasted, in most cases, until one of the brothers died or wished to separate himself more formally. By the tenth–eleventh century, however, undivided lands held by cousins and sometimes more distant relatives were commoner. Indivision at least postponed the necessity of determining fair portions, which could be an acrimonious business, and was always complex. A Lucchese charter of 762 records part of the process by which Bishop Peredeus divided his property with his nephew Sunderad at his brother's death; nearly thirty pieces of land are carefully set out and apportioned, and this was only part of their landholding. But to separate the affairs of Peredeus and Sunderad out entirely they would have had to have exchanged their lands to create independent blocs of properties, and this they certainly failed to do. Such exchanges are in fact very rare in Italian charters. An early example is from the hills above Parma, up the valley from Varsi, in 770, when Audepert son of Auderat exchanged his property in one village for the property of his uncle and cousins in another village. Audepert seems to be separating himself off from his kin, at least in a physical sense. Perhaps more interesting, however, is that his kin, Artemio and his nephews and nieces Rodepert, Gumpert, Asstruda and Paltruda, were still holding their lands undivided; it is Audepert here who was the exception. We are dealing here with two different levels of society, for Peredeus and Sunderad were important aristocrats, and Artemio and Audepert were at best very small landowners, and probably owner-cultivators, but the problems of division and co-operation remained the same.[7]

Kinship was the commonest form of horizontal solidarity, but it was not the only one. Slaves, for example, were regarded in law as being without kin, and when they were freed *en masse*, the resultant group of *colliberti* were regarded as having the same structure and obligations as a kin group. Even slaves sometimes at least had recognisable relatives, however. There survive two remarkable texts from late eleventh-century Arezzo, listing some of the household slaves (including a family of cooks) of the monastery of SS Fiora and Lucilla, and in particular five generations of the descendents of one Petrus, living about 950, through his three daughters, Lucica, Gumpiza, and Dominica, who are described as all being related by kinship (*propinquitate*). Five generations is a big group of kinsmen by any standards, and the suspicion arises that its depth may just be the result of the ownership records of the monastery; but when one of the latest generation, Johannes son of Rusticellus, claimed his freedom in a public court in 1080 (without success), his servile kinsmen came too. Most of the links in these slave genealogies were male-line, as well; the structure of the group was the same as for free men. The links even between household slaves and the free were not entirely lacking. One or two free men married into these families, and some of the slaves had, in fact, once been free, and were only slaves because they could not pay the legal penalties for murder and theft; they may have had free kinsmen too. These texts are, as far as I know, unique, and suddenly let a shaft of light into what is otherwise total darkness. But it is unlikely that the state of affairs they illuminate was unparalleled elsewhere.[8]

Other collective groups are usually generically referred to as *consortes* or *consortia*. *Consors* in classical Latin meant 'partner' or 'co-owner', often 'co-heir', and these words are the basis for its meaning in early medieval Italy, as elsewhere in Europe, with different emphasis in different contexts. In eighth-century Italy it seldom meant 'kinsman' or 'co-heir', and normally denoted a partner in economic activity who was not a kinsman. But in the centuries following the distinction between kin and *consortes* broke down, and kin or heirs are often referred to as *consortes*. The emphasis of the word, however, was still on the co-ownership or co-operative use of property, and it kept its meaning of 'co-operating non-kinsmen' as well. It is in this context that members of village communities are sometimes referred to as *consortes*. We saw in the last chapter that villages which engaged in collective action were usually those in marginal areas, with some co-operative economic activity, such as pastoralism, as a basis for their collectivity. The men of Limonta referred to themselves as *consortes*, but here the economic base was probably a common subjection to the monastery of S. Ambrogio. An instance where the word points to the collective activity of a whole village or area is a courtcase of 824, when the *consortes* of Flexo unsuccessfully contested the rights of the monastery of Nonantola to fishing and pasturage near their territory, even though these rights had been granted to the village by King Liutprand. Flexo was in the Po marshes, and its inhabitants were still small owners, fighting to keep independent of monastic encroachment. It is quite possible that in such areas, village solidarity was more important than kinship, or at least on the same level of importance, and, conversely, that the absence of a powerful village community in settled areas was one of the things that gave the strength of kinship in Italy its whole raison d'être, as the only organising principle there was. Certainly the 'heirs and *consortes*' of the tenth–eleventh-century formularies elsewhere in Italy were rather different from the *consortes* of Flexo. Such *consortes* were, for the most part, extensions of the kin group, more or less artificial modifications of its extent. When in the eleventh century and after, aristocratic families set up contractual relationships inside the kin group to safeguard territorial nuclei and some forms of collective economic activity, these relationships were known as *consortia*, too (see p. 187). Their existence emphasises the continuing importance of kin relationships as the organising principle for most of society.[9]

Royal legislation shows that kings regarded feud and oath-helping as legitimate parts of the law, informal remedies based not on the formal presentation of evidence and the decisions of judges but on the confrontation of kin groups and the bargaining that surrounded the determining of compensation. Feud and its analogues are traditionally associated with crimes of violence and honour. Our court cases, however, were mostly concerned with land and legal status. They were rarely associated with any of the compromises and mediations that we associate with feud. Some examples should give some idea of their flavour.

In 762 Alpert of Pisa and his sister-in-law Rodtruda (with Tasso her legal representative) came to the royal court at Pavia. Tasso claimed that Alpert was illegally occupying the land of his dead brother Auripert, who had willed it to the Church. Alpert in response produced his charter, in which he and Auripert agreed to institute each other as heirs if either died childless, as Auripert had. Tasso replied by stating, first, that the charter was only a copy and so legally invalid; second, that it did not conform to the types of gift legitimated in Liutprand's seventy-third law; thirdly, he produced another charter (also a copy) by which Auripert willed his land to the Church, thus voiding the first one. Alpert asked, in apparently verbatim surprise: 'But, Tasso, if my copy is not legally valid, how come yours is?' Tasso, in something of a coup de théâtre, announced that *his* charter had been countersigned by King Aistulf, and was thus fully valid. Alpert lost.[10]

At some point during King Liutprand's reign, in or near Como, Lucius came to court to claim the legal recognition of his liberty which was being questioned (with violence) by Toto of Campione. Lucius produced his charter of the time of King Cunipert, showing he had been freed by Toto's kin by the ritual of being led around a church altar. But this ritual was only made legally valid in 721, in Liutprand's twenty-third law; a charter predating the law therefore fell. Lucius could not prove that he had been recognised as free for the thirty years previous to the court case, either (his rent and labour service obligations could have been performed either by slaves or freemen). His case therefore fell, for thirty years' renunciation of a right voided a man's claim to that right.[11]

Sometimes, when written evidence was not available, the court could

take oral evidence instead; we have seen examples of this in the
landlord–tenant cases in chapter 4, some of which include instances
where churches demanded witnesses to supplement charters, and
voided the charters when the witnesses were seen to have died. A less
weighted case is perhaps that of Gundi, the wife of Sisenand, a Frank
living in the eastern Abruzzo in 873. The imperial advocate Maio
claimed that she had become a nun after the death of her first husband,
against Sisenand's statement that he had married her legitimately.
Maio found a bishop and fifteen other witnesses who swore that she had
become a nun; she and her property were both forfeit to the state.
Sometimes more subtle legal problems were invoked. In 912 the
Emperor Guy's widow Ageltruda claimed back land that she had given
to the Church in an extant charter, against the protests of the bishop of
Piacenza, on the grounds that the charter was false. She succeeded in
showing this, not on any grounds of internal authenticity, but by
demonstrating that the church to which she had given her property,
SS. Croce and Bartolomeo in Persico, had never been built, so that the
charter fell.[12]

The list could continue. Nearly all court cases are interesting and
illuminating. There are about 10 from the Lombard period, and some
260 in Cesare Manaresi's collection of *placiti*, royal cases, between 774
and 1000 – and he missed several, and excluded large numbers of others
because they were not held by royal officials. They are all different in
style, at least until formulaic procedures and methods of case-recording
crept in in the 880s, and often apparently verbatim. But they are alike in
one crucial respect: a concern for the letter of the law, and for the literal
meaning of charters, where this did not conflict with the law. It is clear
from this that they did not have much to do with feud. Feuds, of course,
were probably not recorded so often in writing; nor did they often
involve churches, the chief preservers of documents. And, as I said,
the sort of disputes that surviving court cases record are much less those
that would involve feud. There are few for theft or crimes of violence,
despite the attention these were given in the Lombard code. A small
percentage show the Church exercising its rights to judge the sexual
misdemeanours of its clerics. A slightly larger group are the disputes
over status that we saw in the last chapter. The vast bulk of surviving
cases, however, concern land. Land is what most written evidence was,
after all, about. Rothari certainly envisaged that oath-helping could be
used in property disputes, as indeed it often was in court cases from
northern Europe, above all Anglo-Saxon England. But already he

allowed that a document could be used as *prima facie* evidence for the existence of a disputed land sale, if there was such a document (charters were much less common in the seventh century). In 746 Ratchis strengthened this. Evil vendors were prepared to swear that they had not been paid the full price for a sale, even though a charter had been made out for it: 'this seems harsh to us and our judges; . . . they can take anything away by such an oath'. Henceforth, no oath could invalidate a properly drawn up charter.[13]

Written evidence was the basis of most of our court cases. Its corollary was the primacy of written law. Rothari, like Germanic legislators elsewhere, was setting down custom (and sometimes updating it); unlike most others, though, he made an attempt to set down all of it, in 388 chapters. His attempt underlay all later legislation, right up to the early eleventh-century *Liber Papiensis*, a compilation by the law school at Pavia of all Lombard and post-Lombard royal law, with comprehensive annotation, cross-referencing, and sample cases, a remarkable and sophisticated tour de force, and the model for the revivals of Roman and canon law a century later. Royal written law was increasingly regarded as supreme in all fields. Liutprand allowed written law to be by-passed in a charter only if both parties agreed – and he excluded the law of inheritance from this. Louis II enacted categorically: 'no-one should dare to judge by his will alone, but should fully teach written law. What is not written about should be offered to us for our decision'. Medieval law in most countries moved slowly from the royal publication of traditional custom to the claim by the king of primacy over all law. In Italy, though, scarcely more than two centuries after Rothari, all law had become written law, at least in the eyes of the kings.[14]

These were, of course, only royal claims, but they seem to have been largely respected by the Italians – Lombards, Romans, and Franks alike. The extent of this respect emphasises the strength of the hegemony of the state in Italy. It also, perhaps, needs some explanation, for Italy was certainly unique in western Europe in the power and all-pervasiveness of written law in the eighth–ninth centuries.

The crucial point relevant here is the high proportion of the inhabitants of the Italian kingdom, at least of the upper classes, that were in some sense literate. Written law and the literal meaning of charters had some reality for them. We might expect this for churchmen and the urban professional strata – scribes, notaries, lawyers, doctors. But we find it among ordinary laymen too, particularly after the beginning of the ninth century. Our evidence comes from the percentage of people who signed as witnesses at the bottom of charters, rather than making crosses. In the Lucca charters of the eighth and ninth centuries, the percentages of signatures climb to remarkable heights. In the 760s, the first decade in which charters become numerous, 47 per cent of witnesses already sign their names; by the 820s this has climbed to 62 per cent, and by the last decade of the century as much as 83 per cent. Clerics and professionals already have a 69 per cent signature rate in the 760s; by the 890s, this has risen to 100 per cent. Even ordinary laymen, though only showing an 11 per cent rate in the 760s, have reached 77 per cent by the 890s.[15] Only men of some standing witnessed charters, and these figures cannot be regarded as valid outside the male members of the landowning classes, but for those classes they are clearly very high, and far higher than anywhere else in the West at the time. The ninth-century rise must, furthermore, provide some indication of the practical effect that the educational concerns of the Carolingian Renaissance had on the urbanised upper classes in Italy. Being able to sign one's name and add a short formula of witnessing is not, of course, a very ambitious criterion of literacy. In some contexts today (where the capacity to make a signature is an essential passport into many occupations) it does not even always prove an ability to read. But in the ninth century, when the symbolism of literacy was totally different, being able to write must at least have entailed an awareness of what written law and written proofs could mean, even if such a 'functionally literate' person could not read particularly fluently, let alone read Virgil for pleasure. Some exceptional men could even do that, in fact. Everard of Friuli, who died in 866, divided his library between his sons in his will. He had over fifty books: bibles, gospels, works of liturgy; Augustine's commentary on Ezechiel, his sermons, the *City of God*; the lives of Martin of Tours, the Oriental Fathers, and Apollonius; works of Isidore, Fulgentius, Martin of Braga, Basil of Caesarea, Orosius; two of the ninth-century Mirrors of Princes, the *Gesta regum francorum*, the *Liber Pontificalis*, a bestiary, Aethicus's cosmography, *De Rebus Bellicis*, and seven law codes, those of the Salian and Ripuarian Franks, the Alemans, the Bavarians, the Lombards, and the Roman codes of Theodosius II and Alaric. Few, if any, ordinary landowners would have even thought of emulating Everard, but the Carolingian Renaissance had some effect on them, too, in its more lowly (but more useful) role as the instigator of some form of schooling.[16]

The fact that written texts had some meaning to and use for the

Italians is amply shown in the number of charters that survive – several hundred in the eighth century, mostly as original texts; several thousand in the ninth century. Law was seen as integral to these texts. Not infrequently, charter-makers (or their scribes) show that they were aware of the explicit terms of laws: a number of common charter formulae across Italy cite the enabling laws of specific kings. In one charter from the territory of Pistoia in 880, the nun Roteruda, when giving what was in fact a legally dubious gift to a certain Widulprand, quoted the whole of Liutprand's 101st law verbatim. Normally, too, charters did not appear involving procedures that had not yet been legitimated by law. We saw king Liutprand rushing through his law to legitimate gifts to the Church in 713 (see above, pp. 43); our run of surviving charters virtually starts from that point. Among the landowning classes, at least, the influence of royal law and legislation was in principle very strong.[17]

This set of attitudes certainly derived from Roman traditions, the practice of comprehensive legislation and the written act alike. We have seen how this influence was felt on the content of some aspects of Lombard law, particularly the law of property (see above, p. 69f.) Respect for written law and abstract rules of evidence was just as Roman. Respect alone, however, was not enough to recreate the terrifying grandeur of the late Roman legal system, based on attitudes to law that we would recognise today – the difference between civil and criminal, the finality of disinterested judicial decision (with provision for appeal) – as well as practices that are in theory less familiar, such as the systematic torture of witnesses. The state was now Lombard and Lombard–Frankish, and the Lombards, though literate and sophisticated, remained a Germanic people, uninterested in recreating the coercive apparatus of the late Roman state, essential for the functioning of late Roman law. It is at this point that the apparently contradictary survival of feud becomes explicable. Formal procedures derived from the Roman period were restricted to the specific spheres of law that we have just looked at, property-owning and status. In other spheres, particularly where one side sought redress for violence, theft or insult from the other, traditional Germanic community methods were used, which hardly involved the state at all. The mixture of formal and informal procedure, of evidence and compurgation, is perhaps best seen in a law of Louis II against conspiracy to robbery, part of his comprehensive measures to restore public order in 850. If anyone was suspected or popularly rumoured to be part of such a conspiracy, he could clear himself by the oath-helping of twelve men, and if he could not, he was to face the standard penalty (normally a composition, half to his victim, half to the state). Wherever such thieves were known to live, however, all the local population had to give evidence to the court in a sworn inquisition.[18] Here the state intervened to clear up illegality in an area; but any specific local suspicions were still dealt with inside the community by standard oath-helping procedures, and the only change Louis made here was a possible doubling of the number of oath-helpers necessary for the accused to clear himself. This is all the response Louis thought necessary to solve what was clearly a serious social problem, and it may have worked – the problem did not recur in his later laws. A society beyond the Alps would probably have resorted here to physical ordeals to supplement community accusations. Louis instead used an inquisition, a fact-collecting device, similar to a British or American Grand Jury – ordeals were rather rare in Italy, apart from duels.

Where kings did intervene, by the enforcement of written law, they had the problem of ensuring that the state had the power to back up judgements that were not accepted by the losing party, particularly when the losing party was a man of influence and power. (How often judges really did judge against the strong is, perhaps, another matter – kings certainly had to legislate too often against corrupt or interested legal decisions to make us certain that the state was wholly effective here.) By what means the state did this is not easy to see. Our court cases merely preserve judgements, and do not tell us how (and if) they were carried out. But it is perhaps significant that the only groups who contest or protest at the decisions of courts in our texts are some of the peasants who lost cases about their status and rights (see above, pp. 109–11); these were the social groups who were excluded from the Lombard–Carolingian political settlement. Inside the landowning classes, the judgements of courts do not seem to have been rejected in this way; for them, the decisions were apparently valid even if they were unfavourable. If this is really so, then it must reinforce the impression we have already of the strength and authority of the Lombard and Carolingian state in Italy by comparison with that elsewhere in Europe, and this must have been substantially linked to the greater hegemony of the state over a literate upper class.

There are a few instances in our cases of winning parties making concessions to the losers, in at least some cases, presumably, in the recognition that they had no chance of making their rights real, even with the formal backing of the state, without the acquiescence of the losing parties. A typical example of such a pay off is a court case of 859, where the Milanese monastery of S. Ambrogio proved that Lupus had no right to the benefice he was claiming in Cologno Monzese, but then granted other land to him.[19] Cases like this became increasingly common up to the eleventh century and beyond, and certainly show the weak position monasteries were sometimes in on the ground, subject to coercion by their lessees/vassals, or at least behind-the-scenes nego- tiation. But the compromise came after the end of the case; it was not part of court procedure. Though the winners of cases may have sometimes found that their victories were hollow, the use of compromise as part of the court case itself was very rare; so was oath-helping (though it was used in Lucca in 840 in the absence of witnesses) and the duel.[20] The duel was, nevertheless, kept by the Carolingians as a last resort if evidence offered by each side in a case was inconsistent, with no way of choosing between it. This was greatly extended by Otto I in the Capitulary of Verona of 967, who, to the alarm of many churchmen and the later legal commentators of Pavia, allowed the authenticity of charters to be challenged by trial by battle, thus resulting, as the legists complained, in 'battle being held for properties possessed for a hundred years . . . and those who possessed them being killed'.[21] With this legislation the state partially drew back from the role it had assumed as the source of law. Otto and many of his advisers were German, foreign to Italian tradition. The state by the 960s was weak, and in many respects had surrendered its functions to units small enough to return to community legal remedies. But what is notable about cases from the 150 years after 967 is not that there are, now, trials by battle in our court cases, but how few of them there are – less than a dozen in the 320 court cases between 967 and 1100 in Manaresi's collection. The idea of absolute justice upheld by the state was devolved to the cities of Italy. The communes inherited this, alongside the trial by battle. They knew that the state was the fount of law, and when they laid claim to *de facto* statehood in the twelfth century, they did so largely by legislating. The duel and even the feud remained part of that law for centuries.

Hierarchy and Lordship: the Upper Classes

IN this chapter, we have so far been counterposing the solidarity of family and village communities to the notion of justice that is associated with the interests of the state. Lordship may seem to have been excluded. The eighth–ninth-century tendency for lay and ecclesiastical landowners to extend their properties at the expense of their smaller neighbours could be regarded, however, as working against the community solidarities we have been looking at. Marc Bloch, one of the greatest of all medieval historians, certainly thought it did: he saw 'feudal society' in France and Germany as replacing an older, slightly more egalitarian society based on the ties of kinship, largely through the inadequacies of such ties, in the tenth century and later. Kinship solidarities may have tightened as the state fell and lordship became more important, but most of the role of kinship was taken over by the feudal bond. More recent work, however, has changed the emphasis of Bloch's picture. Families are now seen as having always had an important part to play in the organisation of feudal society, and to have become considerably more highly organised as feudal hierarchies replaced the state. Kinship was, too, more important the higher one was in society; the wider one's field of action, the more one needed one's relatives. Kinship and lordship certainly could conflict; much of the best literature of twelfth-century France hangs on such themes. But society was complex enough for both to coexist in all except extreme circumstances.

In Italy, as we have seen, kinship and the family seem to have had most importance for day-to-day life and for local support. Lordship and service were more important for wider relationships and social mobility. A man could rise in his lord's service. His need to put himself under the protection of a lord could also demonstrate his fall. Kinship, horizontal links, was most relevant to men when they were in opposition to their equals; lordship, vertical links, when they opposed the powerful (except when the latter were actually their lords). We can see the coexistence of both axes from very early in the Lombard Kingdom: Rothari's law on *farae*, corporate kingroups, deals with what happens to gifts that 'a duke or any free man' has given to a man in his service who now wishes to migrate with his *fara*. They still coexist: Jeremy Boissevain has shown how family links and patronage complement each other in the modern Sicilian Mafia. The fragmented patterns of local landowning and local power that were such a feature of eighth–tenth-century Italy (and later), and the survival of concepts of public obligation all through our period, probably made lordship a less dominant force that it would be in feudal France, but it remained one of the basic bonds that underlay all society.[22]

Lordship and hierarchies undergo much more obvious changes than the kinship patterns I have so far described. This is because they are more closely linked to the shifting structures of the state. Some of this dynamism is more apparent than real – the rise and fall of particular families, for example, or changes in the terminology of lordship – but some is genuine, especially as the state itself alters. This is best seen in the structure of the aristocracy, and in the criteria for its existence.

The aristocracy have appeared as actors in nearly every context so far in this book, without my attempting to define exactly what they were. We have looked at the relationship between great families and the state under the Carolingians; the way that the ideology of the different rulers of Italy could change the titles and the very names of Italian landowners; the urban orientation of the upper classes and their urban building; and the possession by aristocratic families of estates composed, mostly, of small and widely-spaced groups of properties. The common theme at each point has been the ownership of land. Land, almost alone (leaving aside the occasional or not-so-occasional merchant), conveyed wealth and hence status and power. This is the most consistent element in the identity of the upper classes. The ways in which land and its cultivators were exploited could change; so could the way in which landholding was transmuted into political power, as we shall see; but it remained the first key to nobility. Paul the Deacon put the point succinctly in a poem of the early 780s, a plea to Charlemagne on behalf of his brother Arichis, a hostage in Francia: *nobilitas periit miseris, accessit aegestas*, or, rather less succinctly: 'nobility is lost to the poor; indigence has come in its place'. The Lombards and their successors had little concept of a 'nobility of blood', a status that could persist even when its holders were landless – Paul's use of *nobilitas* is as a very vague term indeed, and 'eminence', or 'notability', might be a better word.[23] Social mobility was quite possible for the lucky or unlucky in Italy – even for the Carolingians. The male-line descendants of King Bernard settled down in the tenth century as fairly undistinguished counts of Parma and Sospiro (as well as slightly more distinguished counts of Vermandois in France). Families adapted fairly easily to changed economic positions.

Land was not the only criterion for the establishment of an aristocracy. Two other variables were also relevant: the attitudes of aristocrats to each other, and the intervention of the state, royal patronage. To be aristocratic, one needed the recognition of others. The jockeying for status among the upper classes of late Roman and early medieval cities is easily visible in the building that went on in them, as we have already seen (see above, pp. 83–4). Such pressures were equally strong even for those, like bishops and abbots, who were, in theory at least, out of the secular hierarchy altogether. Royal patronage was, however, the key to political recognition. Though hierarchies were based on land, the stages in each hierarchy were always public offices, senators or prefects under the Empire, tribunes or dukes under the Byzantines, dukes, counts, or marquises in the Lombard–Carolingian kingdom. Their whole organisation was determined by the ideology and orientation of the state. Kings were in a position to give landowners so much more status and power, largely through the granting of public offices, that no one could easily reject royal patronage, and the power that this in turn gave the king. The tension between landowning and the interests of the state, between private and public power, largely worked in the state's favour for most of our period. In the early ninth century the balance began to shift in Benevento (cf. below, pp. 159–63), and in the early tenth century in the kingdom of Italy too, until, by the late tenth century, the system had entirely changed, and the state itself had more or less ceased to exist in its old form. How this occurred will be examined in the last chapter of this book; but the preconditions, the changing patterns of the upper classes, we will look at here.

The Lombards certainly had a social hierarchy of some sort when they first came into Italy. We can see it crystallising in the first decades of the occupation, with the establishment of Lombard dukes in the cities, and their sovereign power during the interregnum. Some of these dukes came from named noble families. Rothari, at the beginning of his Edict, listed all his sixteen predecessors as king of the Lombards. These kings were not all related to each other, so, for the kings of each new *genus* (family or clan – quite possibly *fara*), he gave its name – Audoin, *ex genere Gausus*, or Arioald, *ex genere Caupus*, or Rothari's own *genus*, Harodos; here he gave a list of his eleven male-line ancestors. These may have been in some sense a nobility of birth; but if so, the groupings did not have the staying power of, for example, the six noble lineages listed in the eighth-century Bavarian law code, whose prominence in Bavarian history is undisputed. The names never recur among the Lombards, and nor do any other family names until the very different world of the eleventh century. The laws themselves do not mention an aristocracy at all, merely free warriors, called interchangeably *liberi homines, exercitales,* and *arimanni.* These were clearly regarded as the formal and public basis of the Lombard state. The only evidence in the laws for any sort of hierarchy is that the composition for killing a free man is not given as a specific sum; it is to be paid *in angargathungi,* a Lombard term glossed in Latin as 'according to the quality of the person', and cognate with Anglo-Saxon *gethynge,* 'honour'. This is a specific criterion of status, but it is strikingly vague. We cannot produce a coherent picture of sixth and seventh–century Lombard hierarchies. All we can say is that status differences probably produced a differential share-out of land and booty at the time of the invasion. The dukes and gastalds and the richest landowners were doubtless for the most part those most important among the Lombards before 568. The *de facto* meaning of 'quality' or 'honour' in Rothari was probably, however, already the amount of landed property a man possessed. In the eighth century, this became explicit, for Aistulf in 750 divided those liable to army service exclusively by property ownership: those who had eight or more tenant holdings, those who had seven, those who had no tenants but forty *iugis* (twenty-four acres) of land, and *minores homines* who had less than that. The Lombards had titles too, borrowed from the Romans, such as *vir devotus* and *vir magnificus,* but it is difficult to show that they meant anything more precise than 'soldier' and 'important man' respectively. The precision of titles that went with the complexity of the late Roman state and its various aristocratic hierarchies had by now disappeared.[24]

When our charters begin, in the eighth century, important men are clearly all landowners. We have seen some of these already, such as Taido of Bergamo (living in 774) and Gisulf of Lodi (dead by 759). Taido was a royal *gasindius* and Gisulf a *strator* (his daughter Natalia was firstly wife of another *gasindius,* Alchis *vir magnificus,* and secondly wife of Adelpert *antepor regine*; his kinsman Arichis had been gastald of Bergamo). Both held positions at court. Gisulf, at least, was a royal official – *gasindii* had a less formal role as king's retainers, as we shall see. Their positions became part of their titles, and certainly contributed to their personal status. Arichis of Bergamo was no longer gastald there when he was mentioned in a 769 charter, but the text still refers to his former office. Office-holding brought land with it. Although in theory such land went on to the next holder, in practice officials could appropriate some of it or give it to dependents, as Liutprand complained. Unscrupulous officials could also profit from selling justice, as we see in the laws of Ratchis.[25] And, finally, officials were the most common lay recipients of royal patronage, gifts of land. Office-holding was fairly profitable, then. It did not, however, define an aristocracy. We can scarcely doubt that we are in the presence of the highest Lombard aristocratic circles when reading the charters of these men and women, and their witness lists are sonorous with *gasindii* and *viri magnifici*. But their chief basis was less their offices than their possessions of family land.

Taido's will makes this point most clearly. As a royal retainer, he had a particularly close link with the king; but his will was almost all composed of land he had inherited from his father. There is not a single reference in it to land he had acquired in any way, and in particular nothing from the king. This is perhaps a little exceptional, and we do find references to gifts of royal land to laymen, in charters and laws. These were, certainly, very often to officials and *gasindii*, like Aistulf's gifts to Desiderius when he was duke of Brescia, though not nec-essarily.[26] They were, however, more or less always to men who were already landed. Landowning was not only the main entry to official positions, but to royal attention at all. Kings could, of course, give land to favourites, no matter what their former status, and some of the officials at Pavia were probably from obscure backgrounds. We only very seldom have instances of kings actually doing this, however – a rare exception is Gregorius Grecus, Liutprand's jester, who received some land in gift from the king near Bologna. The professionals of the king's court, such as the *referendarii* and notaries, the most likely officials to have had lesser origins, did not make charters that survive. The only one who did, Gaidoald, doctor to Liutprand and Aistulf, had a large amount of family land, and was in fact one of the largest landowners in Lombard Tuscany.[27] It was this, rather than his medical qualifications, that initially made him an aristocrat. Paul's dictum about nobility being the opposite of poverty was written in these very decades.

Royal patronage, then, principally favoured already established landowners. Furthermore, royal gifts were not particularly generous, (cf. above, pp. 51–2 for the Carolingians), and they rarely matched the scale of property that a man already possessed. Grimoald, Paul the Deacon tells us, gave rich gifts to the army from Benevento with which he seized the throne in 662, when he sent them home. He kept some people with him, though, giving them enormous possessions. This may have been necessary to give material bases to men whose own lands were far away, and it is the last example of lavish royal gift-giving that we know from Italy until the early tenth century.[28] Later kings gave generously to churches, but even then, not on the scale of kings in Francia; and laymen were, it seems, satisfied with a few tenant holdings, a wood, a stretch of uncleared land, the occasional whole estate, and presumably the perquisites of office-holding. It may be for this reason that these Lombard aristocrats do not strike us as being very rich. Eight tenant houses was Aistulf's criterion for political importance. Taido and Gisulf had very much more than that, but in no sense the scale of landowning that a Roman senator had had or a Frankish imperial aristocrat would have in the next century. Their lands were as scattered, though, as those of the Supponids. Taido's landowning consisted of eight estates and ten or so tenant houses in four city-territories, shared with his two brothers. This was scarcely giant personal wealth, and each portion was already divided into three – the fragmentation would have been greater and the scale even smaller in the next generation. The vast wealth and power of the kings quite overshadowed such landowners. Though office and association with the king did not bring much material benefit, it at least brought more political power. It was this that the Lombard kings had to offer their aristocrats, above all, and it was less expensive than land.

This circle of links shows how Lombard kings patronised their aristocrats. It also, however, shows that kings who did not create new nobilities by gift had inevitably to use the nobility that was already there. The chain between landowners and the king was not perhaps very strong. It did not, however, break. This was doubtless mostly because of the wealth and power of the state and the relative absence of opposing power centres. It was underpinned by the strong sense that kings and, in part, their upper classes had of the public nature of the kingdom, part of the Roman legacy to the Lombard state: office-holding gave power and status in its own right, independent of the private wealth an office-holder already had, or might improperly obtain. Such a sense of the public pervades all Lombard legislation. The state was, nonetheless, based on less secure foundations than that of the late Empire. It could no longer – if it had ever been able to – rely on disinterested service. More personal links were by now necessary. Public hierarchies based on status and landowning were reinforced by lordship, personal links between people of different social positions. These already existed under Rothari. In the eighth century they were extended. Royal *gasindii* appear in our laws and charters: king's companions or retainers, linked to the king by *fidelitas*, loyalty sealed by an oath. Liutprand mentioned them in his sixty-second law, of 724, when he updated Rothari's law on compensation for killing, and defined the 'quality of the person' more tightly. The 'smallest' *exercitalis* was to be worth 150 *solidi*, the 'first' 300 *solidi*. 'But concerning *gasindii* we enact that if even the most insignificant of that order is killed, he should be compensated for with 200 *solidi*, since he is seen to serve us,' rising to 300 *solidi* again for the most important. The direct personal link between the *gasindius* and the king was important to Liutprand and his successors. Fraud by Liutprand's administrators was bad enough, but frightful when perpetrated by one of his *fideles*: 'what sort of *fidelitas* is it, when he colludes with a judge or an administrator or an *aldius* or a slave and takes over our property against our will?' Such men are guilty of the crime of perjury as well as fraud.[29] Even so, the gasindiate was never a particularly prominent part of Lombard society. The striking feature of Liutprand 62 is not the recognition of a legally privileged stratum of king's retainers, though this is there, but the tiny difference this made to the wergilds of his men. A hierarchy stretching from 150 *solidi* to 300 *solidi* to cover all free men from cultivators to aristocrats is not very highly accentuated by medieval standards. And, as Taido's will shows, the gasindiate did not necessarily bring permanent material advantage, either. To our eyes, accustomed to the concrete returns for loyalty in the better-known societies of feudal France and England, this whole pattern may seem rather frail – some have regarded the military failures of 755–6 and 773–4 as showing just such frailty. This, however, is to fall into the idealist trap of regarding the logical neatness of classic military feudalism as the product of historical inevitability. We cannot use the 'lack of development' of formal personal links to the king as an explanation for the fall of the Lombard state. The Franks were, simply, militarily more powerful and more experienced. How the Lombard state would have developed must remain unknown.

Lower down in society, several levels of lordship already existed. Not only kings had *gasindii*; dukes and other aristocrats could as well. A law of Ratchis envisages a man entering into the service of a royal *gasindius* or his *fidelis*; we have as many as four levels here. How normal this was we cannot tell, but it was not a new feature of the eighth century. Rothari mentioned men in the service (*gasindium*) of dukes or other free men, and indeed from 568 onwards every aristocrat must have had some sort of armed following, based on gifts that will have included land. Judging by royal parallels, such gifts were usually outright. References to revocable or even non-heritable gifts are rare in Italy before 774.[30] But, though lordship was important, it was still a relatively informal part of Italian social structure. The formal basis of the social system of the Lombard kingdom was still the public position of free men, *exercitales* or *arimanni*. These men were for the most part small and medium landowners, working the land themselves or through tenants. The informality of lordship is probably to be linked to the rarity of leases for anyone except a small number of cultivators before the ninth century. Relationships of lordship among the upper classes in the ninth century and later were, as we shall see, regularly expressed in the granting of leases.

The Frankish kings made few deliberate alterations in this pattern. They patronised Franks, of course, as we have seen, and probably gave them the lands of rebel Lombards. The balance of landowning in some areas slowly became Frankish. Dependents were now called *vassi*, vassals, instead of *gasindii*. But the state remained much as it had been in the Lombard period. Society continued to change, however, and by the end of the ninth century had greatly altered. We shall look at two aspects of this in turn: the development of the ideal and reality of the public position of the free owner, the *arimannus*, and the changes in the nature of lordship and landowning itself.

We owe most of our current ideas on *arimanni* to Giovanni Tabacco, who elaborated them most fully in 1966 in a major book, *I liberi del re nell'Italia carolingia e postcarolingia*. The Carolingian kingdom maintained the Lombard tradition in its reliance on the public responsibilities of the free warrior people, the *arimanni*, otherwise referred to now as 'sons of the Church' or 'private men', or even just 'Lombards' – we saw that the ideal was closely associated with a consciousness of being Lombard (see above, pp. 71–2f.), though the stratum certainly eventually included Romans and, after 774, Franks, who had similar traditions at home. The detailed obligations of *arimanni* were determined by their status and ownership of property. By Aistulf's time, some of them had even slid into tenancy, but they still owed services to the state, not through personal bonds to lords but through their own public position. These services were principally military, though not wholly, for the kingdom was by no means always at war either under the Lombards or later. A court case of 864 refers to the obligations of owners as *oste et ponte et placito*, the army, bridge maintenance (including public works in general) and attendance at court; Carolingian legislation mentions the latter two quite as much as the former.[31] *Arimanni*, like aristocrats holding public office, were in a direct relationship to the state, in theory still unmediated by the levels of lordship that were increasingly part of Italian society in the ninth century. The Carolingians regarded this relationship as extremely important. The power of large landowners at the local level, especially counts and bishops, was very great and increasing, but the kings expended considerable effort in their legislation to keep up their direct links with the free. There were two dangers to kings in the expansionist activities of the powerful. The first, which we have already seen evidence of (pp. 61–108ff.) was the simple oppression of their neighbours by the rich, which, combined with the traditional weakness of the poor in times of economic calamity, drove the smaller *arimanni* into tenancy and so potentially out of the public domain altogether. The second was the tendency of lords to form their own retinues from men who should be performing public duties, thus privatising the channels of state service, and directing them to their own benefit instead of that of the state.

The responses of the state to both of these trends tended to be rather inconsistent. Kings did not need every free man in the kingdom to fight their wars, and it was not unreasonable to take only those who could afford to arm themselves, and who did not need to cultivate the land. Liutprand in 726, at the start of his wars, allowed judges to release a certain number of 'the smallest men, who have neither houses nor lands' to do public labour service of an unspecified kind for the period of the war. Lothar in 825 required free men who had insufficient property to serve in his Corsican expedition to gather in groups of two to four or more and send only one of their number (this was a common European practice). Louis II in his orders for the Beneventan war of 866 excluded men with less than 10 *solidi* worth of property (not necessarily land) from all obligations, and poor men with more property than that had to stay behind as a kind of home guard for the period of the war.[32] The poor were too insignificant to be of great military advantage to kings, and even when vast numbers were mobilised, as in 866–7, kings tended to feel that the less important could be written off. But on the other hand they were worried that the unscrupulous activities of the powerful might exclude the state from an ever greater proportion of the population. Freedom and army service had been closely bound together among the Lombards, and the other obligations of the free, such as participation at court, might be lost if poor freemen fell too far. In 813, 'newly created' *libellarii* (see above, p. 107) were subjected to the control of their landlords when performing services for the state, at least if they 'have cut themselves off from the public domain, not by fraud or improper activity, but only through poverty and the need for land'. Public duties tended to be associated with the ownership of land, and not with leased property. It is in the early ninth century, too, that we first find references in charters to tenants becoming liable to the private jurisdiction of their lords for minor disputes and misdemeanours (major cases, though, remained public).[33]

Lothar (or his advisers) was the first to react against this growing privatisation of tenants' services. In 822, men who had alienated the whole of their property (and thus presumably became tenants) were henceforth to be liable to counts for their public services. The provisions of 813 were replaced by a reassertion of the public rights represented by comital authority. The ninth century was, too, full of laws designed to prevent the small free owner from being pushed over the border into tenancy by improper exactions by the powerful, right up to the capitularies of the last legislators in the Carolingian manner, Guy and Lambert in the 890s. Guy in 891 even reasserted the full public obligations of all *arimanni*, apparently whether or not the owners of land, to serve in the army. Guy was, however, rather consciously reviving Carolingian tradition; *arimanni* were certainly not by now any less oppressed. In fact, the list of oppressive acts perpetrated on them is rather wider in the 890s laws than before. And Guy's and Lambert's laws make one point abundantly clear: that the people who were most likely to oppress the poor were above all the public authorities themselves, counts and their deputies. In 898 Lambert even legislated against the habit of counts of handing over the public services owed by *arimanni* in benefice to their vassals.[34] The rearguard action of the *arimanni* of Cusago in 900 (see above, p. 109f) against the count of Milan illustrates these dangers very clearly. And they were dangers against which kings were virtually powerless. The only counters to the power of counts, judicial immunities for churches over their tenants, removed the poor from the immediate reach of the state even more firmly.

This discussion has been based almost entirely on the legislation of the Carolingians. Its validity is difficult to test. Private documents by their nature tell us less about the relationship between the free and the state, and almost nothing about the oppressions of the powerful. We cannot tell how many concessions in them were the result of coercion. But, conversely, the shrillness of the laws, though it tells us that the Carolingians felt they were not being obeyed, does not tell us how common oppression was. As we saw in chapter 4 (pp. 107–9), it is unlikely that all small owners lost their lands. It is also clear that free tenants for the most part retained their legal freedom, and we see from numerous hearings that they at least sometimes had access to public courts, even if they seldom won their cases. What seems to be appearing by about 900 is a two-tier system of freedom: free tenants had lost their public obligations, though they still retained some public rights to set against their economic subjection; free peasant proprietors mostly maintained their obligations and their rights for the moment, though there were now fewer proprietors. The Carolingians could do little to save small freemen who were in danger of subjection to the powerful, but they could at least maintain the existence of the public responsibilities of *arimanni* for those who remained independent enough to claim them.

One suspicion remains here, however: precisely because we only know of the full extent of these threats to the position of the free from Carolingian legislation, they may not have been such an especial feature of ninth century developments as is sometimes thought. Late Rome was certainly full of such threats, and the prologue to Rothari's Edict of 643 declared that Rothari was actually issuing it largely on account of the 'extra exactions [taken from the poor] by those who have more strength, using force'. The peasant cultivator is at risk in all societies from the rich, even when they are not deliberately out to attack him, but especially (as is usually the case) when they are. What was new in the Carolingian period was partly the greatly extended landowning of the Church, the product of a century of gift-giving, which as we have already seen tilted the balance of local power firmly in the direction of large owners; but particularly the new threat that the local power of the rich posed to the *public* position of the poor. It is possible that this new development was the product of Frankish aristocratic attitudes. The concept of public authority was certainly weaker in the Frankish kingdom than that of the Lombards. It may genuinely be, though, that it was only from the late eighth century onwards that enough free peasants were beginning to become tenants for legislators to be concerned about it. Whether this was so, and if so why, are not problems that we can yet answer.

The development of clienteles (groupings of the personal dependents of a lord) among surviving free owners was, however, something that was visibly associated with Frankish social patterns. We saw that in the Lombard period aristocrats had retinues, and that these personal links often went against the interests of the state. Under the Carolingians such links were greatly developed, through the institution of vassalage, apparently a much stronger personal bond than the gasindiate, though also based on the oath of fidelity. Certainly the laws make far more reference to the vassals and entourages of aristocrats than Lombard laws had. Kings were not wholly averse to this development, either. It allowed for quicker mobilisations of troops, and, though emphasising the local armed power of counts, at least strengthened their authority in those circumstances when they were acting in the interests of the state.[35] Kings relied on their own vassals, and expected both them and the vassals of counts and bishops to be prompt in service. They do not seem to have been wholly disappointed: vassalage, far from weakening royal authority, in many ways strengthened it, especially in the crisis of public power that followed Louis II's death.

On the other hand, private relationships inevitably weakened the whole fabric of public obligations, especially the more kings relied on them for the reliability that public obligations did not always provide. Small *arimanni* who survived the ninth century did so, for the most part, because of the support they were given by patrons, either lay or ecclesiastical. By 900, kings were left with few small men who recognised no lord between themselves and the king. Italy had become a network of clienteles, patronage groups dependent either on counts, or on non-comital families focused on small office-holding (both secular and clerical), or, increasingly, on bishops. The upper classes acted as intermediaries between the state and all other strata of society. Though this was less immediately contrary to state interests than the expropriation of the lowest stratum of the free, it hit at public relationships in a much more fundamental way. Central government became less and less relevant to the affairs of localities. The groundwork was beginning to be laid for the full localisation of power in cities and rural *castelli* (castles and fortified villages) that came about in the tenth century as the state itself lost and gave away all its powers.

As the free non-aristocratic owner was pushed onto the defensive, the aristocracy itself took on a more complex pattern. Wealth and status had hitherto depended on the outright ownership of land; tenants were for the most point unfree or barely free peasants. As large landowners extended their ownership, this was no longer practicable. The ninth century was a peak for ecclesiastical landowning, and the greatest Frankish families were larger owners than Lombard aristocratic families had been. The gap between them and lesser owners was increasing. But the growth of clienteles of vassals and their political influence raised the problem of how to reward them and keep their loyalty. The Frankish answer is well known: the conditional benefice granted in return for military service, the basis of 'feudal tenure'. In Italy, such benefices appear in our sources from the early ninth century onwards, and quickly become naturalised. As early as 816 the abbot of Monte Amiata rented out to peasants a house and land 'which Inghipert our vassal previously had in benefice', showing the recognition, at least sometimes, of the normal Frankish link between vassalage and the benefice.[36] The Italians never, however, fully accepted the implications of the benefice, that the only return a lord needed from his lands was military service. Far more common were native forms of Italian conditional tenure, ordinary land leases.

We have seen the bishops of Rome and Ravenna building up support from the seventh century onwards by leasing land to aristocrats and soldiers. From the beginning of the ninth century our ecclesiastical records show churches doing the same in Lombard Italy. The only difference between the two areas is that the non-Lombard parts of Italy still had a particular type of lease for large-scale long-term grants, the *emphyteusis*, and that the Lombards did not. It is not, therefore, always easy to tell whether a lease in Lombard–Frankish Italy was to a cultivator or to a vassal or aristocrat, except by incidental information – the size of the property leased, the amount of rent required. It is not necessarily the case that people would even have regarded the two levels of lease as fully distinct. Even peasants could, if of sufficient standing, lease extra property which they cultivated indirectly, and there was a steady gradation upwards from there. Large leases were normally for money rents, which were, though often more than nominal, small in proportion to the size of the property. One of the earliest leases to the Aldobrandeschi family in southern Tuscany, for example, from 809, required a rent of 120 *denarii* every 1 October, a fair sum, but small as the rent for a very large estate with two attached monasteries.[37] Such leases say nothing about military service or even, for the most part, political loyalty. They are public documents, however, and valid in court. This concern to keep the economic side of personal relationships, even between members of a clientele, inside the domain of public law is very characteristic of the Italians. The written evidence of proprietorial rights was at least as important as the unwritten, perhaps merely understood, recognition of personal obligations. These were still for the most part the product of personal links alone, particularly the oath of vassalage. Land was the *quid pro quo*, but was not directly associated with these personal obligations, unless it was a benefice. When the state began to fall in the tenth century, and clienteles became more and more important, the lease remained the dominant form of concession. Benefices themselves came to be merely a form of lease, and increasingly similar; divisible between heirs, for example, as was leased land, and not necessarily linked to military service. The forms came together, however, as they both more and more turned in effect into outright cessions of property, which neither of them was originally intended to be.

Large-scale leases were made by churches in return for political support, but it would be an error to imagine that they were ever made wholly voluntarily. Bishops and abbots needed support against the appropriations of lay aristocrats (sometimes, as under Lothar, encouraged by the state). The best way to do this was to lease out land to other aristocrats – sometimes, as an admission of defeat, the same ones. Franks may have been the major offenders, taking advantage of state patronage to establish themselves on the land; certainly the ninth century court cases that show the claims of churches against such men are mostly directed against Franks. Churchmen gave out leases to their supporters, while at the same time seeking to void those that had been given under duress. Jeremias of Lucca obtained diplomas from Louis II in 852 to cancel any leases or written cessions he chose (not benefices – they cannot have been an important part of episcopal gift-giving in this period in Lucca). He used them in 853 against a small family who had leased an episcopal church (see above, p. 61). But even Jeremias gave large leases to others, particularly his own family.[38] And, by the early tenth century, a whole set of aristocratic families had grown up in Lucca who, though possessing some property outright, were largely based on episcopal leases, and are referred to in our sources as vassals of the bishop. These families were mostly Lombard, and sometimes apparently descended from property-owning families of the Lombard kingdom. The 'Cunimundinghi' of the Garfagnana, in the Appennines above Lucca, who first appear in the tenth century, were probably the descendents of Pertuald *vir magnificus*, protégé of King Liutprand in the early eighth century and father of a bishop of Lucca, Peredeus. Such families, regularly receiving leases from bishops, were clearly a stable part of episcopal clienteles; as in Byzantine Italy two centuries before, some of them supplied the holders of episcopal office too. But the whole basis for their power had shifted. Status in the eighth century was based on landowning. By the tenth century it was simply based on possession, whether through outright ownership or a lease. By the end of the tenth century whole lordships could be based on such leases, usually centred on the lease from the bishop of the tithes of a baptismal church (*pieve*) and its dependent churches. The Cunimundinghi, for example, controlled the *pieve* of S. Pancrazio from 940 onwards.[39]

The Cunimundinghi and others like them were the new petty nobility of the tenth century and onwards. Many of them soon ceased to be dependent on the bishops, their original patrons. Throughout the tenth century, conscientious or ambitious churchmen can be found complaining that they found their patrimonies dispersed when they took up office. A well-placed cleric, like Gerbert, made abbot of Bobbio by Otto II in 982 and pope (as Sylvester II) by Otto III in 999, could have some effect. Gerbert sent off numerous letters to Otto II complaining about the state of Bobbio after the leasing policies of his predecessors. Otto III eventually voided them all for him in 998, and even issued a capitulary generalising it. Bishop Rather of Verona, the major littérateur of tenth-century Italy, found himself in a similar position in the 960s, if one can trust his extensive and highly-coloured complaints. He too was rewarded by a royal diploma in 967 voiding disadvantageous leases, though he was unlikely to have been able to use it, as his enemies got him removed from office, not before time, in 968.[40] But despite the efforts of these luminaries, the petty aristocracy continued to base themselves on episcopal leases, eventually emerging as the strongest section of the upper classes by the eleventh century (cf. below, pp. 187ff.).

This concentration on the lands of the Church is the product of the ecclesiastical bias of our evidence, but all the signs are that counts and other lay aristocrats were doing similar things. This was also true of the state. Kings made use of outright gifts, which, as we have seen, were not over-generous to the laity (churches could not do this; it was against canon law to lessen Church property by gift). They do not seem to have made use of leases, but after 774 they certainly gave out benefices to their vassals, perhaps still on a fairly small scale. In the tenth century, however, as many new families were royal vassals as episcopal ones, including several new comital families in Italy. This must reflect the increasing generosity of kings after the death of Louis II, which reached stunning proportions under Berengar I (see pp. 172ff.). Whether these families were based on outright gifts of land or benefices is often unclear, but they do not seem to have regarded their tenure as particularly conditional; by now it may not have made much difference, as the power of the state waned. Even the status of count, or viscount, and the lands pertaining to such offices, often became hereditary private property in the tenth century, as they were now increasingly regarded as permanent cessions of rights to a family. In this respect, office-holding became assimilated to the holding of benefices, as in northern Europe. Unlike in northern Europe, however, it did not remain inside the loose hierarchy of military feudal obligations; both office-holding and the benefice became the unconditional property of individual families. The public lands of a count began to be divided up between his heirs. By 1000, even the title of count, or marquis, often became common to all members of a family. By this time, the structure of power that the Carolingians depended on had been all but forgotten.

By the tenth century, the hierarchies of Italian society had substantially changed. The public rights and responsibilities of all free men, graded according to landowning and headed by rich landowners who were usually public officials, the ideal basis of the Lombard–Carolingian state, had been replaced by a system of clienteles, linked to a great lord (lay or ecclesiastical) by ties of vassalage, and by more or less freely conceded leases, gifts, and benefices of land. The public obligations of the free in the eighth–ninth centuries were largely military, but they extended to all sorts of other things, especially the administration of justice. The clienteles of the tenth–eleventh centuries, by contrast, were almost entirely military.

The contrast was not, however, complete. Even the Lombards had had armed followings associated with their lords, as befitted one of the more active groups of the barbarian invaders of the Western Empire. And in the tenth century not everything had become privatised. Most justice remained public. The status of the free was still in principle a public matter; the state still existed as a concept in public law. Lordship never became so strong as to become the organising principle for all, or even most, of society, unlike, for example, in northern France. As in France, military service was more and more the prerogative of the aristocracy. In the eleventh century, *miles*, soldier or 'knight', became a technical term for a petty noble. Ordinary inhabitants of cities still fought, however, often with some effect as the cities lurched towards independence and communal status. And one important element of the 'feudalisation' of northern Europe in the tenth century and onward did not occur in Italy: the growth of the concept of a closed noble caste. Paul the Deacon had expressed its absence in the eighth century. Rather of Verona assumed the same in the tenth:

Let us look at the son of a count, whose grand father was a judge; his great-grandfather was a tribune or a *sculdahis*, his great-great-grandfather just a soldier. But who was the father of that soldier? A soothsayer or a painter? A wrestler or a fowler? A fishmonger or a potter, a tailor or a poulterer, a muleteer or a packman? A knight or a peasant? A slave or a freeman?[41]

Significantly, Rather saw social mobility as occurring inside the ranks of the official hierarchy. There is no doubt that the possibility of such mobility (however rare it actually was) was related to the continuing survival of the public ideology of the state, in which every free man in theory had the same rights. This ideology was to persist, above all, in the cities, and after a century and a half would be a strong tool in the hands of the communes. The real power of the state had long gone by then, however, partly as a result of the developments I have outlined above. We shall see how in the final chapter.

6. The South

In 839 Prince Sicard of Benevento heard a court case between the bishop of Benevento and the monastery of S. Maria in Locosano over the possession of a baptismal church, S. Felice. The advocates for the two sides argued over the history of the church in the last century or so, and then Justus, the bishop's advocate, decided to appeal to principle: all baptismal churches belong to the bishop, by canon law. This does not matter, said the monastery's advocates, 'for the princes and bishops [of Benevento], putting into oblivion both canon law and the edicts of our own Lombard people, have always judged [our possession] to be the custom of our state' – and if it were not, many monasteries would be destroyed. If the bishop wants to observe the canons, they said, why does he keep control over the diocese of Siponto, which he has done ever since Duke Romoald I gave it to S. Barbatus of Benevento in the seventh century? Ordain a bishop in Siponto first, they said, and then tell us who is breaking canon law. Sicard seems to have found this argument acceptable; at any rate, S. Maria kept its church.[1] Benevento's autonomy was sufficient justification for ignoring, when necessary, not only the Lombard law of the North, but the law of the church itself.

Benevento in the ninth century was different from the North, and felt itself to be. Erchempert, writing his history in Capua in about 890, regarded Lombard history after 774 as being nothing other than the history of Benevento and its successor states; in the North, it had ceased to exist. This sense of Lombard legitimism underlies all the ideology of the rulers of the southern states, from the time Duke Arichis II assumed the title of prince in 774 onwards. Arichis may have begun to wear a crown; certainly his successors did. Princes were under some circumstances prepared to offer allegiance to Frankish kings and emperors, as in 788, 812, 867, and 963, but this was only the recognition of superior armed force. Rather more often, in fact, they recognised the hegemony of the emperor of Byzantium, particularly in the years when Byzantine power was at its height, c. 880–960. For decades at a time, princes of Benevento and Salerno accepted the title of patrician from Constantinople, sometimes going there in person to receive it. But the development of the Lombard South, and at least parts of the Byzantine

South, ran along lines independent of developments elsewhere, and had begun to since well before 774. Except for the last four decades of the Lombard kingdom, Benevento had always been in effect an independent duchy; and the Byzantine territories of Rome, Gaeta and Naples were only nominally under Eastern control after the seventh century.

Southern documentation is not the same as in the North, and the traditional emphases of historians have been different. The first reason for this is that southern Italy had a better tradition of history-writing. Until the end of the tenth century, we have access to detailed narratives of political events, such as are rather rarer in the North, and these are often more than competent. Erchempert has a claim to being the best historian, along with Agnellus, of our entire period in Italy; the anonymous author of the *Chronicon Salernitanum* of the 980s to being, at least, the most imaginative.[2] A temptation to concentrate on pure political history is more feasible in the South, and, owing to the large number of sovereign states there, fighting incessant wars, there is perhaps more political history to analyse. This temptation is encouraged by the patchy survival of documents before the twelfth century. There are some very large collections of documents indeed – the monastic archives and cartularies of Farfa, Montecassino, Casauria and Cava each run into thousands of pre-twelfth-century documents, and the secular archives of some of the Apulian cities and especially Naples are substantial too. But for large tracts of southern Italy we have almost no evidence at all, and even the archives we have have barely begun to be exploited, Farfa, S. Vincenzo and Naples excepted.

In these circumstances, detailed treatment of the development of southern Italy to compare with the North is barely yet possible, especially as political and geographical fragmentation has resulted in such a number of totally different histories. I will set out, first, an outline of the economy of the South, and then a brief political narrative up to about 1000. We will then look at two of these different histories, which will provide some parallels for our theme in chapter 7, the fall of the state in the North: first, the Byzantine Catepanate, where a strong government lasted well into the eleventh century; second, Benevento, where collapse began in the early ninth century. Finally, we will look at the context of major changes in settlement and local control in tenth–eleventh-century Rome and Campania.

THERE is not much flat land in the South of Italy. The Campagna

Romana, Liburia (the modern Terra di Lavoro, the plain of Capua), and the Apulian plain were the most important areas; others, such as the plains of Metaponto, Sibari, and the Sele, are ill-documented and were probably largely uncleared or degraded marshland. Between these areas of relatively fertile and populous land stretch the mass of the southern Appennines, not as high as in central Italy, but even more barren, especially in those tracts where waterless limestone plateaux and eroded clay slopes predominate. Such tracts exist in the North, as marginal land between settled areas; south of Rome, they make up half the total land mass. It is scarcely surprising that political power was concentrated in a small number of areas. Of the seven states that contested power south of Rome, the political centres of five were clustered in the middle of Campania, Capua, Naples, Benevento, Salerno, and Amalfi; the sixth, Gaeta, was close by to the north; the seventh, Byzantium, through a succession of provincial administrations, centred itself on Apulia (see Maps 3, 5, 6). Control of the rich lands that did exist was the chief preoccupation of these states, and largely explains the incessant wars between them. But the mountains could not be ignored. They constituted the chief bulk of the territories of the Lombard states, at least, and an unlucky state, like Benevento in the 880s and 890s, might find itself temporarily restricted to mountain and hill country only. Its control was made more difficult by the absence of viable urban centres to act as bases for local administration.

Louis Duchesne pointed out in 1903 that the Lombard invasions and, to a lesser extent, the Gothic wars had resulted in the annihilation of the great majority of the episcopal sees of the South of Italy.[3] In the duchies of Spoleto and Benevento, out of some hundred bishoprics, only about ten survived in 700: Spoleto and Forcona in the duchy of Spoleto; in the duchy of Benevento, probably Capua and Agropoli, Benevento (after a hundred-year gap), and a handful of Apulian cities conquered late in the seventh century. The Lombards may or may not have been particularly hostile to Catholicism in the South; but all these dioceses were certainly very small, and they were mostly in hill country. The cities they were based on were extremely small as well, and would in many cases barely have counted as villages in northern Italy. Episcopal organisation, and Christianity itself, were probably rather weak in most of them. Any slight dislocation, a war or a hostile duke, would have sufficed to bring them down.

As a typical example of such a city we might take Isernia in the Molise Appennines, a bishopric by the ninth century and a county from 964, which even now, after fast expansion, has barely 15,000 inhabitants. It still lies along a narrow wedge of mountain spur between two torrents, the chief town of a province of broken and poverty-stricken hill country, with almost the same boundaries as the tenth-century county. This county was actually rather large for a southern city-territory in the tenth century, about the size of Bedfordshire, but it was totally insufficient under those conditions as the territorial backing for active city life. Other 'cities' were even smaller. In the tenth century the Byzantines stopped trying to distinguish theirs from fortified villages – the term *kástron* begins to be used indifferently for either in our Greek texts. Acerenza, the most important city in what is now Lucania, could have its site moved at the whim of Grimoald III of Benevento in 788, if we can believe the *Chronicon Salernitanum*.[4] Even Capua, the centre of Liburia, was evacuated to a nearby hilltop castle called Sicopolis in 840. The city's inhabitants only returned to the plain in 856, in a different place, five kilometres away on the Volturno river-crossing. Of the old city (now S. Maria Capua Vetere) only the amphitheatre remained, used as a fortification. Athanasius of Naples cleverly used the time of the vine harvest to sack the new city in 884, for the whole citizen body, including the upper classes, were out picking grapes; at this point, Capua's economy was overwhelmingly agrarian.[5] Capua was the latest of the great plains cities to develop, and by the tenth century it too was flourishing; but outside the plains, cities were never large or pro-sperious, and most hardly had any real urban status at all.

The contrast between the mountains and the plains was heightened by the remarkable sophistication of the major lowland cities. In the seventh–eighth centuries this may not yet have been apparent, except in the Byzantine and Lombard capitals, Naples and Benevento; these were active cities, as fitted their political importance. Arichis II expanded Benevento in the late eighth century, building a *civitas nova*, a new town, there. The new capitals of the ninth century, Gaeta, Amalfi and Salerno, were as yet only *castra*, defence posts. Once established, however, they rose fast. Salerno, too, was virtually refounded by Arichis in the 770s–80s; he quadrupled the size of its walls and built a palace there, making it into the second city of his principate. In the ninth and tenth century it filled out its new walls, more than tripling its population. To begin with, such an expansion was simply the reflection of the new political importance of the city, which by 849 was the centre of a sovereign state. But in the tenth century, when it acquired a port, it quickly set itself alongside Amalfi, Naples, and Gaeta as a trading centre.[6]

Amalfi is the most famous of these trading cities. It seems to have established its position, after breaking free from Naples in the 840s, by more or less consistently siding with the Arabs in their raids on the Italian coast in the ninth and tenth centuries, and thus obtaining special concessions and opportunities in the Arab world. Certainly there is no better reason why the inhabitants of an inaccessible fishing village, some 500 square metres in size, hemmed in by cliffs, should have become the major traders in the western Mediterranean. But the other cities were commercially important too: inhabitants of Salerno and Gaeta appear beside those from Amalfi and Venice in the *Honorantiae* as privileged merchants in Pavia, and the Arab traveller Ibn Hawqāl in 977 put Naples second only to Amalfi as a trade centre.[7] Thanks, ironically, to the Arab raids themselves, a complex set of trade routes between Byzantium, the Arabs, and the West developed, with its western apex in Campania (Venice, of course, had a similar position in the Adriatic, followed by the Apulian cities Bari and Trani). The Campanian cities already had large fleets in the ninth century, probably matching those of the Byzantines; the tenth and eleventh centuries marked their peak. As a counterpart to the will of Giustiniano Partecipazio in Venice (above, p. 90), we have that of Docibilis I, consul (*ypatus*) of Gaeta in 906, who could distribute to his seven children and several other recipients: large quantities of money in gold, silver, and bronze, silk cloth, jewels, 120 *solidi* worth of marble fitments in the church of S. Silviniano, besides much land and many animals. These cities were cosmopolitan, with extensive links with the East, and Jewish quarters; Capua and Benevento had Jews in the administration, too, and Oria in Apulia was a major Jewish intellectual centre.[8] By the eleventh century Salerno had established the chief source of its fame in Europe, its medical school. The cities declined only with the Norman conquest and with competition from the new northern commercial cities, Genoa and Pisa, which had closer links with the trade outlets in Europe.

Exactly how much effect this commercial sophistication had on the hinterland of southern Italy is unclear. The upland cities were politically separate from the trading ports, and, as we have seen, scarcely existed as urban centres. Even the principality of Salerno, which nominally included much hill and mountain country, had no other effective cities except perhaps Nocera. Capua and Benevento certainly prospered, but more in the way we have seen northern cities prosper: as the centres for upper-class and administrative consumption, rather than commerce. The southern coastal cities acted as entrepôts for international trade more than for commercial contact with their hinterlands. Naples produced linen. There seems to have been a development in Liburia from the tenth century towards the cash-cropping of vines. In Campania, at least, the effect on the inland economy of coastal commerce seems to have ended there. In Byzantine Apulia, at least in the eleventh century, there is some evidence of the development of the production of wheat and perhaps oil for the market, and in Calabria we find silk manufacture. Silk was a manufacture that soon spread into Lombard areas too, for there are references to it in late tenth–century leases from the high Appennines in Abruzzo. Monasteries like S. Vincenzo al Volturno were sometimes prepared to improve their most barren properties, presumably for the market (though S. Vincenzo would have had its own needs for silk). But outside Byzantine areas, this was uncommon.[9]

The rural economy of the South inevitably reflected the great contrasts between geographical areas. Land in the plains was fractioned at least as much as anywhere in the North. In 964 Pandulf I of Capua-Benevento gave 300 *modia* (perhaps 67 acres) of land in Liburia to S. Vincenzo, divided into no less than 118 separate fields, each with its boundaries and dimensions given in the text. Some of these were minute, as in this instance:

. . . The fifty-first piece, called *ad cirasa*: on one side, the land of S. Salvatore; on the other, the land of John the Neapolitan; one end gives onto the land of the above-named Ursus; the other on the above-mentioned land of Agimund. It measures on each side 41 paces, and at each end 8 paces.

On the other hand, mountain land could be owned in vast units. The nucleus of S. Vincenzo's land at the sources of the Volturno, the gift of both Duke Gisulf I of Benevento in *c.* 700, and Arichis II in 760, formed a solid bloc of over 500 square kilometres.[10] An area like this, or the contiguous bloc owned by Montecassino, will have been largely forest, with only small-scale settlement. Some of this may have been further reduced too, after the Arabs sacked the monasteries in 881–3 and the monks fled to Capua; in the tenth century, we find large-scale clearance leases for the area to immigrant cultivators, newly settled in fortified villages (see pp. 164–7).

This contrast between fractional and consolidated landowning was far more acute than in the North. It represented great differences in local control. It is doubtful, however, whether the economy as a whole was as differentiated. The pastoral–agricultural divide in the South did not in this period lead to clear regional specialisations. The mountains seem to have produced as much grain and wine as pastoral products. And the organisation of agrarian production did not vary all that much over the South, for the centralised 'manorial system', weak enough in the North, did not exist at all south of Rome. Labour service occurred, rarely, in the ninth century in the Sabina and Abruzzo; further south, it is never recorded. Some land was cultivated directly by slaves; the great bulk, however, over the whole of the South, consisted of tenant holdings in return for rents, in money or (more often) in kind, intermingled with the land of small free owners. Small-scale peasant production was everywhere dominant.

There were probably rather more servile tenants in the South than in the North at first. Why this should have been we do not know, but it probably explains the common sixth–ninth-century practice in southern Italy and Sicily of alienating, not plots of land, but *condumae*, slave families. Land usually came with such *condumae*, so the gift was much the same as that of *casae massariciae* in the North. The latter, however, could have free tenants farming them; a *conduma* was necessarily servile. In the tenth–eleventh centuries, these servile tenants seem gradually to have moved towards freedom, helped partly by the confusion of the Arab wars, and partly, as in the North, by the absence of labour service.[11] From the tenth century, leases with free cultivators began to appear in the South, over a century later than in north or central Italy. Slavery still persisted, but, as in the North, was diminishing. We have an example from Gaeta of a number of slaves claiming their freedom in a court case of 999; though they withdrew from trial by battle to prove it at the last moment, they were granted freedom by the bishop in the end, in return for a pound of gold. Slaves not only desired freedom, but could sometimes afford to purchase it at high prices.[12] This rise in the status of slave cultivators seems to have been absolute; it was not matched by a significant weakening in the position of the free. The slow rise of ecclesiastical property-owning produced a slow attrition of the lands of small free owners, as it did the lands of the upper classes, but we have no parallels to the decline of the *arimanni* in the North in our infrequent southern legislation, and, south of Rome, no documents have so far been analysed that hint at it either. The Arab invasions may in this case, too, have prevented the consolidation of local power that we can see from Rome northwards.

The re-establishment of monastic landowning in the Appennines in the tenth century allowed substantial amounts of local independence to the monasteries' tenants (see pp. 166f.). There were particularly large numbers of small owners in Byzantine Apulia; the power of the Byzantine state must have had something to do with this.

Before we move on to more political problems, it is worth noting one of the more remarkable minor features of the economic life of the South, the ownership of the *tertiatores* of Liburia.[13] This was the object of a complex set of chapters in a treaty made between Arichis II and Duke Gregory II of Naples, probably in 786. The *tertiatores* themselves were apparently servile tenants, paying a partiary rent of a third. They appear in a document probably of 748, when two of them, Mauremund and his wife Colossa, are sold to a Neapolitan monastery, in just the same way as *condumae* elsewhere. The most striking feature of their condition, however, is that they were owned jointly by the duke of Benevento and the duke of Naples, or by various Lombard and Neapolitan aristocrats and churches to whom the dukes made gifts. Liburia must have largely consisted of fiscal and urban communal land under the Empire, and was divided between Benevento and Naples, probably in the seventh century. But the solution they chose to the problem of division, the joint ownership over, and equal rent-taking from, each of the tenants of the area, was a unique response to a territorial problem, and does not seem to have been affected by the numerous wars between the two sides. Arichis provided for the splitting of this joint ownership over much of Liburia, but it persisted in parts of the area until the tenth century and beyond. Of the 118 pieces of land there alienated by Pandulf I in 964 (see p. 151), 57 were held 'in common with the Neapolitans'; and in the eleventh century, when land in Liburia was almost entirely private and wholly fractioned, the *pars militie* (Naples) and *pars langobardorum* remained as two counterpoised groupings of properties, inextricably intermingled. This may serve to emphasise one point: the major socio-economic divisions of the South were geographical, not political. The Lombard and non-Lombard parts of the South were usually at war, in various combinations, but they had the same customs, and indeed mostly spoke the same language. It is not helpful to separate them too ruthlessly in our analyses.

THE political history of the South is just as complex, and, as more work has been done on it, it is rather harder to generalise about.[14] Grimoald I

(649–62) and Romoald I (662–87) of Benevento had fought off Constans II and established Beneventan hegemony in the South. By 774 Arichis II controlled a united principate that stretched as far as the tip of Apulia (only Otranto remained Byzantine) and half-way into Calabria. The duchy of Naples was an independent enclave on the west coast, more or less autonomous from Constantinople. Byzantine Calabria and Sicily were under fuller Eastern control.

Benevento was strong enough to withstand occasional Frankish invasions from the north. More serious for its territorial integrity were the civil war of 839–49 and the beginning of the Arab attacks in the same years. The murders of Grimoald IV in 817 and Sicard in 839 show the growing insecurity of princely power in Benevento, as we shall see (pp. 160f.). By 839, several Beneventan aristocrats regarded themselves as in line for the throne. Radelchis I, the new prince, killed his first rival, but his enemies rallied around Sicard's brother Siconulf and based themselves on Salerno. Only Frankish intervention ended the war, when Louis II and Guy I of Spoleto forced a division of the principality in 849. By that time, the Arabs were attacking all parts of the South. Radelchis began to use them as mercenaries in 841, and installed them in Bari in 843. They seized the city, and used it as the basis of an emirate until the end of the Frankish–Lombard–Byzantine siege in 871. From there, and from later bases on the west coast at Agropoli and on the Garigliano, the Arabs terrorised the South for several decades. The insecurity they produced ate away the relationships at the base of southern society. Every state in the South was frail, except Byzantium, by the time another international alliance ousted the Arabs from the Garigliano in 915.

Naples had its weakest moment early, between 800 and 840. An uncertain leadership remained on the defensive against attacks from Sico and Sicard of Benevento, who besieged Naples twice before making peace in 836, and went on to occupy Amalfi in 838–9. From 839 on we can detect no authority exercised by Naples over the succession of consuls and prefects of Amalfi. The 830s, too, saw the first *hypatoi* of Gaeta, already more or less independent. Docibilis I (867–*c.* 910) certainly owed no allegiance to Naples, and founded a dynasty lasting until the twelfth century. By this time Naples too had acquired a permanent dynasty, just as long-lasting, starting with Sergius I in 840. Sergius and his son Gregory III were very active in the ninth-century wars, though Gregory's son Athanasius II, bishop and duke (876–98) was certainly the most prominent member of the dynasty in these years.

Benevento and Salerno separated in 849, but remained on bad terms, exacerbated by the counts of Capua, who wished to establish their own autonomy from Salerno. Salerno remained unstable until a Capuan protégé, Guaifer I, became prince in 861. By that time Capuan independence was recognised. A brief period of peace was enforced by the presence of Louis II in the South in 867–73; after his departure, the wars started again. They were now complicated, at least in Campania, by the fission of Capua after 879 into several different warring gastaldates. Gaeta, Salerno, and Naples all joined in on different sides until Atenulf I of Calvi, one of the rival gastalds, seized Capua in 887 with help from Athanasius of Naples (cf. below, p. 162). Atenulf's success contrasted with the fortunes of Benevento and Salerno, who were beginning to suffer from a Byzantine revival. In 876 the Byzantines occupied Bari, and in 880 they expelled the Arabs from Taranto. In 885–8 they occupied the whole of Apulia, pushing the Beneventans back into the mountains. Salerno became a client state of Constantinople in 886. Benevento was actually conquered by the Byzantines, and held for three years (892–5) until it was 'liberated' by Guy IV of Spoleto, who occupied it until 897. Benevento enjoyed three years of independence before Atenulf united it with Capua in 900, a union that lasted till 981.

By 900 the Byzantines held the whole of Apulia (though the northern fringe changed hands several times with Benevento thereafter), almost all Lucania, and the whole of Calabria. Benevento and Salerno had lost about half their rural land areas. The Byzantines were not successful everywhere, however. Between 827 and 902 the Arabs had conquered the whole of Sicily, and they used it thereafter for systematic attacks on Calabria. Naples was fully outside the Byzantine sphere, and Sardinia was by now in effect independent, roughly divided into four *iudicati*, ruled by judges. But the Byzantine themes of Langobardia (Apulia) and Calabria, united in the late tenth century under a catepan, remained the most solid units in the South henceforth.

After the Arabs were forced out of the Garigliano in 915, Capua–Benevento and Salerno achieved some sort of territorial stability. War in Campania slackened off, though Landulf I of Benevento (910–43) and Guaimar II of Salerno (893–946) attempted intermittently to show their prowess by fighting in Apulia, partly in response to the first of a series of uprisings in the Apulian cities. In 961 Pandulf I Ironhead became ruling prince in Capua–Benevento, and increased his power with an alliance with the new Italian king-emperor, Otto I. In 967

Otto I came south, leading the first invasion from northern Italy for nearly a century. Pandulf, who had already been given Spoleto and Camerino, was entrusted with Otto's planned conquest of Apulia in 969. He was rather ignominiously captured and briefly taken prisoner to Constantinople, but Otto's support still gave him supremacy in the Lombard South. When a palace revolution overthrew Gisulf I of Salerno in 973–4, Pandulf moved in and reinstated him. He was rewarded by the Salerno succession for him and his son. Briefly, in 974–81, Pandulf ruled Italy from Ancona to the fringes of Calabria. At his death, however, his domains split up. Salerno, after a brief occupation by Amalfi (981–3), acquired a new dynasty; Spoleto reverted to northern rulers; even Capua and Benevento split again. The century ended as it had begun, in a welter of confused wars and invasions from the North – Otto II in 981–2, disastrously; Otto III, rather more effectively in 999, when Capua was briefly put under Spoletan control. The eleventh century was similar: the occasional grand gestures of princes like Pandulf IV of Capua in the 1020s or Guaimar V of Salerno in the 1030s were increasingly overshadowed by the rising power of Norman mercenaries, who by the 1070s were masters of the whole South. Southern history took on a decisive shift of direction from then on.

René Poupardin in 1907 called this history one of 'intestinal struggles as sterile as they were obscure', and has been criticised by historians for this phrase ever since, but it would be hard to say that he was wholly wrong.[15] Every one of the Campanian powers had its moment of glory; each was equally ephemeral. Capua at different times occupied Benevento, Salerno, Naples; Salerno occupied Amalfi and vice versa; Naples and Salerno both held Capua briefly; the Spoletans, in their southern ventures, were at times in control of Benevento and of Capua. Too many powers contested too little territory. The highest point was reached by Pandulf I, superficially the strongest Lombard prince since Sicard, but Pandulf's reign was in reality characterised by an almost total lack of control by the prince over his territories on the ground. Why this was is more interesting than the reasons for his temporary political successes. I will discuss the development of Capua–Benevento as a paradigm for the breakdowns in internal structure of most of the southern states, after we have briefly looked at the exception to this tale of decline, the Byzantine Catepanate, particularly the theme of Apulia.[16]

The Byzantines never achieved a total hegemony over Apulia, in the sense of an unquestioned acceptance of the legitimacy of their rule. Urban uprisings were common, culminating in the series of revolts in 1009–18 that established a certain amount of autonomy for cities like Bari and Trani, as well as for new cities such as Troia (founded in 1019). Greek influence was never dominant in most of Apulia. Lombard law was the most common law professed in charters (Roman law was very rare, though Apulia cannot have been a region where the Lombards ever settled in large numbers). Lombard personal names far outnumbered Greek ones even in the coastal cities. Apulia contrasted in this respect with Calabria, which was very largely Greek in customs, culture and speech, for the Lombards had never conquered it. The tenth–eleventh-century saints' lives of Calabria were clearly written inside a cultural world that looked exclusively to Constantinople. So, for example, when the most famous Calabrian hermit, Nilus of Rossano (c. 910–1005) left Calabria in the 970s, foreseeing renewed Arab attacks, he went to Capua and then Rome, rather than to the eastern Mediterranean, hoping to avoid the limelight of his own reputation by retreating to Latin-speaking lands.[17] Apulia had Greek customs too—even the rebel leader of the 1010s, Meles, wore Greek dress according to Norman accounts – but the Byzantines had little impact on Apulian society. The Byzantines used the Lombard aristocracy as their officials and local administrators. Only the catepans and strategói, the rulers of Byzantine Italy, were invariably Greek, and they, like the exarchs of the seventh-century North, were frequently changed. The Lombard aristocracy seems, however, to have been for the most part loyal. The urban revolts were certainly not in favour of rule by the princes of Benevento and Salerno. They were, rather more, ad hoc hostile responses to individual administrators and to the continuing effectiveness of Byzantine government.

The Byzantine administration showed that a model of government which was still in many essentials that of the late Empire could function as well in the tenth century as the sixth . The Byzantines still taxed, and their taxation network was more centralised than it had been four centuries before. City-territories and village-territories were assimilated together, becoming, simply, fiscal units, kástra (if fortified) or khoría (if open settlements). Urban and rural autonomy was initially strictly de facto, the result of important local families being given a variety of local offices. Cities, however, particularly on the Apulian coast, were complex communities, and can sometimes be seen acting collectively. A charter of 992 for the small city of Polignano refers to 'all the men living in the city of Polignano, the greater, the medium, and the whole people', who collectively consent to a gift. As in northern Italy in the same period (cf. below, pp. 190–1), they began to make claims for autonomy that more properly matched their internal complexity, and the early eleventh-century revolts partially achieved this. Villages, too, seem to have acted collectively, and obtained in some cases some powers of self-government. We should be wrong, however, to see this autonomy as prefiguring the communal movement of the North in any precise way. The Byzantine state kept overall control, and, except where it conceded specific immunities, continued to exact taxes. Troia held out heroically against a siege by the German Emperor Henry II in 1022; in 1024, as a reward, its tax burden was cut to a lump sum of 100 *solidi* yearly, and it was relieved of having to pay market dues. The sum of 100 *solidi*, though, would not have seemed small in the Lombard South for the obligations of what must have been rather more a village than a town, and only five years old at that.[18]

We can even see the Byzantines administering some quite remote parts of their territory. The inhabitants of Tricarico, in the depths of Lucania, petitioned the catepan in 1001 to have their city-territory redefined after Arab devastation; the catepan sent two sets of officials to decide on this, with local help. The state also involved itself in at least the fruits of land clearance. New settlements, privately established, became *khoría*, inscribed on the fiscal registers of the state, and therefore taxable – we have an instance of this (though with some fiscal exemptions) from the monastery of S. Maria del Rifugio, again near Tricarico, in 998.[19] Elsewhere, the state founded its own settlements, particularly along the northern frontier of Apulia. Some of these certainly involved land clearance and the installation of new populations – in the case of Troia, largely from Lombard areas.

The internal structure of the Byzantine state in Italy remained firm, even in the mid-eleventh century, when incessant wars and declining Constantinopolitan interest left more and more of it to the hands of the Normans. This stability was probably very largely achieved through the financial solidity and patronage potential of a state that still extracted taxation from its inhabitants. Late Roman parallels would certainly suggest that even when local aristocrats controlled local offices, they might hesitate to subtract themselves from a state which could hold out so much personal financial advantage to them. Exactly how these processes worked in Apulia, however, and when (or if) they broke down, must await more work on the tenth and eleventh-century documents from the coastal cities.

In Capua and Benevento the patterns of political life were rather different. The principality of Benevento in the eighth century was a strong state, closely modelled on the Lombard state of Liutprand and Aistulf.[20] From Romoald II (706–30) onwards, surviving documents show dukes and then princes making gifts of fiscal land or slaves (usually in small quantities, except the mountain valleys given to Montecassino and S. Vincenzo). They oversaw court cases, and made treaties with Naples much like those the northern kings made with Venice. The court of Benevento was, it seems, modelled on that of Pavia, with the same range of officials, though their functions are even more obscure–the *referendarius* (or *duddus*), *vesterarius*, *marepahis*, *cubicularius*, and the treasurer, the *thesaurarius* or *stolesayz*, who was particularly important, and sometimes achieved the position of prince itself. The dukes and princes were certainly rich. They seem to have had a large amount of land under their direct control, including, as we have seen, much of Liburia, the richest part of their territories. Beneventan coinage was independent of that of the North, and much more developed. Until the mid-ninth century the state minted two gold coins, the *solidus* and the *tremissis*, and after the 780s a silver *denarius* as well. After 851 the Lombards minted only silver, but Byzantine, Arab, and later Amalfitan gold was available all over the South (Naples had bronze coins, too). Especially as Byzantine influence grew, the princes were tempted to imitate the more glorious models of Constantinople rather than Pavia – so Arichis II, throwing off allegiance to the North, built a palace church in Benevento dedicated to S. Sofia, following Justinian's example. This should not take us in: the ceremonial dignity of the Lombard princes was at its highest in the eleventh century when their real influence had virtually vanished. A better indicator of princely control is the fate of the offices of the court administration, almost all of which disappeared after 900.

Beneventan local administration was similar to that of the North, too. The dukes and princes ruled through gastalds, who, under Frankish influence, came increasingly to be known as counts. These were the local representatives of the state in the cities of the principality, and were also, it seems, responsible for the demesne of the state, which was divided into sections corresponding to the gastaldates (more often known as *actiones*). Princes like Arichis II and Grimoald III had clear control over these *actiones*, and we cannot detect hereditary lines of gastalds until the mid-ninth century. Montecassino and S. Vincenzo felt secure enough to acquire land scattered as far off as Lucera, Taranto, and Oria.[21]

Princes were, it seems, elected, at least in the absence of obvious hereditary succession, and after Grimoald III died in 806 the people and aristocracy of Benevento had several opportunities to choose their princes. Grimoald IV the *stolesayz* (806–17) and Sico, gastald of Acerenza (817–32) were elected; and after the murder of Sico's son Sicard (832–9), so were his rival successors Radelchis I the treasurer (839–51) and Siconulf, Sicard's brother (839–51). The princes were, as can be seen, all from the office-holding ranks of the aristocracy, and it is in the relationship between these ranks and the princes that we can see the first beginnings of the collapse of the state.

One aspect of this relationship is certainly that any influential aristocrat could feel himself qualified to become prince. Erchempert and the *Chronicon Salernitanum* (rather less reliably) cite many people as having such ambitions. Grimoald IV was killed through a plot between several aristocrats who aspired to supreme power. Two of these, Sico of Acerenza and Radelchis of Conza, ruled remote and wild gastaldates where central power could not have been very strong. But it is important that gastalds of remote cities should have been interested in gaining the princeship. As in the Lombard kingdom, the possibility of becoming prince kept distant lordships inside the same political structure. Even the 839–49 civil war shows the force of this structure, as rival alliances of aristocrats fought across the whole length of the principality to achieve central power for their protégés.

More dangerous to the survival of princely power was the attitude of aristocrats to the prince once he was in office. Grimoald IV, Sico and Sicard were all attacked as tyrants. Sico may have avoided the fate of the others only because he spent much of his reign fighting the Neapolitans, thus giving his nobles opportunities to expend their energies on someone else. He was certainly in a weak position on his accession in 817, being an immigrant, an aristocratic exile from the North without a firmly based body of support. He had to marry his children into a number of aristocratic houses, and he placated his nobles as much as he could. But these measures, and Sicard's murder when he ignored them, show that princes no longer had the consent of their upper classes to act as autocrats. Radelchis of Conza, Sico's unsuccessful rival, is supposed to have said at Sico's election: 'he is a foreigner; as we wish it, we have him as prince; as long as we wish we will keep him; when we wish, we will put him out.'[22] Whether this conditioning of princely power was a new development of the ninth century is uncertain, as our detailed narratives only begin in 774, but it may have been a delayed result of a decline in the legitimacy of central authority after the end of the traditional Beneventan dynasty in 758. It is clear, though, that the mountainous nature of the principality must have always made it extremely difficult to control, and the *de facto* powers of the fringe gastaldates, especially Capua, Conza, and Acerenza, however much the gastaldates concerned looked to Benevento, must always have been considerable. To dominate them, any prince probably had to act rather more high-handedly than his upper classes might like.

The next development is most visible in Capua, through Erchempert's hostile eyes: the slow but systematic attempt by the members of the comital house of Capua to separate themselves from the principality altogether. Landulf I (815–43), its founder, made his sons promise at his deathbed 'that they should never, if it was in their power, allow Benevento and Salerno to make peace', while they established their own power, safe in their *castello* of Sicopolis. (Sico had been impressed by the honour done to him by this name, but a retainer remarked that 'Rebellopolis' would have been a better title.)²³ As Radelchis and Siconulf and their allies fought over the South, Landulf's heirs gradually took over the gastaldates of the Volturno and Garigliano valleys. When the war ended in 849, Capua, always nominally on Siconulf's side, was part of Salerno, but soon had its independence effectively conceded. The county of Capua was not, however, as both Benevento and Salerno were, a public organism. Landulf had presumably appropriated the fiscal land of the territory. It became the land, not of a state of Capua, but of his family. Landulf's sons controlled it, with some disagreements, as a co-operative group. When the last of them died in 879, Landulf's grandsons split their patrimony up into gastaldates and began to fight. Those gastalds in the area who still did not belong to the family were beginning to privatise their properties too. Rodoald, gastald of Aquino, built the *castello* of Pontecorvo in the 860s against the Capuans. The Frank Magenolf, who overthrew him, reintroduced obligations like tax and army service to the rural population, who 'previously knew of nothing except onions and garlic' – Rodoald's *castello* was certainly not a public one and indeed public obligations seem to have been for some time unknown in the territory of Aquino. The *castello* of Calvi, centre of the gastaldate from which Atenulf reoccupied all Capua and eventually Benevento too, was similarly built by Atenulf himself and his brother Lando with the help of his noble and non-noble followers (the *pars nobilium* and *pars vulgi*). Like Pontecorvo, this looks less like the centre of public authority than of private power.[24]

When Atenulf's dynasty united most of the old Beneventan principality, these tendencies to fission might seem to have been halted. In fact, though, Atenulf and his successors merely carried on the Capuan family tradition, giving their gastaldates to family-members, in the hope that kinsmen would be loyal. These gifts were accompanied by extensive immunities; the role of the state was slowly diminished. The gift by Pandulf I to his second cousin Landulf in 964 of the county of Isernia in what is now Molise is a particularly clear example of this, for the whole county was given over to the private possession of Landulf and his heirs, with an immunity. Landulf still wielded his public powers there as count, but his possession of the county was entirely privatised. The rest of Molise was similarly separated off from the power of the central government in this time. Trivento was ceded in 992 to a comital family in much the same way as Isernia; and, though the princes still had powers in Larino as late as 970, Pandulf's activities there were the last that a Beneventan prince is recorded as having undertaken.[25] Eleventh-century documents for Molise reveal a completely private world of counts freely making cessions to monasteries of what seems to have been public land. Elsewhere, the princes may have been excluded even earlier; very few princely documents survive from outside the near vicinity of Capua and Benevento after 850. When the monasteries of S. Vincenzo al Volturno and Montecassino moved to re-establish their property-holding in the mid-tenth century, the princes confirmed their rights, allowed them to build *castelli* and exercise full authority over them, and even intervened to stop the opposition of counts who objected to the local powers the monasteries were building up.

This development away from public authority and towards private family power associated with fortifications is more like contemporary developments in northern France and the Low Countries than like those we shall see in the next chapter in northern Italy. In France, royal concessions are associated with feudal tenure, the conditional fief; in southern Italy they were outright gifts, for, as Frankish influence was weak there, the fief was more or less unknown before the Normans (the closest the south Italians came was the swearing of temporary oaths of fealty, as Atenulf did to Athanasius of Naples in 887 for a fixed period of fifteen months – Erchempert called this a *foedus gallicus*).[26] Such concessions reveal the same patterns of disintegration and privatisation, however. The main reason for the victory of private power in each of these areas must be the absence of cities, the firm foci of public rights. The social complexity of cities prevented independent powers based on them from turning their powers into private possessions. In northern Italy, where the state collapsed as fully as in the South, urban public authority continued to dominate over the increasing privatisation of rural lordship. In the mountains of the South, there were simply no cities to act as public foci. The unit of political power became the mountain valley, with a small centre such as Isernia or Trivento, dominated by a single family. Only in the coastal cities did public power continue to survive and be strong, but, at least outside the Byzantine provinces, this had no effect on the hinterland.

In one major respect, however, southern Italy was not at all like northern France: in the manner these new local powers exercised control over their subjects. Unlike France (and even parts of northern Italy) aristocrats did not lord it over their cowering peasants from their castles; the peasants lived in these castles too, freely, with binding leases. I have, for this reason, translated *castrum* or *castellum* as '*castello*', the Italian term, for the English word 'castle' is misleading; 'fortified village' would usually be better anywhere south of Siena. The break-up of the state was, over much of the South and Centre of Italy, marked by the rapid concentration of settlement into these *castelli*, the process known to the Italians as *incastellamento*, alongside the establishment of private rights based on the building of their fortifications, the common European context for castle-building. The northern fringes of Capua-Benevento show this phenomenon very clearly, but it has been best studied in Lazio, by Pierre Toubert, and I shall use his region as a basis for a general discussion of *incastellamento* in the South.

The socio-political development of Rome and its territory was superficially unique, but it shared a number of common characteristics with the rest of the South.[27] Owing to the international status of the bishops of Rome (the popes), the Church early acquired a total dominance in the city and its surroundings, and the organisation of the ecclesiastical bureaucracy was far more developed and politically significant than elsewhere, from at least the seventh century. Until the end of the ninth century, and again after about 1050, the control of this bureaucracy was the inescapable prerequisite of all local power, and even in the intervening period it was a force that the most resolutely secular hierarch had to come to terms with. When Rome was on the fringes of an Empire that valued its role as a spiritual centre, that of the Byzantines until the 730s or so, that of the Franks between 774 and the

880s, or that of the Germans, rather more intermittently, after 962, this bureaucracy maintained a certain solidity as an office-holding hierarchy set against that of the lay nobility. When Rome was left to its own devices, as in the mid-eighth century, or after John VIII's death in 882, popes and other ecclesiastical leaders came far more under the control of their kinsmen, the leading noble families of the city and the Campagna Romana. Links between the church and the aristocracy were at all times extremely close, however. The aristocracy after all based much or most of its landed power on leasing church property, as we have already seen (see above, pp. 77–8).

Rome was not a fraction of the size it had been when it was the symbolic centre of the Empire and sustained by the grain tax from Africa, but it was still large in the ninth–tenth centuries, by contemporary standards. The prestige of the city meant that it was the focus for the aristocrats of its entire territory (three or four times the size of a city-territory in the North, and as large as a tenth-century southern principality), even though this territory contained nearly twenty 'cities' on the southern pattern, medium-size settlements with a cathedral and some minimal public authority still. Rome sucked the life from these cities. They were, with rare exceptions, never the centres of activity of major aristocratic families, all of whom preferred to live in Rome, except when on the losing side of one of Rome's innumerable factional disputes, and the cities remained unaffected by the economic revival of central Italy as late as the twelfth century. The privatisation and localisation of public authority in the tenth century took place in Rome, even more than in the far smaller territories of the North, in favour of families that for the most part lived in the city. The only great rural powers were ecclesiastical – the monasteries of Farfa and Subiaco, and the bishops of the more important Lazial cities, Sutri, Tivoli, Velletri, Veroli. These were often very large landowners, however. Farfa, slightly less Arab-devastated than the Campanian monasteries, had absorbed most of its small lay landowning neighbours in the late ninth century, probably precisely because it was the only power on the spot in the Sabina – all potential landowning rivals were in the city. It thus came to dominate the same sort of coherent bloc of land that Montecassino and S. Vincenzo had always had, and several of the other Lazian church-landowners achieved a similar position.

In the tenth century all these institutions began to build fortified villages, either directly or via leases to nobles. So in 966 the abbot of Subiaco leased an estate to the nobles Milo and Anastasia 'in which there is a place where a *castello* is to be newly built at their own expense, and enclosed by a *tufa* [volcanic stone] wall, and men are to be amassed there'. In 972, S. Vincenzo leased a large tract of its central territory to a collective group of sixteen to twenty families; 'they must build a *castello* inside these bounds where they wish, and build houses, courtyards and gardens there, and live there'.[28] The concentration on ecclesiastical landowners in these texts is doubtless merely because they kept their documents; Roman and Campanian aristocrats must have done the same sort of thing in their own lands. So must even the inhabitants of those areas (which must have been a good proportion of the total) where single families did not own solid blocs of land, for sometimes peasant groups seem to be the sole owners in *castelli*. By the mid-eleventh century, virtually the whole of Italy south of Tuscany seems to have been dominated by these *castelli* (though the date and completeness of *incastellamento* certainly varied from place to place, and in certain areas it did not occur at all).

The impetus for *incastellamento* was traditionally thought to be the danger of the Arab invasions, but the process did not really begin until well after the Arab defeat at the Garigliano in 915. The socio-political context was certainly the growth of immunities and the devolution of public powers that marked the retreat of the state. Pandulf I legitimated S. Vincenzo's castle-building, a little late perhaps, in 967; Otto I in 962 had already given the monastery total jurisdiction over its tenants.[29] In Rome, much of the impetus for this localisation and the recently established politics of castle-building was given by Marozia's son Alberic, who ruled Rome as a lay head of state in 932–54 as 'senator of all the Romans' and patrician, and from 936, on the south Italian model, as prince. Alberic did not intend to preside over the disintegration of the territory of Rome, however, as Pandulf would in Capua. There were, in fact, few local public powers in the Campagna to wield, and the counts of the fringes of the Roman territory were comparatively weak. Alberic was not, however, greatly concerned about the public nature of local powers; Rome and its nobility would control the countryside, whether in a public or a private manner. Alberic made sure that countships and monasteries were subject to his supporters (who included several reforming abbots, even Odo of Cluny, as well as important noble families), while recognising that they were going to take control of their properties in the best way they could: by building *castelli*. Private justice was not explicitly granted to them. Lords acquired such powers in a more piecemeal manner, which reached fruition only in the early years of the eleventh century.

This gives a context to the growth of *castelli* in the hinterland of Rome; it does not, however, explain *incastellamento*, the movement of whole populations from the surrounding area into the new fortifications. One answer is that the texts relating to *incastellamento* that we have are very often associated with land clearance. The wastelands of the territory that Farfa dominated were being cleared from the eighth century onwards, and the *castelli* were associated with a final reorganisation of landholding and even, apparently, field patterns, largely connected to the completion of this clearance. S. Vincenzo and Montecassino, further into the mountains, still had whole tracts uncleared, and some of S. Vincenzo's *incastellamento* charters do not require rents for the first three –four years, to give the tenants a chance to build up their crops.[30] This theory fits much of the southern Appennines, and also fits the fact that *incastellamento* was much less complete in the plains, which had already been cleared, and where landowning was much more fragmented. It is not totally satisfactory as an explanation, because we cannot expect every founder of a *castello* to have been involved in land clearance, or in the almost entrepreneurial land reorganisation that is visible in Farfa and Subiaco, and it does not explain why these should necessarily be associated with the concentration of settlement, but it is the best we can do at the moment. We cannot yet entirely solve this problem; more areas will have to be studied in detail before we can get at its roots.

The establishment of groups of families on their own, surrounded by walls, did not in every case represent an unambiguous increase of control over them on the part of their landlords. Rents were contractually fixed, and often low, particularly in the high Appennines where the monasteries were keen to attract colonisers, who came in some cases from long distances and were sometimes men of status. A yearly rent of one *modius* (possibly thirty pounds) of wheat, one of barley, and two of wine per house, plus one pig in every eleven, or twenty, was fairly normal for S. Vincenzo tenants, for example.[31] These rents, and all the other norms of the *castelli*, soon became customary. It would have been difficult to change them, and it is not easy to find lords trying. Conversely, though, the inhabitants of these *castelli* seldom tried to extend their own rights, and achieve autonomy; their lords were too influential. The most common development was, in fact, the opposite: small nobles, sometimes, perhaps, the more successful *castello*-dwellers themselves, began to become lords of single *castelli*, in many cases actually living in them, holding nominal leases from their ecclesiastical landlords. In these cases, the ordinary inhabitants of *castelli* certainly lost some of their social independence, even when economic dues did not become heavier. The only villagers in the South to achieve collective liberties at all frequently were the subjects of the Byzantine Catepanate, the least privatised and most powerful of all the states in the South. To this should be added some of the Montecassino *castelli*, whose exceptional militarisation was perhaps the fuel for more frequent and successful claims for self-rule than elsewhere. But all through the South, the fortified village brought with it stability of tenure and rent, and free status; not small advantages, when landownership was as solid as it was in the mountain and hill-country where such villages predominated. Only in the North, where landowning was more fragmented, could peasants occasionally achieve more, culminating in some places, at the end of the eleventh century, in the beginning of the rural commune (see p. 188).

7. The Failure of the State

Political and Institutional Change in Northern Italy
875–1024

LOUIS II (844–75) was a powerful ruler who could do what he chose inside his kingdom and destroy all his opponents. The German emperors who ruled Italy after 962, like Otto I or Henry II, were as powerful; their opponents, though stronger than those of Louis, lasted no better. Otto or Henry certainly had little power to control what went on at a local level in Italy, except by means of the occasional large-scale court proceeding, but it would be an optimistic analyst of Carolingian government who could claim much more direct power for Louis. All medieval kings had to act inside the parameters set for them by the attitudes of those who served them and through whom royal power was delegated. Between 875 and 962, however, these parameters decisively changed. Louis had ruled through a complex set of organs – the state bureaucracy, *missi*, counts and bishops in cities – which structured their political activity around the king, and tended to balance each other to royal advantage. By the late tenth century, being a count was no longer very different from being an ordinary landowner; the state bureaucracy was dissolving; the concerns of the ecclesiastical and lay aristocracies were directed towards their own power bases, and barely towards the state at all. The Ottonians could pull down bishops and even popes, and elevate new noble families in traditional ways, but their power base was German, not Italian. As kings of Italy they had almost no direct power of any kind. In 1024, the inhabitants of Pavia revolted and burnt the royal palace there; after that, Italy barely even existed as a state. It must be emphasised, however, that these changes did not represent the triumph of dissolution over organisation, anarchy over order. They were changes in the locus of power, rather than in power itself.[1] Local forces became more independent; small nobles, villages, and cities gained autonomies of different kinds; central government was replaced by a pullulation of little powers. Why and how this happened is one of the most interesting and complex problems of medieval Italian history. I shall discuss it from two directions: first, the broad lines of political development and institutional change; second, the interrelation between these and the changing patterns on the ground. To divorce the two is improper, and results in some duplication, but it is the only way of discussing these changes in a relatively coherent way. In 875 Louis II died. He was succeeded by several Carolingians, mostly absentee. At the overthrow of the last of these, Charles the Fat, in 887, the marquises of Spoleto and Friuli fought a series of untidy civil wars that lasted for nearly two decades, complicated by outside claimants from Provence and Germany, until 905. The period 875–905 has a certain unity. It can most usefully be seen as a continuous opposition between two factions of the Italian lay and ecclesiastical aristocracy, one side favouring kings with French or Burgundian links, the other side favouring Germans. Louis II did not leave an heir. The only alternative kings were his uncles, Charles the Bald and Louis the German, who ruled what are now France and Germany respectively. Supporters of Charles included Anspert, archbishop of Milan, and the bishops and counts of north-west Italy. Supporters of Louis included Berengar of Friuli, his kin the Supponids, Wibod, bishop of Parma (Louis II's major episcopal *aide* in his last years), and the bishops of north-east Italy. The opposition here was broadly geographical. The most constant members of each side had strong personal links across the Alps to France/Burgundy and Germany respectively. Each of the kings and claimants of the period to 905 can be associated with one side or the other. Charles the Bald (875–7), Boso of Provence (claimant 879), Guy of Spoleto (889–94), Lambert (891–8) and Louis III of Provence (900–5) had the support of the pro-French side; Carloman (877–9), Charles the Fat (879–87), Berengar I of Friuli (888–924), and Arnulf (894–7), the pro-German. With such a plethora of rulers in quick succession, nearly all of them dying without male heirs, the opportunities for changing sides and exploiting royal rivalries were considerable, and many people indulged in it. The core of support for each side, however, remained considerable, and fairly geographically constant, with Piedmont and Lombardy pro-French, the Veneto and Friuli pro-German, and Emilia wavering. Tuscany and Spoleto for the most part remained more aloof.

Charles the Bald and Carloman only made brief visits to Italy. Charles the Fat was in Italy most of the time between 879 and 886, but it is difficult to show him actually doing much. Pope John VIII (873–82) tempted him to Rome with the offer of the imperial title in 881, but failed to persuade him to emulate Louis II and fight the Arabs. The title of emperor, first given to Charlemagne in 800 and carried by rulers in

Italy fairly constantly after 817, was a useful prestige element in the battle for support in these years – Guy in 891 and Arnulf in 894 derived particular benefit from it. Charles the Fat mainly needed it as an adjunct to his European power; after 884 all other adult male-line Carolingians had died and Charles was the heir to all the realms of Charlemagne. Charles did little enough anywhere in Europe, in fact, but his inactivity is slightly curious in Italy. where he actually spent most of his reign. Instead, Italian politics in the mid-880s were dominated by feuds between Berengar of Friuli, Charles's major lay supporter, and Liutward bishop of Vercelli, his arch-chaplain and arch-minister, who fell in 886. It is not very surprising that at Charles's overthrow the Italian magnates elected Berengar as king, especially as Berengar was himself a Carolingian in the female line.

The period after 887 is a continuation of 875–87, though there were more candidates to choose from after the Carolingians had ceased to be the only possible royal family, and there were thus more wars. Berengar was principally supported by the German faction; the French faction, headed by Anselm, archbishop of Milan, were ready to choose Guy (III) of Spoleto instead. Guy had elevated ambitions. The Guideschi marquises of Spoleto, though prepared to defend their autonomy (Guy had revolted against Charles the Fat in 883), were part of one of the greatest families of imperial nobles, and Guy in 887 seems briefly to have had the idea of gaining the kingship of France and Lorraine. Returning to Italy with a Franco-Burgundian following, he was elected as king against Berengar in 889, defeated him, and boxed him into what was to remain Berengar's solid base in all the troubles to follow, the north-east. In 891 Guy took the title of emperor, the first non-Carolingian to do so, and issued capitularies, for the first time anywhere in Europe for a decade. Guy clearly intended to rule in the Carolingian manner, as did his son Lambert, who legislated in 898. This intention even won over to him old pro-German stalwarts like Wibod of Parma. Apart from legislating, though, we cannot see Guy doing very much; he was prevented by Arnulf of Germany's first invasion in 894, and his sudden death in the same year. Arnulf nominally appeared at the request of Berengar and of Pope Formosus (891–6), but he intended to rule Italy himself, as emperor. The imperial prestige tempted supporters of both sides to him in his two invasions, 894 and 895–6, but in 896 he had a stroke and retreated, leaving his followers to the mercy of Berengar and Lambert.

Lambert died in 898, leaving Berengar as sole king. In 899, though, the Hungarians appeared in Italy, raiding on horseback from the east, in the first of a series of invasions lasting until the 950s.[2] Berengar's army was annihilated by them. Berengar, in fact, in forty years of campaigning, is not recorded as ever having won a battle. The raids of the Hungarians in the Po plain began to be matched, at about the same time, by Arab attacks on Piedmont from their strongholds in Provence. In 900 the magnates of the north-west, now led by the Anscarids, marquises of Ivrea, a Burgundian family installed by Guy, revolted and elected Louis of Provence as king. Louis went to Rome and was crowned emperor, but his support fell away and he left in 902. When he returned in 905, Berengar captured and blinded him. Berengar then ruled unopposed until 922. In 915 he had himself crowned emperor as well, but he remained a reluctant heir to the grander aspects of Carolingian ideology. His interests were firmly bounded by the borders of Italy, and by straightforward power politics inside them. The tradition of making capitularies died with Lambert.

All these kings, and their successors, were either extra-Italian or rulers of Italian marches. This has led some historians to conclude that the Italian state was already so weak that only men with an external power-base had the strength to rule it. It is certainly true that the marquises were the strongest Italian aristocrats; but the preference for external kings was only a product of Carolingian legitimism, initially (after 875, all Carolingians were outsiders), and after 898 the result of a desire by Italians for neutral outsiders who might not stir up internal rivals, as Berengar of Friuli had stirred up Guy of Spoleto. Only after the 940s were native Italians too weak to rule Italy, and much had changed by then. The Italian upper classes do not seem to have preferred outsiders for their own sake; they merely recognised their advantages. Though all these external kings were Frankish by descent, they were definitely perceived as foreign. After 887 the Franks in Italy were beginning to see themselves as Italian rather than Frankish. Thus Berengar's supporters made much of the (somewhat specious) claim that he was a local man, unlike Guy with his Burgundian army. Similarly, one of these Burgundians, Berengar II, would have supporters in the 940s hailing him as the representative of Italian interests against the Provençal protégés of Hugh of Arles. The concept of the coherence of the Italian kingdom remained strong still. It was strong enough for Guy of Spoleto to regard it as worth fighting for after his wider ambitions had failed, despite the traditional distance that Spoleto had from north Italian politics, before and after Guy's brief venture.

Significantly, the only Italian aristocrat to remain aloof from the power struggles in the North was the only marquis not to try for the throne, Adalbert II of Tuscany (886–915), who changed sides continually between 887 and 905, and sometimes (as in 887–9) did not recognise any king at all (see p. 184). Other notables, lay and especially ecclesiastical, seem to have wanted a single king of Italy and a solid and stable state. They just differed, and sometimes changed their minds, about who was to rule it.

Civil wars certainly show that kingdoms were still considered worth fighting for, but as with Benevento in the 840s, the strains of civil war often made such kingdoms rather more frail. One of the first elements of the early Carolingian state to weaken was the bureaucracy. The personal group of professional administrators that ran the state in the mid-ninth century ceased to exist. Instead, the king's major representatives were reliable magnates, Boso of Provence under Charles the Bald, Liutward of Vercelli under Charles the Fat, Arding bishop of Brescia under Berengar. These were, not surprisingly, major representatives of the two opposing political groups. The administrators of the governmental machinery in Pavia were at first less involved, but even they would become political actors in 927, when some of them staged an unsuccessful *coup* against the new king, Hugh.[3] Increasingly the governmental circles of Italy became divided. Kings could not count on a secure basis of unquestioning support, even if they controlled most of Italy. They had to make concessions. Guy and Lambert, despite their programme of capitularies against the depredations of the powerful, in the manner of Louis II (see above, p. 6of.), were not in a very strong position to put their laws into operation. Even their most faithful followers were tempted to defect to Berengar of Friuli, when the kings moved too strongly against their illegalities. Almost all we know of the actual concrete activities of any of these kings are their concessions of land and legal rights to their lay and ecclesiastical supporters. These reached their height in the years of the sole rule of Berengar I, 902–22.

Berengar was the fulcrum between royal power and royal impotence. Before 902 a lucky king might have re-established the centralised state of Louis II. From 902 onwards, though, in some hundred surviving diplomas, Berengar alienated away fiscal land, fortifications, rights over town walls, juridical powers, tolls, and other immunities, as outright grants, on a larger scale than any Italian king in history. It has been quite credibly claimed that under Berengar the public institutions of the state were so weakened that no future king would be able to re-establish them. Exactly why Berengar did this is the basis for an understanding of the developments of these years.[4]

The immediate context was the threat of the Hungarians. The charters by which Berengar allowed the building of *castelli* were often glossed with phrases about the Hungarian danger. The *castello* of Sperongia was given to the monastery of Tolla in 903 'since it was founded for the use of the monastery against the persecution of the pagans and other plunderers'. In 912 S. Maria Theodota in Pavià obtained authority to build *castelli* anywhere on its property 'on account of the persecution and invasion of the pagans'.[5] The Hungarians had left in 900, but returned again in 904 and then 921–4. Berengar knew he could not field an army against them, still less defend the whole population from their diffuse and unpredictable raiding. Indeed, so low was his military reputation that every Hungarian incursion triggered off a revolt against him. We saw in chapter 5 (pp. 139–40) that under the Carolingians public army service tended more and more to be channelled through the clienteles of office-holding aristocrats, slowly privatising it. These clienteles had gained ground during the civil wars, and the concession of public rights of fortification to private persons under Berengar both recognised an irreversible development and crystallised it. Private defence replaced the public obligations of the Carolingian period. Berengar gave the deacon Audebert the right to build the *castello* of Nogara in fiscal land on the Veronese plain in 906 with a wide concession of tolls, market rights, and a complete judicial immunity. By 920, the abbey of Nonantola had acquired half the *castello*, and is seen making an agreement with twenty-five of its inhabitants which specifies their obligations to defend it, and to pay a low money rent (1 *denarius* per year per family), in return for houses, lands, pastures, and the right to collect wood in a neighbouring forest 'since we do not dare to take wood for our hearths anywhere else, for fear of the pagans'. Defence was now the subject of a private contract between owners and tenants. When, in the mid-eleventh century, Nogara became the centre of a lay lordship, defence obligations would be restricted further, to the military aristocracy.[6]

Castelli like Nogara bear an obvious resemblance to those we have seen in the central and southern Appennines, with free tenant inhabitants owing fixed rents and obligations of defence. Rather more common in the North, though, were smaller fortifications containing fewer permanent inhabitants, which just served as places of refuge, and increasingly as the administrative and judicial centres of private estates.

Most villages were not owned by a single owner, and so a lord could not very easily found a *castello* for permanent occupation by all the inhabitants of a village, as many lords could in the South.[7] *Incastellamento*, the process of castle-building, thus had a very diverse effect on the settlement patterns of different areas in the North. For the most part, however, particularly in the plain, new *castelli* were just an addition to the concentrated or dispersed village patterns of each area. They rarely replaced the old population centres entirely; sometimes they just consisted of new walls around such centres. *Castelli* continued to be founded into the eleventh and twelfth centuries, seldom with royal sanction, becoming a common element in the social patterns of every region. The local power relations that they created and reflected were very various, as we shall see in the next section.

The crucial point about Berengar's concessions was that the collective public responsibilities of the inhabitants of the kingdom could no longer be relied on. This largely explains his indifference to Carolingian ideological traditions; they no longer had much meaning. In the face of a real and unpredictable military threat, and Berengar's unpopularity among sections of the aristocracy, the whole of the hegemony traditionally enjoyed by kings of Italy crumbled. Berengar's best-known concessions are the *incastellamento* charters, with their demonstration of military weakness and their wide judicial immunities that broke up the coherence of comital jurisdiction in the countryside, but he alienated away wide sections of the fisc too, accounting for perhaps a third of all the known fiscal grants from the whole period 700–1000, at least in Lombardy and Piedmont.[8] Berengar, for the first time in Italy, needed to make systematic gifts in order to gain and maintain support from the notables of the kingdom. And one aspect of these concessions is particularly clear: the great bulk of them were to the Church, above all to bishops. This fits with the Carolingian practice of balancing the power of counts and bishops, for counts controlled the military clienteles over which Berengar had lost authority. Bishops, however, were themselves by now not politically weak, with their own followings of tenants and vassals and their vast lands. Berengar's cessions, and those of his successors, tipped the balance decisively and permanently in favour of bishops.

This was most visible in cities. Bishops began to be conceded full comital powers in their cities, restricting counts to the countryside. Guy gave these powers to the bishop of Modena in 891, and Louis III to Reggio in 900. Berengar added Bergamo and Cremona; many more followed. After 962, Otto I and his successors granted comital powers to some bishops for up to five miles around the city walls too.[9] By the end of the century, bishops were dominant in most of the cities of Emilia and the Veneto, and many of those of Lombardy. Only those of Piedmont and Tuscany remained predominantly lay. The context of these grants was often explicit. In 904 the bishop of Bergamo was granted the city walls of Bergamo, and the right to rebuild them with the help of the citizens and the refugees from the Hungarians, along with full comital rights in the city; Bergamo had just with difficulty withstood a Hungarian siege. Berengar cited 'the great incursion of the savage Hungarians' as a reason for his grant, but also, given equal weight, 'the serious oppression of the count and his officials'.[10] Henceforth, kings almost invariably took the episcopal side in disputes between counts and bishops. Bishops were less likely to be politically partisan, and thus dangerous, than counts. They were themselves usually from noble, even comital, families, of course, but their offices were not hereditary, and they were not, as counts were, defined by their military responsibilities. As the century continued, the whole structure of comital power in northern Italy was ceded away. Cities were in the hands of bishops. Even in the countryside comital authority was undermined by immunities, for Church lands and, increasingly, for *castelli*, which were becoming autonomous bases for completely new concentrations of authority and lordship (see pp. 186ff). Kings like Berengar, and after him Hugh, seem to have regarded the great comital families as their main enemies and to have worked fairly consistently to undermine their power.

The results of this transfer of authority were complex, and in the long run dangerous for the state, as society became more localised. The tenth-century kings were doubtless aware of this, but regarded the risk as worth taking. By making concessions, they could attach the loyalties of the new local powers to their own persons. Berengar and his successors certainly prevented one development: that of the haemorrhage of public power into the hands of the secular aristocracy, as occurred in France and in Benevento. It is true that, by the eleventh century, the office of count had become assimilated to the private property of comital families, and was often conceded by kings in benefice. By that time, though, the official powers of counts were far weaker. Cities and *castelli* were the independent foci of public authority, though in *castelli* this authority was becoming privatised in the hands of lay owners. Power in the countryside was thus too fragmented to offer an alternative to that of the bishop in the cities. Kings, having granted this power to bishops, were often asked to confirm it in successive reigns; their authority was still recognised. This is important. Berengar may not have been able to prevent the collapse of the authority of the state, but he could at least, through his grants, determine into whose hands his authority was devolved, and obtain suitable recognition from his protégés. Bishops, in this respect, were undoubtedly more reliable than counts.

Cities were, as we have seen, the best centres for the survival of the public relationships of free society. Bishops were not able, for the most part, to maintain a private hegemony over urban society in the North; it was too socio-economically complex, and the sources of power there were too strong. They could do no more than take on the roles of patron and judicial arbiter, and hope to survive with their power uncontested. But this was not a product of episcopal rule. It is doubtful that a reasonably prosperous city (as nearly all the cities in the North were) could ever have passively become the private possession of a lay family as they did in the South, even if counts had kept control of their cities. In 1014 the citizens of Mantua obtained a diploma from Henry II recognising their public rights and properties, and giving them an immunity against all lay officials and bishops. Mantua was not a city that had ever received an episcopal immunity, and its counts were members of the house of Canossa, the most influential family in the kingdom, who used the city as a major base. Nevertheless, its citizens had retained enough sense of their coherence to resist the Canossa and obtain this text, and they were even sufficiently aware of their public position to call themselves *arimanni*.[11] The granting of rights to bishops elsewhere may instead have created the problem of the political separation of the countryside from the city, for the restriction of counts to the countryside and the fragmentation of rural authority created a strong rural aristocracy with judicial rights, for the first time in Italy. The 'rural counts' that the city communes of the twelfth century had to conquer, one by one, were only two centuries old.

Other consequences of these royal concessions were less ambiguous. The official powers of counts, however unreliably exercised, were at least public powers that kings had granted to them, and could in principle remove, either by granting them piecemeal to bishops or by dispossessing the family that exercised them. Once powers were granted to bishops, however, they were permanently lost. Kings could at times reclaim land that they had handed over to the Church, but once the state had abandoned its authority over an area in a diploma giving juridical immunity, it could never get it back. A comital city still had a bishop in it as an independent counterweight; an episcopal city had no balancing force at all. The state was henceforth directly dependent on the goodwill of bishops. Kings who attempted to retreat from this dependence, as did the leader of the 'feudal reaction', Arduin of Ivrea (1002–15), fell as a result. And the relative political neutrality of bishops, so reassuring to hard-pressed kings, was not all to their advantage. Bishops were officials in a different hierarchy; if the state fell, their office would still have the same status. Their power was not like that of the great ninth-century lay families like the Supponids, who had land scattered across the whole Po plain (see above, pp. 57–8). Episcopal property-owning rarely stretched far beyond the borders of the bishop's own diocese, and did not need the umbrella of a strong state to protect it. By now, lay property-owning too, with some notable exceptions, was restricted to smaller geographical areas. Political preoccupations became more localised. As they did so, the very existence of the state became slowly more marginal. The political consequences of this were not slow to show themselves.

Berengar gained over fifteen years of unopposed rule while he put these developments into motion. His second successor, Hugh of Arles (926–47) found that they were already irreversible. His accession marked a new step in the changing politics of Italy. Berenger had in 920 brought in Hungarian mercenaries to strengthen his weakened military forces, but this stirred the magnates of the north-west to defy him and invite in Rudolf II, king of Burgundy (922–6). In 923 Berengar was defeated at Fiorenzuola and retreated to Verona; in 924 the Hungarians burnt Pavia, and shortly after, perhaps as a consequence, Berengar was assassinated. In 925, however, the Italians revolted against Rudolf too and defeated him, offering the crown to the count of Provence Hugh, who established himself in 926. The 922–4 period was the last time one can see the North being split along geographical lines. Berengar kept his support in Emilia and the Veneto right up to his death. Hugh began his reign with broad-based support. He soon found, however, that none of it was unconditional. Hugh's reign marks the beginning of a general crisis in royal hegemony. There were too few forces he could trust.

Hugh intended to be an active king. An active Carolingian king made laws and tried to see that they were kept, and attempted to keep checks on the misuse of power by his officials. Already, though, this was no longer possible. A king could no longer intervene directly in local affairs, without making his intervention into a political enterprise. Hugh's activities seem, rather, to have been restricted to the patronage or destruction of particular individuals and families in an attempt to strengthen his loyal power base. Even though we have a narrative history for Hugh's reign, the fullest parts of Liutprand of Cremona's *Antapodosis*, Hugh cannot be seen doing anything else, and Liutprand does not seem to have expected him to. Hugh's clearest aim was to bring the marches of Italy under his firm control, as they had not been since 875. Friuli had ceased to exist during Berengar's reign, but Tuscany and Spoleto were fully autonomous; Ivrea, too, Guy's creation, had become a powerful force. In 931 Hugh deposed his half-brother Lambert of Tuscany and blinded him. Hugh's full brother Boso became marquis, only to be deposed in turn by Hugh in 936, and replaced by the latter's illegitimate son Hubert. In 928, he appointed his nephew Teobald as marquis of Spoleto, and in 932 he attempted to extend his control over Rome by marrying its ruler, the *senatrix* Marozia, but in this case Alberic, Marozia's son, drove him off and established his own hegemony there. In 936, at Teobald's death, Hugh put Anscar II of Ivrea into Spoleto, Anscar's brother Berengar count of Milan becoming marquis of Ivrea. In 940, though, he changed his policy towards the house of Ivrea and overthrew Anscar. In 941 Berengar of Ivrea fled to Otto I in Germany and Hugh abolished his march.

It is clear just from this bald outline that Hugh's standard solution for problems of loyalty was to appoint members of his own family to offices. Boso and then Hubert ruled Tuscany; Hubert in 943 was given Spoleto as well; Hubert's brother Boso became bishop of Piacenza and arch-chancellor; Hugh's cousin Manasse archbishop of Arles was given the bishoprics of Verona, Mantua and Trento, and the new march of Trento too. This last gift is a striking collection of offices (Liutprand devoted a whole chapter to satirising Manasse for taking them all, totally against canon law),[12] but it emphasises Hugh's concern to combat his chief external danger, invasion from Germany. Manasse's appointment in 935 followed an unsuccessful incursion in 934 by Arnulf of Bavaria, at the request of the count and the bishop of Verona, Milo and Rather. Milo survived as count, but Rather was deposed and imprisoned in Pavia, where he wrote his first major literary work, the *Praeloquia*, to justify his actions (he returned to Verona as bishop in 946–8, and then again in 962–8). Hugh may well have felt that such treachery showed that only his kinsmen were reliable supporters. Hugh's violence and aggression in claiming his rights as king undoubtedly alienated potential supporters from the lay aristocracy. Hugh in response penalised them all the more. In the last years of his reign there seem to have been almost no counts in Emilia at all, for example. Hugh just relied on the bishops there, although at least one, Guy of Modena (c. 943–67), became a firm enemy too.[13] When Berengar of Ivrea came across the Alps in 945 with a small German army, Hugh's support melted away. Milo and Manasse, the frontier defenders, went over to Berengar at once (Manasse was promised the archbishopric of Milan), and the whole aristocracy of the North including most of Hugh's nominees, followed him or remained neutral. Berengar took over the government, assumed the title of *summus consiliarius*, head counsellor, and waited for Hugh to die, which he did in 947. Hugh's son Lothar, already co-king, died suddenly in 950, and Berengar had himself crowned king.

In 945 Berengar of Ivrea led the final rejection by the Italian aristocracy of the only type of strong king the Italian political system still allowed. Hugh was violent and interfering, but this was only because society had already localised itself so much that any intervention from above looked like interference, and any removal of a count or bishop looked like high-handedness. Italy had not just become a network of private lordships; even public power had devolved to localities, leaving the king outside. Hugh was not weak, even in 945. His property as king was still, despite Berengar I's (and his own) concessions, immense, and his personal property was considerable too. In a more private, 'feudalised' world like tenth-century France, Hugh might, paradoxically, have been in a better position to rule than he was in Italy. But Hugh's magnates did not hold their land from him, for the most part, and their only links to him were private links of personal loyalty. These were, by now, inadequate. When put under pressure, Hugh's support all disappeared. Berengar II was left in sole command of a political power structure that was virtually worthless to him. Berengar made one gesture towards the public traditions of the kingdom, one fitting for this unheroic period, when he taxed the whole kingdom with a poll tax, for the first and last time since the Lombard invasion, to pay off a Hungarian attack in 947. This tax, in the same tradition as Charles the Bald's Danish tribute in France in 877, and the late tenth-century Anglo-Saxon danegeld, largely went into Berengar's own treasury (if we can believe Liutprand's report), but Berengar did not have the political weight to attempt to collect it again, and the gesture stopped there.[14]

Berengar II ruled in the shadow of German invasion, even more than Desiderius had, two centuries earlier. Otto I, having established control over his German kingdom, appeared in Italy in 951–2 and proclaimed himself king. Berengar had to go to Germany to be recognised as king under Otto's protection. He kept this position until 961–2, when Otto finally annexed Italy and was crowned emperor. But Berengar's state was by now nothing like that of Desiderius. Any action Berengar took to establish his power stirred up new opposition, particularly from the Church. Like Hugh, he found aggression to be his only practicable expedient. The traditional resources of the kingdom were contracting rapidly. The most important focus of public authority, the comital court, seems to have disappeared altogether in Berengar's reign. After 922, the area in which official court proceedings were held had already shrunk to include little more than the central parts of the Po plain, western Emilia and eastern Lombardy. Between 945 and 962, there are none recorded at all.[15] By 962, the independent Italian kingdom had virtually dissolved.

Otto I undertook some temporary restoration work which was for the most part accepted by the Italians. Otto, after all, was at least politically neutral between rival Italian magnates. But, more importantly now, he had a strong army that Italian disloyalty could not undermine, and was militarily invincible, not only in the North, but also in Rome (where he overthrew hostile popes, Alberic's son John XII in 963, and John XIII in 972) and Capua–Benevento.[16] Otto raised up several new noble families, such as the Obertenghi and the Canossa. He reinstated counties (but also gave more grants of rights to bishops) and began to hold court proceedings again. In 967 he even legislated, though the Italians were less enthusiastic about this (see above, p. 128). But Otto's state was somewhat artificial, and only held up by his external military strength. When, after his death in 973, the rulers of Germany virtually stayed away from Italy until 996, the central administration could not carry on as it had done under the early Carolingians. Under Otto I, the state dues described in the *Honorantiae Civitatis Papiae* (see above, pp. 89f.) were still collected by Gisulf, King Hugh's chamberlain. In the late 980s, his grandson was removed from the office and the assets of the state began to be sold off or given away. This process may have been halted while Otto III ruled in Rome (996–1002), but it continued again under his successors. This partial loss of the fiscal rights of central government by the state after c. 990 fits with the slow breakdown of public control over local government since c. 900. It also gives a perspective to the burning of the palace at Pavia by the people in 1024, for even the people of Pavia, long privileged by exemptions, no longer felt that the state was of any advantage to them.[17] Henry II (1004–24) was still influential enough to destroy the king the Italian aristocracy crowned against him in 1002, Arduin of Ivrea, without a battle, barely finding it necessary to come into Italy at all. After his reign, however, the military strength of German emperors was not matched by a significant positive response by any section of their Italian subjects; the state was by now irrelevant. Supporters of Conrad II (1024–39) and his successors were magnates (and later cities) calling on external German support to pursue their own private and local advantage, rather than embattled adherents to the traditions of the kingdom. Rulers after 1024 were left posturing in a vacuum; the history of Italy lay elsewhere.

The New Aristocracy and the Growth of Urban Autonomy

VERY few of the important aristocratic familes of 1000 had been important a century before. The Arduinici of Turin, the Aleramici of southern Piedmont, the Obertenghi of the north-west Appennines, the Gisalbertingi of Bergamo, the Canossa of the Po marshes, the comital families of Tuscany (Guidi, Cadolingi, Gherardeschi) were new arrivals, the protégés of Hugh and Otto I. The first two of these were recent immigrant families from the north; all the rest were Lombard. The great Frankish families of the Carolingian period had nearly all died out, leaving only a few, ruling single counties, like the Bernardingi in Parma, or concentrated in limited areas, like the Berardenghi east of Siena. The 'new' families, though in many places long grounded in their localities, had no previous association with the state, and no memory of its Carolingian ambitions. Anyone wishing to recreate the the authority of the Carolingian state would get little response from them. This, however, was less significant than it looks. The local interests of these families were the product, not of their ideological outlook, but of the organisation of their landowning. They were, for the most part, successful members of the second rank of the late and post-Carolingian nobility, the vassals and tenants of Carolingian magnates and bishops, whose original landed bases had been the leases of these magnates to their clienteles (see above, pp. 141–3). They were not owners of vast scattered estates, but of lands inside smaller areas, where the wider concerns of the kingdom were less visible. Even when they were the objects of extensive royal patronage, as were, it seems, the

Obertenghi under Otto I, their lands remained largely concentrated in a single region. And though they held offices, their power was not for the most part based on their office-holding at all. Offices certainly brought land, as they always had, but they did not bring a great access of public authority, for, as we have seen, the public powers of counts were now decisively fragmented and diminished and the title of 'count' or 'marquis' became after 1000 little more than a claim to personal status.[18] These changes can best be seen through examples: first, Emilia, a reasonably typical part of northern Italy, and the subject of much recent work, especially by Vito Fumagalli; secondly, Tuscany, outside the mainstream of the developments I have set out in this chapter, the region where the force of the state remained longest.

The dominant family in Carolingian Emilia was that of the Supponids, who we have already seen associated with Brescia (see pp. 57–8). They were in many ways the archetype for a family of king's men in the ninth century, and remained firmly in the camp of their kinsman Berengar I during the civil wars. They then fell out with him, however; Boso (probably count of Parma) revolted in 913, and his brother, Wifred of Piacenza, may even have sided with Rudolf II in 922. After 925 they are barely heard of again. The last known family member, Suppo IV count of Modena, is last recorded in 942. They seem to have died out, and this is in itself not surprising. Noble families do die out quite often, if they are restricted to male-line family links. But their wide power base must long have been difficult to sustain, across several decades of civil war and temporary partitions of the kingdom, and they were heavily reliant on the power associated with holding public office, which had begun to dissolve as Berengar gave more and more of it away. Berengar's hostility may have weakened them more directly, too. By the reign of Hugh, their last family members seem to have begun to concentrate on a single province, that of Modena, where Suppo IV's uncle Arding was bishop as well. Hugh, as usual, was suspicious of them and even forced them to give him land. Their power was clearly in decline well before they physically died out.[19]

Berengar had other protégés in Emilia, however, and these families began to acquire bishoprics and counties in the first decades of the century. They were all local. The Lombard 'da Gorgo' family (based on the new *castello* of Gorgo by the Po) supplied a bishop and a count of Piacenza and a bishop of Reggio under Berengar. It was in bishop Guy of Piacenza's territory that Berengar fought his final battle of Fiorenzuola in 923. Hugh may have been suspicious of the da Gorgo, too; there were no counts of Piacenza in his last years. The family survived, however, and, linked with similar families such as the Frankish Gandolfingi, dominated western Emilia in the late tenth century, with Ottonian patronage. The da Gorgo and the Gandolfingi were in origin small families of vassals and officials in the Emilian countryside, about as far removed from the Supponids as can easily be imagined, but already under Berengar they were becoming equivalent in status, and they had a far better rate of survival. It is important that several of them should be found as bishops. Episcopal and comital office, though institutionally at odds, had become equally valid alternatives for family ambition (though Lombard families had, of course, looked to the episcopacy at least since the eighth century). By Berengar's reign, episcopal office was already the firmer of the two, as well. Although counts still ruled inside the city at Piacenza, bishop Guy was a more important figure than his brother count Raginer, and the strongest figure in Emilia in the middle of the century was certainly Guy, bishop of Modena and abbot of Nonantola, traitor first to Hugh, then Berengar II (for whom he had been arch-chancellor), then, with less success, Otto I.

Only one major family in Emilia chose to restrict itself overwhelmingly to comital office-holding, and that was the house of Canossa.[20] Their brief but dramatic history (their male line died out in 1055, their female line in 1115) shows what changes an enterprising family could make inside the new social order. Their founder was Adalbert-Atto, a member of a family of small Lombard nobles, probably from the Appennine borders of the territory of Lucca, and an active opponent of Berengar II. Otto I rewarded him with the attenuated counties of Reggio and Modena, and later Mantua. Adalbert-Atto seems to have spent the 960s–970s building up large blocs of land in the Po marshes, often exchanging for them smaller, dispersed estates in the long-cleared lands of the plain. The marshes became the focus for the power of the Canossa. The Appennines (where Canossa itself is) were somewhat less important, and the plain, the focus of the landowing of others, took third place. The Canossa saw that land clearance and a firm coherent lordship (or *signoria*, to use the Italian term) were a secure route to political power, and already in the first decades of the eleventh century they had visibly obtained it. By then, Adalbert-Atto's grandson, the monstrous and violent Boniface (marquis c. 1013–52) wielded vast proprietorial power from Cremona and Mantua into the fringes of Tuscany, and royal patronage increased this still further. The title of marquis was inherited from his father, and seemed to have carried no official status, but Boniface was in a good position to be made marquis of Tuscany by Conrad II in 1027.

Boniface ruled his lands firmly from his rural castles (except the city of Mantua, where he had a palace). His uncle and brother were bishops, but the influence of the Canossa on most cities was from the outside. This rural control may have been the background to a remarkable revolt against Boniface by, it seems, the citizens and small nobles of the Po valley, whom he had to defeat in a pitched battle in 1021. The Canossa were certainly exceptional – only the Obertenghi, and the Aldobrandeschi in southern Tuscany, operated in the country-side on quite such a scale. But they showed that independent rural power was possible, if based on non-urbanised areas like marshes and mountains, even in northern Italy. The Canossa could not have done this, however, under the Carolingians. The rejection of the cities was only possible in the brief period between the end of city-based Carolingian administration and the beginning of the power of the city communes. Even then, few great families did it. *Incastellamento* and residual office-holding could be the bases for real rural power, but the most important prizes, the episcopacy and its patronage network, remained under the control of cities.

Tuscany had a rather different development.[21] We saw that Adalbert II kept aloof from the civil wars of the North; and, after a lucky escape in 898 when he did, unsuccessfully, stage a revolt against Lambert, he avoided any hostility from the kings. Adalbert ruled the Tuscan march autonomously, as his father had (see above, pp. 59–60), with his capital at Lucca. Very few of Berengar's diplomas concern Tuscany at all, and none of those involving *incastellamento*. Adalbert kept public powers in the march under his own control. But the build-up of smaller families on fiscal and episcopal land in Lucca continued. And even before Adalbert's death in 915 private *castelli* began to appear, without any diplomas or Hungarians to justify them. Early *castelli* were episcopal; bishops were very powerful, even in the lay stronghold of Tuscany. The bishops of Lucca had a *castello* at S. Maria a Monte, south-east of Lucca, as early as 906, and one at Moriano to the north by 915. Others soon followed. They were, for the most part, strongpoints for the bishop to protect and administer his properties, and were not yet explicitly associated with immunitarian jurisdiction – only in the 1070s is Moriano recorded as a centre for civil jurisdiction by the bishop over its surrounding area.[22]

After 915 Adalbert's heir, Guy (915–30) was a minor. Berengar I, influential in Tuscany for the first time, was probably responsible for a new development from the 920s, the institution of counts in the Tuscan cities, probably as rivals or balances to the marquises: the Cadolingi and Guidi in Pistoia, followed in the 940s by the Gherardeschi in Pisa and, later, Volterra. These families were Lombard, and apparently city-oriented. They seem to have been the most successful of the vassals of king and marquis, and they quickly established themselves as the dominant families of the region, next to the marquis. Their possessions were not, however, visibly concentrated in single city territories (which were smaller than those of the North), but interconnected across the whole of the north of Tuscany. Only after the end of the tenth century did more localised, much smaller families appear. These were mostly based on *castelli*.

Tuscany's political coherence remained greater than in the North, though the seeds of its collapse were already present. King Hugh, who overthrew Guy's brother Lambert and re-established royal officials there, did not destroy the march. Hugh's son Hubert (936–c. 69) was left in control, and his son Hugh (969–1001), a firm supporter of the Ottonians, re-established Tuscany as an organised unit, actually extending marchesal powers, and going to great lengths, according to Peter Damiani, to ensure that his rule was just.[23] Tuscany avoided collapse largely because it avoided most of the disturbances of the North. The marquises ruled through the rich cities of the Arno valley, and kept vast landed estates, as the childless Hugh's gifts to monasteries at the end of the century showed. But when Hugh died, his state began to break down. The Canossa, marquises in 1027–1115, did not inherit his mantle; they were based too much in the North, and had too few links with the Tuscans. The hegemony of the marquis vanished. Lucca and Pisa fought a war in 1004. The Cadolingi began to build up their rural power outside Pistoia, and others followed them. Tuscany soon became much more like the North. The Lucchesi hated Boniface of Canossa as much as the Emilians did, and in 1081 had his 'perverse customs' and all the surviving marchesal and royal infrastructure inside the city abolished by Henry IV.[24] The example of Tuscany shows how a small portion of the kingdom of Italy could, quite adequately, support the devolved powers of the state without weakening them – indeed by tenth-century standards, even strenthening them. The Tuscan march was concentrated on a heavily urbanised area, and this must explain its survival. No other part of the kingdom had such a history, as far as can be seen at the moment.

Aristocratic families in northern Italy and Tuscany changed their structure very little when the state fell, particularly when one contrasts them with the apparent changes in family structure in tenth–eleventh-century France and Germany. They were always, for example, organised patrilineally (cf. above, p. 118), and even Frankish families conformed to this, as Winigis count of Siena showed when he founded the monastery of Fontebona in 867 and entrusted it to his male-line heirs in perpetuity. The increasing dependence on patrilineal links in the rest of Europe would not be very visible in Italy.[25] We should not expect family organisation to have changed much when the state fell, though. The basis for the aristocracy was and remained their lands, and the way they distributed their power on the ground was as important to them, in the same ways, in 800 as in 1100. Noble families practised partible inheritance in 800, and continued to do so in the eleventh century. Strategies of proprietorship did not change, and, as we have seen (pp. 141ff.), these strategies absorbed leaseholding and benefices too. The only novelty was a developing sense that family members had of the coherence and identity of their lineage. Surnames began to appear in the last decade of the tenth century in Tuscany, and by the mid-eleventh century they were common there, though in the North they were still unusual. Men interested in the past began to trace their families back to Carolingian ancestors, where they could.

This conceptual focus was strengthened by the new tendency for family nuclei to form, around proprietary monasteries, *pievi* (baptismal churches – above, p. 143), and *castelli*. These were fixed points, in a way that estates were not. A proprietary monastery or a *pieve* could be controlled by a grouping of kin as large as the whole lineage, if necessary. It was not necessary to subdivide ownership, though this could happen. Land given to such churches by individual family members was not subject to division, and might even be increased by gifts from outsiders if the church had enough religious prestige. Family control of *pievi* was a tenth-century development; family monasteries began to be common in the early years of the eleventh century, after a near-total break of two centuries.[26] But *castelli*, the classic new development of this period, were the most important foci. As pieces of property they were, indeed, subject to division; as the bases for territorial jurisdiction, however, they had a greater solidity. In the ninth century, as we saw (p. 137f), landlords began to acquire private jurisdiction for minor crimes and lawsuits over their tenants. With the *castelli* of the eleventh century, such jurisdiction often came to cover the whole of a territory under the authority of the *castello*, whether this territory was owned by the holders of the *castello* or not. Smaller families, in particular, began in the eleventh century to base their landed power entirely on such control, and began to try to fuse the juridical rights of *castelli* with landed possession over the whole territory of the *castello*, to create a firm territorial *signoria*, much as they did at the same time in northern France. This was seldom successful, but even when it was, the rules of inheritance meant that such *signorie*, too, began to split up. It was in response to this that families began to unite themselves by formal contracts into *consortia*, which controlled the central nucleus, at least, of their property-holding, the *castello* in the countryside and increasingly the tower-house in the city. This produced some stability. The interplay between the force of partible inheritance and the *consortium* contract continued to pattern noble family links right into the late Middle Ages.

Not all the great aristocratic families and ecclesiastical magnates sought to link their landowning and their *castelli* as closely as their vassals and tenants, the lesser nobility, did. As a result, some of them began by about 1000 to lose control of their lands to their vassals.[27] We have seen how the active churchmen of the late tenth century found that their tenants had begun to establish themselves on church property, to the exclusion of effective ecclesiastical authority (see above, p. 143). The military clienteles of the early tenth century began under the Ottonians to be recognised as a distinct stratum of the aristocracy with different interests from the great landowners, and with a distinct name, varying from place to place – *secundi milites* in the North, *lambardi* in Tuscany; in Milan, where the landowning power of the archbishop was immense, there were two strata, the *capitanei* (with *pievi* as their centres) and their vassals, the *valvassores*. Their *castelli* were different, too. The early tenth-century *castelli* were set down in areas where landowning was complex, and remained so. They were comparatively large, and some *castello*-owners even exploited the popularity of house plots inside the walls by selling or exchanging them for high prices.[28] The *castelli* of a century later, the strongholds of the petty nobility, were often much smaller, and principally served as family seats. They were the foci for much more aggressive policies of proprietorial organisation. Some of the new greater nobles were aggressive too (the Gandolfingi were examples); others suffered from it. So did the peasantry. As at the time of the extension of the manorial system, the peasantry began to resist, sometimes with success.

We have seen that the manorial system had moreorless disintegrated by c.1000 (pp. 111ff.), with widespread commutation to money rents, the abandonment of labour service, and the gradual disappearance of slavery. Tenants often even had the right to sell the land they leased, and many of them owned land outright as well.[29] Independent peasant owners had by no means ceased to exist, either (indeed, some of the most successful succeeded in reaching the ranks of the petty nobility). Although landlords had by no means lost their authority, it was an increasingly open peasant society that the owners of *castelli* were attempting to control by means of the local power the new units of jurisdiction gave. The range of exactions demanded by some *castello*-owners was very considerable, and the obligations pushed many cultivators back into dependence. Others, however, seem to have had the independence and cohesion to fight back, especially in areas where *castello* jurisdictions menaced the landholding of other aristocrats, as well as the independence of the peasantry. A minor oddity is that we can first see this cohesion in a sequence of imperial diplomas confirming the rights of peasants; the state perhaps still felt the threat of uncontrolled private power as much as peasants did. In 970 Otto I gave toll immunities to the tenants of S. Maria in Organo, in the village of Zago in the Veronese. In 983 the (landowning) peasants of Lazise on Lake Garda received fishing rights from Otto II. The slaves of S. Ambrogio, in Bellagio, close to Limonta, were given pasture rights by Otto III in 998. Fifteen named slaves of S. Antonino in Piacenza were given a toll immunity in the same year. In these cases peasants were being granted public rights by the state, even though they were mostly the dependents of monastic owners – some monasteries still kept tight hold over their properties, and they are much better documented than the lay nobility. Such collective rights, though a small part of the peasant economy, were the basis for the possibility of collective action by a community that could be very scattered. As in the ninth century, peasant resistance was at first best organised on the margins of Italian society; but when, in 1058, the abbey of Nonantola ceded a charter to the inhabitants of the *castello* of Nonantola, in which it granted them freedom from excessive rents and all aggression (except when exercising its judicial rights), the way towards the rural commune of the twelfth–thirteenth centuries was open.[30]

The other focus for autonomous activity after the fall of state power was the city. Cities had been acting as collectivities, at least informally, since the late seventh century, and the citizens of Milan had an assembly place in front of their cathedral by 879. The bishop had for several centuries acted as the focus of city politics, as we have seen. His office was the major urban office that important city families could aspire to. When the tenth-century kings gave comital rights in cities to bishops, they retreated from a political sphere that had always been dominated by the episcopacy. But the first responsibilities of a bishop were to his church and city not to the state (cf. above, pp. 175ff.), and when the state ceased to make its presence felt most bishops did not pursue it, except the most ambitious imperial bishops, like Otto III's German appointee, Leo of Vercelli (998–1026), or, more ambiguously, Aribert II of Milan (1018–45). Cities began to develop much more localised politics, and city rivalries began to be much more visible, beginning with the Pisa–Lucca war of 1004.[31]

It is clear that on one level the cession of city government to bishops was a logical step in urban political development. But it was not all to the bishop's advantage. Cities were not collectivities that could easily be controlled, particularly the most important urban families, who were also, for the most part, the major rural landholders too. Only one family could provide a bishop at any one time. And if the clerical hierarchy was functioning in a properly moral, that is to say meritocratic, manner, as began to be more common into the eleventh century, bishops might not be chosen from aristocratic families at all. But city families had no other way of achieving official power and status, now that the offices of state had moved out of cities. Faction-fighting became more intense, in the absence of such outlets, and only began to be resolved with the development of independent communal government and thus new urban offices at the end of the eleventh century. This development, to which all the previous history of medieval Italy has been seen by too many historians as a mere prelude, is not our concern here. But the complexities of urban autonomy were largely the product of the end of the state, and some of them are relevant.

Episcopal *signorie* over cities were in themselves quite similar to private lay *signorie* based on *castelli*. The royal diplomas that granted them were often almost identical. Even the most symbolic feature of cities, their walls, were sometimes granted away piecemeal to private persons. Berengar I gave a section of the wall of Pavia to the monastery of S. Maria Theodota in 913, and Otto II did the same in Como for an urban merchant, Baribert, in 983.[32] But even the most seigneurialised of northern Italian cities maintained some public institutions, as we have seen in the case of Mantua (see above, p. 176), as they were too complex to control by any other means. The germ of the commune lay in these institutions and the professionals that ran them, judges and notaries. These groups were already well established in the eighth century, and by the eleventh had become dominant and influential families, inextricably interrelated with the activities of the clerical bureaucracy and the new landowning merchant stratum (see above, p. 91). The urban landed aristocracy were already finding it necessary to be associated with these groups, too; it was becoming hard to tell them apart. They became the leading citizens of the tenth-eleventh century, the *cives*, usually appearing in our sources without any other description. *Cives* assisted the bishop of Mantua in running the mints he was given by Lothar in 945; the citizens of Genoa were the recipients of a charter of liberties from Berengar II in 958, the first charter to a citizen body that survives.[33] Sometimes the citizens were divided into strata – *maiores*, *mediocres*, and *minores*, or (as at Cremona in 996) 'all the free Cremonese citizens, rich and poor.' Exactly what these strata meant in economic terms is wholly obscure in this period; the leaders of the citizens, however, were always the professional strata and the landed aristocracy. Some of the latter were sometimes distinguished from the citizens as *milites*, episcopal vassals, but they can seldom be seen in opposition to their civilian counterparts (Milan is the clearest exception). Nor were they the only people who fought. The city uprisings of the eleventh century show that ordinary people were prepared to fight and were not unpractised at it. In the urban context, fighting had not become restricted to an élite, and, in pursuit of civic identity, the poor were mostly still prepared to follow the rich.

Uprisings were not a necessary or immediate prelude to the commune, but they show most clearly the force that civic identity began to take on once cities became autonomous political centres. After the mid-tenth century they became much more common. All the citizens of Verona came together to oppose Bishop Rather in 968. In 983 the Milanesi expelled Archbishop Landulf II from the city, and he had to make many cessions to the civic aristocracy to return. The Cremonesi rose against their bishop in or around 1030, and, in Conrad II's words, 'threw him out of the city with great ignominy, despoiled his goods, and destroyed to the foundations a tower of the castle . . . . They also demolished the old city walls to their foundations, and built another, larger, wall against Our state.' The Cremonesi had been on bad terms with their bishops, especially over river tolls for Cremonese merchants, ever since 852 (see above, p. 90), but by 996 the disputes had already come to involve the entire citizen body. Otto III was tricked by them into issuing a diploma that granted them rights and full immunities, though he cancelled it on hearing from the bishop, who already possessed these rights. Cities with strong episcopal rule (Cremona had never had a count) could react against it early. The 1030 Cremona revolt was, however, also against the state, and here it fits in with those of Parma and Milan later in the 1030s, and, earlier, Pavia in 1004 and 1024 and Ravenna in 1027. All of them were, at least in part, risings against what remained of imperial authority.[34] In this respect they were as much part of tenth-century history as of the run-up to the communes; they were local rejections of the hegemony of the state, just as uprisings by individual lay nobles were. The strength of the Italian state had once been derived from its network of cities, but by Conrad II's reign the cities were the standard-bearers of local autonomy, more opposed to him than any other force in Italy. It is at this point that the urban aristocracy detached itself most firmly from the state office-holding traditions of the rural aristocracy, and began to direct its concerns exclusively into urban life. When it did so the force of episcopal hegemony inside the city could not resist it for long; the combined landed power of the urban aristocracy was far greater than that of the bishop. Civic ideology in particular became entirely localised. The Milan praise-poem of 739 (see above, pp. 82–3) honoured King Liutprand and Archbishop Theodore at its climax. But when the Pisans raided Palermo in 1063 and built their new cathedral with the booty, their pride was for themselves alone, 'the Pisan citizens, powerful in their renowned strength', as they wrote on its walls.[35] The commune, here, was clearly close.

THESE examples of autonomy, in *castelli* and cities, by nobles, peasants, bishops, and citizens, look so much more interesting than the sterile history of the late tenth–eleventh-century state that the replacement of the state by these new forces might seem inevitable. Italy was and is very localised. As I have tried to indicate, every different locality has its own history and individual dynamic. Wider forces like the state are, at least initially, imposed on each of these localities from outside. There were, for each of the autonomous forces of the eleventh century, long historical traditions. But the solidarity and cohesion of their ideologies were the product of the fall of the state, not its cause. The conception of a single people or a single state, the *gens Langobardorum* of Paul the Deacon, the *regnum Italicum* of Liutprand of Cremona, lasted as long as the state did. It is only after the state fell that they were replaced, in the minds of Italy's ruling classes, by the explicit affirmation of local loyalties. In another sense, though, it is at least not surprising that the state fell before these new local forces. The Lombard and Carolingian states were monuments to the force of the ideology of the Roman Empire, for the four centuries after it vanished in the mid-sixth century. The Lombard and Carolingian kings tried to rule through large-scale public institutions, without the economic backing of the taxation network of the Empire that produced them. They had large landed bases, in a new world where landowning was the only key to power; but so did their delegates, dukes, counts, and bishops, and the land of their delegates was independent of royal authority, or soon became so. The strongest force that allowed the kings to keep control of their kingdom was simply the consent of their aristocracies to the public ideal of the Roman state that their rulers wielded, and, as a result of this consent, the fact that the landowning classes structured their political action around the state. The state patronage network was, after all, extremely profitable to them. But, despite this, the private activities of these men slowly whittled the public power of the state away, and the state could do little to stop it. Consent the state could keep; but real control, equally part of the ideology of the Empire, was harder. The fact that the state survived only through the consent of the upper classes was mirrored, too, in the equally important fact that the state barely ever made its presence felt among the different strata of the peasantry, the vast majority of society, except as a distant coercive force. The political settlement of the Lombard-Carolingian state was restricted to the aristocracy, and was largely irrelevant to everyone else. The most one could say would be that state control was more effective in northern Italy and Tuscany than in the South, or elsewhere in Europe, largely thanks to the complexity of north Italian cities and of the landowning around them, which enabled the state to exploit local rivalries and make interventions, and which lessened the possibility of any one family gaining local control and seceding from the state. But local intervention required the use of the politics of landowning, and this was not public, but private. The state exploited private links of dependence, too, but in doing so, it strengthened these links. At the crisis point, at the beginning of the tenth century, these links, based firmly on landholding, proved themselves stronger than the public ideology of the state. In this sense, the tenth century (or, in the South, the ninth) does see a victory of localities over the state, for the private bonds of society, personal dependence, community, and the coercion of the peasantry, were local ones. Even public institutions became localised now, in cities and *castelli*. The ideology of the integrated state was replaced by the real force of local society. Italy sprang apart. The localities went their separate ways (though often on parallel lines), fortified by a growing sense of their own separate identities. It would take the ideology of nineteenth-century Romantic nationalism and the socio-economic transformations of the Industrial Revolution to force them back together again.

Bibliographies

Abbreviations

A.S. . . .	*Archivio Storico . . .*
B.I.S.I.	*Bollettino dell' Istituto Storico Italiano per il Medio Evo*
M.G.H.	*Monumenta Germaniae Historica (A.A: Auctores Antiquissimi; S.S.: Scriptores; S.R.L.: Scriptores rerum Langobardicarum; Dipl: Diplomata, either Carolingian (Kar.) or German (by emperor); Epp.: Epistolae)*
Migne, P.L.	J-P. Migne, *Patrologia Latina*
Q.F.	*Quellen und Forschungen aus italienischen Archiven und Bibliotheken*
R.S.I.	*Rivista Storica Italiana*
S.M.	*Studi Medievali*
Sett.	*Settimane di Studio* (Spoleto)

Introductory Note

This bibliography has been divided into English and non-English sections. It is not complete; a complete bibliography would be out of place here, and almost impossible to construct, given the bewildering variety of Italian local journals and the long-standing interest in Italy of the whole range of the international academic community, particularly, for our period, the Germans.

To make cross-referencing easier, the English section (A) and the non-English section (B) have both been divided into the following sections:

1. ORIENTATION AND GENERAL WORKS
2. SOURCES
3. POLITICAL HISTORY
   (a) Late Rome and the Ostrogoths
   (b) Lombard and Byzantine Italy
   (c) Carolingian Italy
   (d) Post-Carolingian Italy and the German Empire
   (e) Southern Italy
   (f) Local Studies
4. SOCIAL HISTORY
5. ECONOMIC HISTORY
   (a) General
   (b) Urban Studies
   (c) Rural Studies
6. THE CHURCH AND CULTURE
   (a) General Religious History
   (b) The Papacy and Rome
   (c) Culture

Cross references will be given in abbreviated form, e.g. (B3–d).

A. Select Bibliography of Works in English

1. ORIENTATION AND GENERAL WORKS

English has not been the language of much major work on early medieval Italy. The only subjects on which English-language scholarship competes on anything approaching equal terms with the best scholarship abroad are the late Roman-Ostrogothic period, the papacy, and, more recently, settlement and field archaeology. Otherwise, one has to bridge the gaps with fragmentary and mediocre analyses, or brief sections in works on other topics. One can only except from these strictures the works of Donald Bullough, principally on Carolingian Italy.

As a general problem, the history of early medieval Italy has no English-language analyses at all; see, however, D. A. Bullough, *Italy and her invaders*, Nottingham University inaugural lecture, 1968. Among narrative histories, the massive eight-volume history to 814, T. Hodgkin, *Italy and her Invaders* (Oxford, 1892–9), is unsuperseded; the best sections are on the fifth–sixth centuries. *The Cambridge Mediaeval History* (Cambridge, 1911–) is the only alternative.

2. SOURCES

Most of the late Roman-Ostrogothic texts are in translation, particularly in Loeb (the *Anonymus Valesianus* comes at the end of the Loeb Ammianus Marcellinus). Cassiodorus's *Letters (Variae)* is available in an abridged translation by T. Hodgkin (London, 1886). *The Theodosian Code* is trans. C. Pharr (Princeton, 1952). About half of Gregory the Great's letters are translated in vols. XII and XIII of *Nicene and Post-Nicene fathers* (Oxford, 1895–8); this series and the Catholic University of America's *Fathers of the Church* translate most of the major patristic texts.

Paul the Deacon's *History of the Langobards* is available in a translation by W. D. Foulke (Philadelphia, 1907); the *Lombard Laws* are trans. K. F. Drew (Philadelphia, 1973).

After 774, sources in translation are much scarcer; the only exceptions are the capitularies and a few court cases in H. R. Loyn and J. C. Percival, *The Reign of Charlemagne* (London, 1975), and Liutprand of Cremona, *Works*, trans. F. A. Wright (London, 1930). Texts on commerce, including a number of Italian documents from the eighth–tenth centuries, and most of the *Honorantiae Civitatis Papiae*, are translated in R. S. Lopez and I. W. Raymond, *Mediaeval Trade in the Mediterranean World* (London, 1955).

3. POLITICAL HISTORY

(a) Late Rome and the Ostrogoths

The master work on the subject in any language is A. H. M. Jones, *The Later Roman Empire*, 3 vols (Oxford, 1964). The fullest narrative in English is J. B. Bury, *History of the Later Roman Empire*, 2 vols, 2nd ed. (London, 1923), older than Stein (B3–a), but comparable. For socio-political history to 425, J. Matthews, *Western Aristocracies and the Imperial Court* (Oxford, 1975) is basic. The second and third volumes of the *Prosopography of the Later Roman Empire* (Cambridge) will be the major research tool of the next decades. For the period up to 490, extremely detailed prosopographical and textual analysis is producing some results: J. Matthews, 'Continuity in a Roman Family: the Rufii Festii of Volsinii', *Historia*, XVI (1967) pp. 484–509; B. L. Twyman, 'Aetius and the Aristocracy', *Historia*, XIX (1970) pp. 480–503; F. M. Clover, 'The Family and Early Career of Anicius Olybrius', *Historia*, XXVII (1978) pp. 169–96; M. McCormick, 'Odoacer, the Emperor Zeno, and the Rugian victory legation', *Byzantion*, XLVII (1977) pp. 212–22.

On the Ostrogothic period, there is also A. H. M. Jones, 'The constitutional position of Odoacer and Theoderic', *Journal of Roman Studies*, LII (1962) pp. 126–30. Theoderic's government is discussed by W. G. Sinnigen, 'Comites consistoriani in Ostrogothic Italy', *Classica et Mediaevalia*, XXIV (1963) pp. 158–65; 'Administrative shifts of competence under Theoderic', *Traditio*, XXI (1965) pp. 456–67.

See also A6–c.

(b) Lombard and Byzantine Italy

For the Lombards, there is little except Hodgkin's (A1) most rhetorical sections, though the chapter in the *Cambridge Mediaeval History*, II, pp. 194–221, is by L. M. Hartmann, the great narrative historian of the period (cf. B1). The short, succinct account of D. A. Bullough, 'The Ostrogothic and Lombard Kingdoms', in D. Talbot Rice (ed.) *The Dark Ages* (London, 1965) pp. 167–74 is valuable; it gives weight to art and archaeology. There is also a chapter in J. M. Wallace-Hadrill, *The Barbarian West* (London, 1966).

On Lombard archaeology, there is now I. Kiszely, *The Anthropology of the Lombards* (London, 1979). A careful survey of one detail of Lombard administrative history gives good insights: D. A. Bullough, 'The Writing-office of the dukes of Spoleto in the 8th century', in *idem*. (ed.) *The Study of Mediaeval Records* (Oxford, 1971) pp. 1–21.

Ravenna is now better covered, with important new work by T. S. Brown, 'The church of Ravenna and the imperial administration in the 7th century', *English Historical Review*, XCIV (1979) pp. 1–28, and *Social structure and the hierarchy of officialdom in Byzantine Italy* (London, 1981); see also, perhaps, A. Guillou, 'Demography and culture in the exarchate of Ravenna', *S.M.*, x.1 (1969) pp. 201–19.

(c) Carolingian Italy

Italy is covered in this period in aspects of general works on the Carolingian Empire: H. Fichtenau, *The Carolingian Empire* (Oxford, 1963); L. Halphen, *Charlemagne and the Carolingian Empire* (Oxford, 1977); D. A. Bullough, *The Age of Charlemagne* (London, 1965); see also *idem*, 'Europae Pater', *English Historical Review*, LXXXV (1970) pp. 59–105.

For Carolingian administration, see D. A. Bullough, 'Baiuli in the Carolingian *regnum Langobardorum* and the career of abbot Waldo (†813)', *English Historical Review*, LXXVII (1962) pp. 625–37; *idem*, 'The counties of the *regnum Italiae* in the Carolingian period, 774–888: a topographical study. I', *Papers of the British School at Rome*, XXIII (1955) pp. 148–68; K. F. Drew, 'The Carolingian military frontier in Italy', *Traditio*, XX (1964) pp. 437–47; and the latter's useful survey, 'The immunity in Carolingian Italy', *Speculum*, XXXVII (1962) pp. 182–97.

There are also a few contributions to more straightforward narrative history, T. F. X. Noble, 'The revolt of King Bernard of Italy', *S.M.*, XV (1974) pp. 315–26; C. Odegaard, 'The Empress Engelberge', *Speculum*, XXVI (1951) pp. 77–103; F. E. Engreen, 'Pope John VIII and the Arabs', *Speculum*, XX (1945) pp. 318–30.

(d) Post-Carolingian Italy and the German Empire

More or less nothing in this category of any value. There are sections on Italy in G. Barraclough, *Origins of Modern Germany* (Oxford, 1947) and *The Crucible of Europe* (London, 1976). *Cambridge Mediaeval History* has useful articles by C. W. Previté-Orton, 'Italy in the 10th century' (III, pp. 148–78); 'The Italian cities to *c.* 1200' (V, pp. 208–41). After 1000, there is, however, work of quality; see the companion book in this series, J. K. Hyde, *Society and Politics in Medieval Italy, 1000–1350* (London, 1975).

(e) Southern Italy

One or two texts are edited with introductions and commentaries in English: U. Westerbergh, *Chronicon Salernitanum* (Lund, 1956), and *idem*, *Beneventan 9th century poetry*

(Stockholm, 1957) which includes useful comments on ninth-century history; M. Salzman, *The Chronicle of Ahimaaz* (New York, 1924).

Pre-Arab Sicily is discussed by M. I. Finley, *Ancient Sicily* (London, 1968); on Arab Sicily there is A. Ahmad, *A history of Islamic Sicily* (Edinburgh, 1975). See also A5–*b*.

(f) Local Studies

There is one large-scale local study in English, R. Schumann, *Authority and the Commune. Parma 833–1133* (Parma, 1973). At the end of our period, on eleventh-century Milan, see H. E. J. Cowdrey, 'Archbishop Aribert of Milan', *History*, LI (1966) pp. 1–15; 'The papacy, the Patarines, and the church of Milan', *Transactions of the Royal Historical Society* v ser. 18 (1968) pp. 25–48. Lucchese episcopal history is discussed in E. G. Ranallo, 'The bishops of Lucca from Gherard I to Gherard II (868–1003)', *5° Congresso* (B1) pp. 719–35.

4. SOCIAL HISTORY

Despite its title, C. E. Boyd, *Tithes and parishes in Mediaeval Italy* (Ithaca, 1952) gives many important insights on the social history of the entire period.

On law, two contributions to early medieval law in general are important for understanding Italian legal history: the fundamental E. Levy, *West Roman Vulgar Law, The Law of Property* (Philadelphia, 1951), and C. P. Wormald's stimulating article, '*Lex Scripta* and *Verbum regis*', in *Early Mediaeval Kingship*, ed. P. H. Sawyer and I. N. Wood, (Leeds, 1977) pp. 105–38.

On family structure, see D. Herlihy, 'Family Solidarity in Mediaeval Italian History', in *idem.*, R. S. Lopez, V. Slessarev (eds.) *Economy, Society and Government in Mediaeval Italy* (Kent, Ohio, 1969) pp. 173–84; D. O. Hughes, 'Urban Growth and Family Structure in Mediaeval Genoa', *Past and Present*, LXVI (1975) pp. 3–28. On women, D. Herlihy, 'Land, Family and Women in Continental Europe 701–1200', *Traditio*, XVIII (1962) pp. 89–120 points up some international contrasts.

5. ECONOMIC HISTORY

(a) General

There are good introductions in the *Cambridge Economic History*: P. J. Jones, 'Italy' in I, 2nd ed., (1966) pp. 340–431 – on the thirteenth century, but with valuable insights on agrarian history throughout the Middle Ages; C. E. Stevens, 'Agriculture and rural life in the Later Roman Empire' *ibid* pp. 92–124; R. S. Lopez, 'The Trade of Mediaeval Europe – the South', II (1952) pp. 257–354. G. Luzzatto, *An economic history of Italy* (London, 1961) is the best general survey.

On problems of early medieval economics in general, G. Duby, *The Early Growth of the European Economy* (London, 1974); P. Grierson, 'Commerce in the Dark Ages: a critique of the evidence', *Transactions of the Royal Historical Society* v ser. 9 (1959) pp. 123–40. The somewhat alienating B. Hindess and P. Q. Hirst, *Precapitalist Modes of Production* (London, 1975) contains important analyses.

F. Braudel, *The Mediterranean and the Mediterranean World in the Age of Philip II* (2 vols London, 1972–3) is a crucial text for the Mediterranean in all periods.

(b) Urban Studies

On ancient cities, A. H. M. Jones (A3–*a*), supplemented by his articles in *The Roman Economy* (Oxford, 1973), pp. 1–60. For early medieval cities, D. A. Bullough, 'Social and Economic Structure and Topography in the Early Medieval City', *Sett.*, XXI (1973) pp. 351–99; P-A. Février, 'Towns in the Western Mediterranean', in M. W. Barley (ed.)

European Towns (London, 1977) pp. 315–42. All these are general works, giving prominence to Italian material. Specific analyses of Italian urban topography are M. Cagiano de Azevedo, 'Northern Italy', in Barley, pp. 475–84, and D. A. Bullough's major article, 'Urban change in Early Mediaeval Italy; the example of Pavia', *Papers of the British School at Rome*, XXXIV (1966) pp. 82–131. For the archaeology of the abandoned city of Luni, see B. Ward-Perkins, 'Luni: the decline and abandonment of a Roman town' in Blake (see below, A5–c) pp. 313–21.

On commerce, apart from Lopez and Raymond (A2) and Lopez (A5–a), there is R. S. Lopez, 'An aristocracy of money in the Early Middle Ages', *Speculum*, XXVIII (1953) pp. 1–43 on moneyers, and two articles by A. O. Citarella on Amalfi, 'The relations of Amalfi with the Arab world before the crusades', *Speculum*, XLII (1967) pp. 299–312, and 'Patterns in Medieval Trade – The commerce of Amalfi before the crusades', *Journal of Economic History*, XXVIII (1968) pp. 531–55. A. R. Lewis, *Naval power and trade in the Mediterranean, 500–1100* (Princeton, 1951) is useful; A. Guillou, 'Production and profits in the Byzantine province of Italy', *Dumbarton Oaks Papers*, XXVIII (1974) pp. 89–109, is essential.

(c) Rural Studies

P. J. Jones, 'An Italian estate, 900–1200', *Economic History Review*, VII (1954) pp. 18–32 discusses developments in the territory of Lucca. There are some interesting ideas in general articles by D. Herlihy, 'Agrarian revolution in Southern France and Italy, 801–1150', *Speculum*, XXXIII (1958) pp. 23–41; 'History of the rural seigneury in Italy, 751–1200', *Agricultural History*, XXXIII (1959) pp. 58–71; 'Treasure hoards in the Italian economy', *Economic History Review*, X (1957) pp. 1–14.

Medieval archaeology is taking great strides in Italy at the moment, and excavations and field surveys by British archaeologists are making a major contribution to it. In general, H. M. Blake, T. W. Potter, D. B. Whitehouse, (eds), *Papers in Italian Archaeology*, I, (London, 1978) sets out recent work, especially the important article by Blake, 'Medieval pottery: technical innovation or economic change?', pp. 435–73. For field work, see T. W. Potter, *The changing landscape of South Etruria* (London, 1979), C. J. Wickham, 'Historical and topographical notes on Early Mediaeval South Etruria', *Papers of the British School at Rome*, XLVI (1978) and XLVII (1979), and G. W. Barker (ed.), *A Mediterranean Valley* (Cambridge, to appear).

6. THE CHURCH AND CULTURE

(a) General Religious History

Boyd (A4) is our best guide here, though only discussing a part of the subject.

(b) Rome and the Papacy

For Rome, we actually have too many English-language works to list. For general narratives, P. Llewellyn, *Rome in the Dark Ages* (London, 1971), and J. Richards, *The popes and the papacy in the early middle ages, 476–752* (London, 1979). The territorial history of the papacy is given good coverage by P. Partner, *The lands of St. Peter* (London, 1972). All these contain bibliographies. See also L. Duchesne, *The beginnings of the temporal sovereignty of the popes 754–1073* (London, 1903). For more detailed topics, see P. A. Llewellyn, 'The Roman church in the 7th century', *Journal of Ecclesiastical History*, XXV (1974) pp. 363–80; *idem*, 'Constans II and the Roman Church', *Byzantion*, XLVI (1976) pp. 120–6; D. H. Miller, 'The Roman revolution of the 8th century', *Mediaeval Studies*, XXXVI (1974) pp. 79–133; J. T. Hallenbeck, 'The Lombard party in 8th century Rome', *S.M.*, XV (1974) pp. 951–66; B. Hamilton, 'Monastic revival in 10th century Rome', *Studia Monastica*, IV (1962) pp. 35–68.

F. Homes Dudden, *Gregory the Great*, 2 vols (London, 1905) has still not been fully superseded as a biography.

(c) Culture

For the Ostrogothic period, we have A. Momigliano, 'Cassiodorus and the Italian culture of his time', *Proceedings of the British Academy*, XLI (1955) pp. 207–45; see the extensive bibliography for other work on the period. For pre-Carolingian learning, see M.L.W. Laistner, *Thought and Letters in Western Europe 500–900* (London, 1957). For one aspect of the urban ideology of the eighth century and onwards, see J. K. Hyde, 'Medieval descriptions of cities', *Bulletin of the John Rylands Library*, XLVIII (1966) pp. 308–40. For learning in the South, see Westerbergh (A3–e).

B. SELECT BIBLIOGRAPHY OF WORKS IN OTHER LANGUAGES

I. ORIENTATION AND GENERAL WORKS

Italians are more conscious than the British of their own ideological standpoints, and as a result many of the books and articles in this bibliography include analyses of historiographical traditions and methodological criteria. The recent collective history, *Einaudi Storia d'Italia* (Turin, 1974–   ), is the most explicit of recent contributions, as well as including easily the best introductions to early medieval socio-political and socio-economic history, G. Tabacco, 'La storia politica e sociale', II pp. 5–167, and P. J. Jones, 'La storia economica', II pp. 1469–1681. Other general histories are more interested in political narrative, especially that of Vallardi; the relevant volumes are G. Romano and A. Solmi, *Le dominazioni barbariche in Italia* (Milan, 1940–5), now somewhat outdated, and C. G. Mor, *L'età feudale* (Milan, 1952). A new series issued by UTET, aimed at a lower level but incorporating recent work, is appearing, starting with vol. II, V. Fumagalli, *Il regno Italico* (Turin, 1978), on the ninth-tenth centuries. The only single-author general history of the whole period is L. M. Hartmann, *Geschichte Italiens im Mittelalter*, 4 vols, (Gotha, 1900–23) which is still classic. An introductory survey is G. L. Barni and L. Fasoli, *L'Italia nell'alto medioevo* (Turin, 1971). F. Sestan, *Stato e nazione nell'alto medioevo* (Naples, 1951) contains some interesting insights about Italian development up to *c.* 800. For modern schools of thought about the period, the simplest access is probably to follow references to major authors such as Bognetti, Violante, Tabacco, Fumagalli in the bibliography.

The Italians, under the aegis of the Centro Italiano di Studi sull'Alto Medioevo, run annual conferences at Spoleto on the early medieval period in the whole of Europe, published as *Settimane di Studio*. These are the best places to look for recent work. The Centro also runs less regular congresses on Italy, the *Congressi Internazionali di Studi sull'Alto Medioevo*; these are often disappointing, with the exception of the fifth, on early medieval Tuscany (Spoleto, 1973).

Bibliographies: on economic history, Jones's article, already cited, is the fullest that is easily imaginable; the UTET series will provide up-to-date general bibliographies.

2. SOURCES

The *Monumenta Germaniae Historica* (*M.G.H.*) provide what are usually the best editions of late Roman sources (*Auctores Antiquissimi*), narrative histories (*Scriptores*), diplomas from the Carolingian and German emperors (*Diplomata*); letters, poetry, etc. The *Fonti per la storia d'Italia* (Rome, 1887–   ), are the Italian equivalent for texts that do not deal so specifically with periods of transalpine rule, especially the diplomas of the native Lombard and post-Carolingian kings, and other national collections of charters and court cases (C. Manaresi (ed.), *Placiti* [Rome, 1955–60]). For local charter collections, see the list in Fumagalli (B1) pp. 306–7, especially the series *Regesta Chartarum Italiae* (Rome, 1914–   ), G. Porro-Lambertenghi, *Codex Diplomaticus Langobardiae* (Turin, 1873), and

D. Barsocchini, *Memorie e documenti per servire all'istoria di Lucca*, v (Lucca 1837–41). From the eleventh century, the vast second edition of Muratori's *Rerum Italicarum Scriptores* (Bologna, 1900–) becomes the fundamental collection of sources.

3. POLITICAL HISTORY

For a general introduction, see Tabacco and Hartmann (B1).

(a) Late Rome and the Ostrogoths

E. Stein, *Histoire du Bas-Empire*, 2 vols, (Bruges, 1949–59) is still the best and most detailed narrative up to 565. The period before 476, in particular, lacks more recent analysis except M. A. Wes, *Das Ende des Kaisertums im Westen des römischen Reiches* (The Hague, 1967). See also K. F. Stroheker, 'Der politische Zerfall der römischen Westens' in *idem, Germanentum und Spätantike* (Stuttgart, 1965), pp. 88–100. For the aristocracy, the works of J. Sundwall are basic, *Weströmische Studien* (Berlin, 1915) and *Abhandlungen zur Geschichte des ausgehenden Römertums* (Helsinki, 1919), with A. Chastagnol, *Le Sénat romain sous le règne d'Odoacre* (Bonn, 1966). On 476, the most subtle guide is A. Momigliano, 'La caduta senza rumore di un impero nel 476 d.c.', *R.S.I.*, LXXXV (1973) pp. 5–21.

For the Ostrogoths, W. Ensslin, *Theoderich der Grosse* (Munich, 1947) is important; those who read Russian might try Z. V. Udal'tsova, *Italiya i Vizantiya v VI veke* (Moscow, 1959), which is, despite its title, more or less all on the Ostrogothic period. On the archaeology of the Ostrogothic settlement, see V. Bierbrauer, *Die ostgotischen Grab- und Schatzfunde in Italien* (Spoleto, 1975). For the economy of the Ostrogothic period (and the fourth-fifth centuries), see Ruggini (B5–*c*).

(b) Lombard and Byzantine Italy

For all post-Roman political history: on royal revenues, C. R. Brühl, *Fodrum, Gistum, Servitium Regis* (Cologne, 1968); P. Darmstädter, *Das Reichsgut in der Lombardei und Piemont 568–1250* (Strasbourg, 1896); F. Schneider, *Die Reichsverwaltung in Toscana (568–1268)*, 1 (Rome, 1914). For political biographies, the multi-volumed *Dizionario Biografico degli Italiani* (Rome, 1960–) has only reached C, but an amazingly high number of early medieval political figures have names beginning with A or B.

On the Lombards, the classic author is G. P. Bognetti, most of whose works on the Lombards are collected in *L'Età Longobarda*, 4 vols (Milan, 1966–8). This collection contains a wide variety of articles, serious and generalised; subtle and far-fetched; first, second and third thoughts on a number of topics; and so on. vol. II, 'S. Maria di Castelseprio e la storia religiosa dei Longobardi', is the fundamental text; then see, as a beginning: in vol. I, 'Longobardi e Romani' and 'Il gastaldato longobardo'; in vol. III, 'I ministri romani dei re longobardi', 'Processo logico e integrazioni delle fonti nella storiografia di Paolo Diacono', 'I *loca sanctorum*', and 'Tradizione longobardo e politica bizantina nelle origini del ducato di Spoleto'; in vol. IV, 'La proprietà della terra', 'L'editto di Rotari come espediente politico', and 'La continuità delle sedi episcopali'.

For the Lombards before 568: J. Werner, *Die Langobarden in Pannonien* (Munich, 1962). Lombard archaeology is discussed, region by region, in a series of handlists in *S.M.* from XIV (1973) onwards. For Lombard metalwork in Italy, see S. Fuchs, *Die langobardischen Goldblattkreuze* (Berlin, 1938); S. Fuchs and J. Werner, *Die langobardischen Fibeln aus Italien* (Berlin, 1950); for pottery, O. von Hessen, *Die langobardische Keramik aus Italien* (Wiesbaden, 1968). Some major archaeological sites: R. Mengarelli, 'La necropoli barbarica di Castel Trosino' *Monumenti Antichi*, XII (1902) cc. 145–380, and P. Pasqui and R. Paribeni, 'La necropoli barbarica di Nocera Umbra', *Monumenti antichi*, XXV (1918) cc. 136–352; G. Fingerlin, J. Garbsch, J. Werner, 'Gli scavi nel castello longobardo di Ibligo-Invillino', *Aquileia Nostra*, XXXIX (1968) cc. 57–135. For place names, E. Gamillscheg, *Romania Germanica*, II (Berlin, 1936) is a start.

Historical narrative is found in Bognetti's 'S. Maria' above; L. Schmidt, *Geschichte der deutschen Stämme: die Ostgermanen* (2nd edn, Munich, 1934), up to 590; G. Fasoli, *I Longobardi in Italia* (Bologna, 1965). For the Lombards and the papacy, see B6; but a large number of valuable articles for this and Lombard religious history in general are collected in O. Bertolini, *Scritti scelti*, 2 vols (Livorno, 1968). Lombard-Frankish relations are discussed in G. Tangl, 'Die Passvorschrift des Königs Ratchis', *Q.F.*, xxxviii (1958) pp. 1–66; K. Schmid, 'Zur Ablösung der Langobardenherrschaft durch die Franken', *Q.F.*, lii (1972) pp. 1–35. The duchy of Benevento up to 774 is discussed by F. Hirsch, *Il ducato di Benevento sino alla caduta del regno longobardo* (trans. of German original, Rome 1890).

Paul the Deacon has a large historiography, much of it rather bad; the best guides are Bognetti, 'Processo logico', above, and E. Sestan, 'La storiografia dell' Italia longobarda: Paolo diacono', *Sett.*, xvii (1969) pp. 357–86.

On the Lombard state, the best introduction is C. R. Brühl, 'Zentral- und Finanzverwaltung im Franken und im Langobardenreich', *Sett.*, xx (1972) pp. 61–94. See also Bognetti, *passim*; P. S. Leicht, 'Gli elementi romani nella costituzione longobarda', *A. S. Italiano*, lxxxi (1923) pp. 5–24; C. G. Mor, 'I gastaldi con potere ducale nell' ordinamento pubblico longobardo', *I Cong. Internat. di Studi Longobardi* (Spoleto, 1952) pp. 409–16; R. Schneider, *Königswahl und Königserhebung im Frühmittelalter* (Stuttgart, 1972). For local administration, see section (*c*) below. For prosopography, see J. Jarnut, *Prosopografische und sozialgeschichtliche Studien zum Langobardenreich in Italien* (Bonn, 1972).

Byzantine Italy: A. Guillou, *Régionalisme et indépendence dans l'empire byzantin au 7ᵉ siècle* (Rome, 1969) for Ravenna and A. Simonini, *Autocefalia ed esarcato in Italia* (Ravenna, 1969). For Agnellus, G. Fasoli, 'Rileggendo il *Liber Pontificalis* di Agnello Ravennate', *Sett.*, xvii (1969) pp. 457–95. For all Ravennate documentation and much else, J-O. Tjäder, *Die nichtliterarischen lateinischen Papyri Italiens*, i (Lund, 1955).

For Umbria, S. Mochi Onory, *Ricerche sui poteri civili dei vescovi nelle città umbre* (Rome, 1930); for Venice, R. Cessi, *Venezia Ducale* (Venice, 1940); for Rome, see B6–*b*.

(*c*) *Carolingian Italy* (See also (*f*))

Basic introductions are E. Hlawitschka, *Franken, Alemannen, Bayern und Burgunder in Oberitalien 774–962* (Freiburg, 1960); J. Fischer, *Königtum, Adel und Kirche im Königreich Italien 774–875* (Bonn, 1965); P. Delogu, 'Strutture politiche e ideologia nel regno di Ludovico II', *B.I.S.I.*, lxxx (1968) pp. 137–89.

For central government: see D. A. Bullough, 'Leo *qui apud Hlotharium magni loci habebatur* et le governement du *Regnum Italiae* a l'époque carolingienne', *Le Moyen Age*, lxvii (1961) pp. 221–45; H. Keller, 'Zur Struktur der Königsherrschaft im karolingischen und nachkarolingischen Italien', *Q.F.*, xlvii (1967) pp. 123–223; *idem*, 'Der Gerichtsort in oberitalienischen und toskanischen Städten', *Q.F.*, xlix (1969) pp. 1–71; O. Bertolini, 'I vescovi del *Regnum Langobardorum* al tempo dei Carolingi', *Vescovi e diocesi in Italia nel medioevo* (Padua, 1964) pp. 1–26; F. Manacorda, *Ricerche sugli inizii della dominazione dei Carolingi in Italia* (Rome, 1968), mostly on capitularies.

For local government, V. Fumagalli, 'Città e distretti minori nell' Italia Carolingia. Un esempio', *R.S.I.*, lxxxi (1969) pp. 107–17; *idem*, 'L'amministrazione periferica dello stato nell' Emilia occidentale in età Carolingia', *R.S.I.*, lxxxiii (1971) pp. 911–20; A. Castagnetti, 'Distretti fiscali autonomi o sottoscrizioni della contea cittadina? La Gardesana veronese in epoca Carolingia', *R.S.I.*, lxxxii (1970) pp. 736–43; P. Delogu, 'L'istituzione comitale nell' Italia Carolingia', *B.I.S.I.*, lxxix (1968) pp. 53–114. For the marches, A. Hofmeister, 'Markgrafen und Markgrafschaften im italischen Königreich', in *Mitteilungen des Instituts für österreichische Geschichtsforschung, Ergänzungsband*, vii (1906) pp. 215–435. For Tuscany, see section (*f*); for Spoleto, E. Taurino, 'L'organizzazione territoriale della contea di Fermo nei secoli 8–10', *S.M.*, xi (1970) pp. 659–710;

E. Saracco Previdi, 'Lo *sculdahis* nel territorio longobardo di Rieti', *S.M.*, xiv (1973) pp. 627–76.

For the Carolingian state and its inhabitants, see Tabacco (B4).

(d) Post-Carolingian Italy and the German Empire

See Mor (B1); Hlawitschka, Hofmeister, Keller (B3–c). The major text is S. Pivano, *Stato e chiesa da Berengario I ad Arduino 888–1015* (Turin, 1908); also G. Fasoli, *I re d'Italia 888–962* (Florence, 1949). For political history to 905, P. Delogu, 'Vescovi, conti, e sovrani nella crisi del regno italico', *Annali della scuola speciale per archivisti e bibliotecari dell'Università di Roma*, viii (1968) pp. 3–72. For the eleventh century, C. Violante, 'L'età della riforma della chiesa in Italia', *UTET Storia d'Italia*, i (Turin, 1959); and, for the movement towards urban independence, G. Fasoli, *Dalla 'civitas' al comune nell'Italia settentrionale* (Bologna, 1969), and W. W. Goetz, *Le origini dei comuni italiani* (trans. of German original, Milan 1965), the best guides to the complexities of the problem.

Pivano established the tradition of the episcopal takeover of cities in the tenth century, and this has had several good recent analyses, especially E. Dupré Theseider, 'Vescovi e città nell'Italia precomunale', *Vescovi e diocesi in Italia* (Padua, 1964) pp. 55–109; V. Fumagalli, 'Vescovi e conti nell' Emilia occidentale da Berengario I a Ottone I', *S.M.*, xiv (1973) pp. 137–204; G. Rossetti, 'Formazione e caratteri delle signorie di castello e dei poteri territoriali dei vescovi sulle città nella *Langobardia* del s.10', *Aevum*, xlviii (1974) pp. 1–67. C. Manaresi, 'Alle origini del potere dei vescovi sul territorio esterno delle città', *B.I.S.I.*, lviii (1944) pp. 221–328 advises caution.

A. Solmi, *L'amministrazione finanziaria del regno italico nell' alto medioevo* (Pavia 1932) and C. R. Brühl, 'Das Palatium von Pavia und die Honorantiae Civitatis Papiae', 4° *Cong. Int. di Studi sull'alto Medioevo* (Spoleto, 1969) pp. 189–220 discuss the decline of Pavia as a capital; G. Tabacco, 'La dissoluzione medievale dello stato nella recente storiografia', *S.M.*, i (1960) pp. 397–446 sets the break-up of Italy in an international context.

Most of the best analyses of this period are local histories, which are covered in section (*f*).

(e) Southern Italy

For Byzantium, the major narrative is still J. Gay, *L'Italie méridionale et l'empire byzantin* (Paris, 1904). For social and institutional analyses, V. von Falkenhausen, *Untersuchungen über die byzantinische Herrschaft in Süditalien* (Wiesbaden, 1967); A. Guillou, *Studies on Byzantine Italy* (London, 1970), a collection of articles, mostly in French; *idem*, 'Italie méridionale byzantine ou Byzantins en Italie méridionale?', *Byzantion*, xliv (1974) pp. 152–90. There is an Italian devotional translation of the Greek life of S. Nilus, G. Giovanelli, *Vita di S. Nilo* (Grottaferrata, 1966).

The independent Byzantine territories of the South all have historical surveys, of varying value. The best are the contributions of G. Cassandro and N. Cilento to the *Storia di Napoli*, ii (Naples, 1969), the starting-point for Neapolitan history. See also, for Gaeta, A. Leccese, *Le origini del ducato di Gaeta* (Gubbio, 1941), and for Amalfi, M. Berza, 'Amalfi preducale', *Ephemeris Dacoromana*, viii (1938) pp. 349–444. On Sardinia: E. Besta, *La Sardegna Medioevale* (2nd ed. Palermo, 1908–9). The only work on the Arabs in Bari is G. Musca, *L'emirato di Bari* (Bari, 1964). The major work on Arab Sicily is, however, genuinely classic: M. Amari, *Storia dei musulmani di Sicilia*, 3 vols. 2nd ed., (Catania, 1933–9).

On Lombard southern Italy, N. Cilento, *Italia meridionale longobarda* (2nd ed. Milan, 1971) is the best beginning, and his *Le origini della signoria capuana* (Rome, 1966), on ninth-century Capua, is also the best recent study of any part of the South. Benevento is analysed well in R. Poupardin, *Les institutions politiques et administratives des principautés lombardes* (Paris, 1907), and by barely anyone since, though see H. Belting, 'Studien zum beneventanischen Hof im 8 Jht', *Dumbarton Oaks Papers*, xvi (1962) pp. 141–93. Salerno is more fully studied; for narrative, M. Schipa, *Storia del principato longobardo di Salerno* (Naples, 1887); for socio-religious history, R. Ruggiero, *Principi, nobiltà e la chiesa nel Mezzogiorno longobardo* (Naples, 1973), a survey of a single Salerno monastery; for the city itself, P. Delogu, *Mito di una città meridionale* (Naples, 1977), a genuinely stimulating book. For North-South relations, see O. Bertolini, 'I papi e le relazioni politiche con i ducati longobardi di Spoleto e di Benevento', *Rivista di storia della chiesa in Italia*, VI (1952) pp. 1–46, VIII (1954) pp. 1–22, IX (1955) pp. 1–57 for the Lombard period; *idem*, 'Carlomagno e Benevento', in H. Beumann (ed.) *Karl der Grosse*, I (Düsseldorf, 1965) pp. 609–71; several articles in *3° Cong. Int. di Studi sull'alto Medioevo* (Spoleto, 1959); R. Ruggiero, 'Il ducato di Spoleto e i tentativi di penetrazione dei franchi nell' Italia meridionale', *A.S. per le province Napoletane*, LXXXIV–LXXXV (1966–7) pp. 77–116. The tenth century has received far less attention; see the *3° Congresso*, above, and Mor (B1). This is true for the internal history of the Lombard states, as well – there is no adequate discussion of Pandulf I, for example; for some beginnings of analysis of the break-up of Capua–Benevento, see F. Scandone, 'Il gastaldato d'aquino dalla metà del s.9 alla fine del s.10', *A.S. per le provincie Napoletane*, XXXIII (1908) pp. 720–35, XXXIV (1909) pp. 49–77; A de Francesco, 'Origini e sviluppo del feudalesimo nel Molise', *ibid.* XXXIV pp. 432–60, 640–71; XXXV (1910) pp. 70–98, 273–307.

(f) Local Studies

Much of the best recent Italian historiography comes into this category, above all for the period after 900, but, increasingly, for the ninth century too. Most of these works cover two or three centuries, and many aspects of social and economic as much as political and religious history.

Several collective urban histories contain important studies of our period: *Storia di Milano*, II (Milan, 1954) and *Storia di Brescia*, I (Brescia, 1963) include some of Bognetti's best work; *Verona ed il suo territorio*, I–II (Verona, 1964) and *Storia di Genova*, II (Genoa, 1941) have useful material.

For Piedmont, there has been much recent work, taking up the long-abandoned mantle of turn-of-the-century masters like Gabotto, much of it in the Torinese local periodical, *Bollettino storico-bibliografico subalpino* (*B.S.B.S.*) – several important articles on Asti in *B.S.B.S.*, LXXIII (1975), for example; a range of major articles on Piemontese settlement by A. A. Settia, since the early 1970s; R. Comba, 'La dinamica dell'insediamento umano nel Cuneese (sec. 10–13), *B.S.B.S.*, LXXII (1973) pp. 511–602. For Alemannic settlement in Asti: R. Bordone, 'Un'attiva minoranza etnica nell'alto medioevo', *Q.F.*, LIV (1974) pp. 1–57. For political history, see G. Sergi, 'Una grande circoscrizione del regno italico: la marca arduinica di Torino', *S.M.*, XII (1971) pp. 637–712.

For Lombardy, there is more evidence, and works tend to be longer. C. Violante, *La società milanese nell'età precomunale* (Bari, 1953) is one of the classics of the discipline; for a paradigmatic local study, on Cologno Monzese, G. Rossetti, *Società e istituzioni nel contado lombardo*, I (Milan, 1968). For Mantua: P. Torelli, *Un comune cittadino in territorio ad economia agraria*, (2 vols. Mantua, 1930–52).

Emilia is the focus for much work by V. Fumagalli, especially *Le origini di una grande dinastia feudale. Adalberto-Atto di Canossa* (Tübingen, 1971), and *Terra e società nell'Italia padana*, (2nd edn, Turin, 1976), which sums up the recent historiography.

For Tuscany, the best recent overall survey is the collection of articles in *5° Cong. Int. di Studi sull'alto Medioevo* (Spoleto, 1973), especially those by Keller, Schwarzmaier, Tabacco, Rossetti, Kurze, Belli Barsali. On the march, in addition, see articles in *Dizionario Biografico degli Italiani s.vv.* Adalberto, Bonifacio; and A. Falce's books, *La formazione della marca di Tuscia* (Florence, 1930), *Il marchese Ugo di Toscana* (Florence, 1923), and *Bonifacio di Canossa*, I (Reggio, 1927). For individual areas, see G. Volpe, *Toscana medievale* (Florence, 1964) for Luni and Volterra; H. M. Schwarzmaier, *Lucca und das Reich bis zum ende des elften Jhts* (Tübingen, 1972), with H. Jakobs's review (in Italian) in Q.F., LIV (1974) pp. 471–82; E. Conti, *La formazione della struttura agraria moderna nel· contado fiorentino*, I (Rome, 1965); P. Cammarosano, *La famiglia dei Berardenghi* (Spoleto, 1974); all of these are excellent.

For Spoleto and the fringes of Rome, see P. Toubert, *Les structures du Latium médiéval* (Rome, 1973), one of the most important and remarkable books on Italian history in recent years; cf. reviews by H. Hoffmann in Q.F., LVII (1977) pp. 1–45; V. Fumagalli in R.S.I., LXXXVIII (1976) pp. 90–103.

For the South, see above, (B3–e); for Rome itself, below, (B6–b).

4. SOCIAL HISTORY

See, once more, Tabacco (B1). All the analyses of regions and localities of Italy I have placed in the immediately preceding section, (B3–f); what follows are all more general discussions. Italian social history has traditionally been dominated by legal historians, and was for a long time the history of social institutions, rather than social structure. The turning points were Violante's book on Milan (B3–f) and G. Tabacco, *I liberi del re nell'Italia carolingia e post-carolingia* (Spoleto, 1966), on the public services of Carolingian freemen, which pointed the subject into new directions. The works that postdate 1953 in the previous section and 1966 in this section tend to have much more sociologically sophisticated terms of reference, though some of the more legalistic texts, especially those of P.S. Leicht and G. Salvioli, are still of the greatest value.

As an introduction, one can single out two works that have long ruled the subject, P. S. Leicht, *Studi sulla proprietà fondiaria nel medioevo*, 2 vols, (Padua, 1903–7), and F. Schneider, *Die Entstehung von Burg und Landgemeinde in Italien* (Berlin, 1924).

For the Lombard period, military organisation has dominated the historiography. Recent work includes O. Bertolini, 'Ordinamenti militari e strutture sociali dei Longobardi in Italia', *Sett.*, XV (1967) pp. 429–629; P. M. Conti, *Devotio e viri devoti in Italia da Diocleziano ai Carolingi* (Padua, 1971); and, breaking fresh ground, G. Tabacco, 'Dai possessori dell' età carolingia agli esercitali dell'età longobarda', *S.M.*, X.1 (1969) pp. 221–68; *idem*, 'La connessione tra potere e possesso nel regno franco e nel regno longobardo', *Sett.*, XX (1972) pp. 133–68, 207–28. See also A. I. Nieussychin, *Die Entstehung der abhängigen Bauernschaft* (trans. from Russian, Berlin, 1961).

For the Carolingians, see Tabacco, *Liberi del re*, above, and *idem*, 'Il regno italico, 9–11s.', *Sett.*, XV (1967) pp. 763–90. For Italian feudalism, P. S. Leicht, 'Il feudo in Italia nell'età carolingia', *Sett.*, I (1953) pp. 71–107; for the decline of the free in the Carolingian period see also V. Fumagalli, 'Le modificazioni politico-istituzionali in Italia sotto la dominazione carolingia', *Sett.*, XXVII (1979).

The socio-juridical aspects of *incastellamento* have a large historiography, stemming from P. Vaccari, *La territorialità come base dell' ordinamento giuridico del contado nell'Italia medioevale* (1921; 2nd ed. Milan, 1963). See, especially F. Cusin, 'Per la storia del castello medievale', *R.S.I.*, L (1938) pp. 492–541; G. Fasoli, 'Castelli e signorie rurali', *Sett.*, XIII (1965) pp. 531–67; G. P. Bognetti, 'Terrore e sicurezza sotto re nostrani e sotto re stranieri', in *Storia di Milano*, II (B3–f) pp. 808–41. See also (B3–f) for *castelli* as an element in local history, and (B5–c) for settlement changes.

For the social history of the city, see Fasoli and Goetz (B3–d), and two other articles by Fasoli, 'Che cosa sappiamo delle città italiane nell'alto medioevo?', *Vierteljahrsschrift für Sozial- und Wirtschaftsgeschichte*, XLVII (1960) pp. 289–305; (with R. Manselli and G. Tabacco) 'La struttura sociale delle città italiane del 5 al 12 secolo', *Vorträge und Forschungen*, XI (1966) pp. 291–320. For legal institutions, G. Mengozzi, *La città italiana nell'alto medio evo*, 2nd ed. (Florence, 1931).

For the family structure of the upper classes, *Famille et Parenté*,ed. G. Duby and J. Le Goff (Rome, 1977) is now the starting point, especially the article by Violante. For the *consortium* in this period, G. Salvioli, '*Consortes e colliberti*', *Atti e memorie di storia patria per le provincie modenesi e parmensi* III ser. 2 (1884) pp. 183–223. For family monasteries, see Cammarosano (B3–*f*) and Kurze in *5° Congresso* (B3–*f*), and Kurze's other articles on Tuscan monasteries, especially 'Der Adel und das Kloster S. Salvatore all'Isola', *Q.F.*, XLVII (1967) pp. 446–573.

On law, see the introductory surveys by P. S. Leicht, *Il diritto italiano preirneriano* (Bologna, 1933), and the multi-volumed *Storia del diritto italiano* (latest edns, Milan, 1941–50). F. Schupfer, *Il diritto privato dei popoli germanici con speciale riguardo all' Italia*, 4 vols, 2nd ed., (Rome, 1914) is still useful, though very wordy. After a gap, the minute analysis of the legal wording of the Lombard code has begun to be practised again: for an example, P. L. Falaschi, 'La successione volontaria nella legislazione longobarda', *Annali della facoltà giuridica: Università degli studi di Camerino*, XXXIV (1968) pp. 197–300. More fruitful is the analysis of the relation between law and society: for a beginning, see F. Sinatti d'Amico, 'L'applicazione dell '*edictum regnum langobardorum* in Tuscia', in *5° Congresso* (B3–*f*) pp. 745–81. For a mass of insights on a variety of problems, P. S. Leicht, *Scritti vari*, 3 vols (Milan, 1942–9).

5. ECONOMIC HISTORY

(a) General

P. J. Jones (B1) is the starting-point, with other articles in the same series, in *Einaudi storia d'Italia*, V and *Annali*, 1 (Turin, 1973, 1979). There is much recent material in several of the *Settimane di Studio*, especially VI (the city), VIII (money), XIII (agriculture), and XXI (urban topography). The best short survey has been translated into English, Luzzatto (A5–*a*).

There are some general economic surveys of individual periods, which link urban and rural material. P. S. Leicht, *Operai, artigiani e agricoltori in Italia, 6–16 ss.* (Milan, 1946) is one of the best. F. Carli, *Il mercato nell'alto medioevo* (Padua, 1934) is a classic of its kind, and the best introduction to the study of all types of exchange across our period. For the late Roman-Ostrogothic period, there are Hannestad and Ruggini, best listed under (B5–*c*), as they stress agriculture, for the Lombard period, there is Fasoli (B5–*c*) and E. Bernareggi, *Il sistema economico e la monetazione dei Longobardi nell'Italia superiore* (Milan, 1960).

(b) Urban Studies

For individual cities see (B3–*f*). For an essential topographical introduction, with reference to further material, see P-A. Février, 'Permanence et héritages de l'antiquité dans la topographie des villes de l'occident durant le haut moyen age', *Sett.*, XXI pp. 41–138. A model urban topography is I. Belli Barsali, 'La topografia di Lucca nei ss. 8–11', *5° Congresso* (B3–*f*) pp. 461–554. For the economic history of the cities of a particular region, Campania, see the important article by G. Galasso, 'Le città campane nell'alto medioevo' *A.S. per le provincie Napoletane*, LXXVII (1959) pp. 9–42, LXXVIII, 1 (1960) pp. 9–53 for more on Campania, see (B3–*e*). For Venice, the early sections of G. Luzzatto, *Storia economica di Venezia* (Venice, 1961). The economic history of single cities and regions, however, is still a little hard to write – the evidence is mostly absent in our period.

For the history of commerce in the strict sense, one can single out, alongside Carli, several of the articles in L. M. Hartmann, *Zur Wirtschaftsgeschichte Italiens im frühen Mittelalter. Analekten* (Gotha, 1904), especially that on the Po trade route; and A. Schaube, *Storia del commercio dei popoli latini del mediterraneo sino alla fine delle Crociate* (trans. from German, Turin, 1915). On industry, there is U. Monneret de Villard's fundamental article 'L' organizzazione industriale nell'Italia langobarda durante l'alto medioevo', *A. S. Lombardo* v ser. 46 (1919) pp. 1–83, with an addendum on *Magistri Commacini* in 47 (1920) pp. 1–14, a subject that has inspired much controversy – see the summary by

M. Salmi, 'Magistri Comacini o Commàcini', *Sett.*, xviii (1970) pp. 409–24. On money, there is a large and diffuse technical bibliography, again starting with Monneret de Villard – cf P. Grierson, *Bibliographie numismatique* (Brussels, 1966) pp. 76–78, 104–10; all Grierson's own work on Italy (in several languages) is now collected in *Dark Age Numismatics* (London, 1979).

(c) Rural Studies

It is notable that, while agrarian history of the communal and post-communal period in Italy has languished, a high percentage of the best economic analyses of our period are of agriculture and rural life.

In general, see the problematic posed in P. J. Jones, 'L'Italia agraria nell'alto medioevo', *Sett.*, xiii (1965) pp. 57–92. G. Salvioli, *Città e campagne prima e dopo il mille* (Palermo, 1901) is still surprisingly interesting. E. Sereni, *Storia del paesaggio agrario italiano* (Bari, 1961) is curiously literature and art-based for the then agricultural organiser of the Italian Communist Party. More recently, a series of articles by V. Fumagalli have general significance, though based mostly on empirical evidence from Emilia. On land clearance: 'Note per una storia agraria altomedioevale', *S. M.*, ix (1968) pp. 359–78, 'Storia agraria e luoghi comuni', *ibid.* pp. 949–65, 'Colonizzazione e insediamenti agricoli nell 'occidente altomedioevale: la Valle Padana', *Quaderni Storici*, xiv (1970) pp. 319–38, and several more detailed articles in the important agrarian journal, *Rivista di storia dell' agricoltura* *(R.S.A.)*, especially in vi (1966) and vii (1967); on leases: 'Coloni e signori nell'Italia superiore dall' 8 all 10 secolo', *S.M.*, x.1 (1969) pp. 423–46, 'I patti colonici dell'Italia centro-settentrionale nell'alto medioevo', *S.M.*, xii (1971) pp. 343–53, 'Precarietà dell' economia contadina e affermazione della grande azienda fondiaria nell'Italia settentrionale del 8° al 11° secolo', *R.S.A.*, xv (1975) pp. 3–27.

For the late Roman-Ostrogothic period: L. C. Ruggini, *Economia e società nell'Italia Annonaria: rapporti fra agricoltura e commercio dal 4 al 6 secolo d.c.* (Milan, 1961), a complex and fascinating book, not wholly convincing; it is well summarised in *idem*, 'Vicende rurali dell'Italia antica dall'età tetrarchica ai Longobardi', *R.S.I.*, lxxvi (1964) pp. 261–86. Alternatively, K. Hannestad, *L'evolution des ressources agricoles de l'Italie du 4ᵐᵉ au 6ᵐᵉ siècle de notre ère* (Copenhagen, 1962).

For the Lombards, Bernareggi (B5–*b*); G. Fasoli, 'Aspetti di vita economica e sociale nell'Italia del secolo 7°', *Sett.*, v (1957) pp. 103–59; P. Toubert, 'L'Italie rurale aux 8ᵉ–9ᵉ siècles. Essai de typologie domaniale', *Sett.*, xx (1972) pp. 95–132.

For the Carolingians, G. Luzzatto, *I servi nelle grandi proprietà ecclesiastiche dei secoli 9 e 10* (Pisa, 1910), reprinted in *Dai servi della gleba agli albori del capitalismo* (Bari, 1966), is classic. On leases, P. S. Leicht, *'Livellario nomine'* (1905), now in *Scritte Varie* ii.2 (Milan, 1949) pp. 89–146 is equally basic, to be put beside the Fumagalli articles, above, and the articles on Lucca, below. For Bobbio, there is material in Hartmann (B5–*b*).

For the post-Carolingian period, there is less general work, apart from the Fumagalli articles already cited; but see G. Luzzatto, 'Mutamenti nell'economia agraria italiana dalla caduta dei Carolingi al principio del s. 11' *Sett.*, ii (1954) pp. 601–22, G. Cherubini, 'Qualche considerazione sulle campagne dell'Italia centro-settentrionale', *R.S.I.*, lxxix (1967) pp. 111–57, and L. A. Kotel'nikova, 'I contadini italiani nei ss. 10–13', *R.S.A.*, xv (1975) pp. 29–80. Kotel'nikova has written a number of articles in Russian, some with Italian summaries, especially in *Sredniye Veka*, x (1957) pp. 81–100, xvii (1960) pp. 116–40; see also A. Lioublinskaia, 'Les travaux et les problèmes des médiévistes soviétiques', *S.M.*, iv (1963), especially pp. 733–44.

On individual regions: for the North, see Comba and Fumagalli in (B3–*f*); A. Castagnetti, 'Dominico e massaricio a Limonta nei secoli 9 e 10', *R.S.A.*, vii, 1 (1968) pp. 3–20.

For central Italy, see Conti and Toubert in B3–*f*; for Lucca, two important articles on leases are R. Endres, 'Das Kirchengut im Bistum Lucca von 8 bis 10 Jht', *Vierteljahrsschrift für Sozial- und Wirtschaftsgeschichte*, xiv (1917) pp. 240–92; B. Andreolli, 'Contratti agrari e patti colonici nella Lucchesia dei secoli 8 e 9', *S.M.*, xix (1978) pp. 69–158. For southern Italy, the starting-point is A. Lizier, *L'economia rurale dell'età prenormanna nell'Italia meridionale* (Palermo, 1907), a tour de force of compression, with barely a wasted word; see also M. Del Treppo, 'La vita economica e sociale in una grande abbazia del Mezzogiorno: S. Vincenzo al Volturno nell'alto medioevo', *A. S. per le province Napoletane*, lxxiv (1955) pp. 31–110; Guillou (B3–e); and a number of articles in Russian by M. L. Abramson, again usually with Italian summaries, in *Vizantiyskiy Vremennik*, vii (1953) pp. 161–93, and *Sredniye Veka*, xxviii (1965) pp. 18–37, xxxi (1968) pp. 155–79, xxxii (1969) pp. 77–96.

On peasant diets, see a number of recent articles in *Studi medievali*: G. Pasquali, 'Olivi e olio nella Lombardia prealpina', xiii (1972) pp. 257–65; A. I. Pini, 'La viticoltura italiana nel medioevo, xv (1974) pp. 795–884; M. Montanari, L'alimentazione contadina nell'alto medioevo', xvii (1976) pp. 115–72; *idem* 'Cereali e legumi nell'alto medioevo. Italia del nord, secoli 9–10', *R.S.I.*, lxxxvii (1975) pp. 439–92.

The effect of *incastellamento* on settlement has had a lot of important work in the last few years – see the already outdated summary by C. Klapisch-Zuber, 'Villaggi abbandonati ed emigrazioni interni' *Einaudi Storia d'Italia*, v (1973) pp. 311–64. See also the articles in *Quaderni Storici*, xxiv (1973); R. Francovich, *Geografia storica delle sedi umane: i castelli del contado fiorentino nei ss. 12 e 13* (Florence, 1973); Settia, Conti and Toubert (B3–*f*); T. Mannoni *et. al.*, 'Il castello di Molassana', *Archeologia Medievale*, i (1974) pp. 11–53; I. Ferrando Cabona, A. Gardini, T. Mannoni, 'Zignago I', *Archeologia Medievale*, v (1978) pp. 273–374. Medieval archaeology is a fast-growing discipline in Italy, and nearly everything gets into *Archeologia Medievale* in some form or other. For an important small-city excavation in the South, see *Caputaquis Medievale*, i, by P. Delogu *et al.* (Salerno, 1976), and volumes to follow, on Capaccio Vecchia.

6. THE CHURCH AND CULTURE

(a) General Religious History

The *Settimane di Studio* have a number of volumes of relevance here: iv (1956) on monasticism, vii (1959) on the Church before 800, xiv (1966) on conversion, and xxiii (1975) on symbolism.

Much of section B3 has reference to religious history, for the episcopate in particular, has always played an important political role in Italy. Bognetti and Bertolini (B3–*b*) gave particular weight to religious matters, and to the conversion and reconversion of the inhabitants of Italy, above all. The major surveys of the effect of the invasions on Italian Church institutions are contained in L. Duchesne, 'Les évêchés d'Italie et l'invasion lombarde', *Mélanges d'archéologie et d'histoire*, xxiii (1903) pp. 83–116, xxv (1905) pp. 365–99; F. Lanzoni, *I diocesi d'Italia al principio del s. 7* (Faenza, 1927). For a later period, the episcopate is discussed in the conference *Vescovi e diocesi in Italia nel medioevo, s. 9–13* (Padua, 1964). Parishes are discussed, most recently, in A. Castagnetti, *La pieve rurale nell'Italia padana* (Rome, 1976), with an extensive bibliographical guide; see also Toubert (B3–*f*).

(b) Rome and the Papacy

Basic political narratives are O. Bertolini, *Roma di fronte a Bisanzio e ai Longobardi* (Bologna, 1941), and P. Brezzi, *Roma e l'impero medioevale* (Bologna, 1947), in the same series, dividing at 774; E. Caspar, *Geschichte des Papsttums*, 2 vols, (Tübingen, 1930–3), with *idem*, *Das Papsttum unter fränkischer Herrschaft* (Darmstadt, 1956).

For Rome and the papacy early in the fifth century, see the massive study (in French) by C. Pietri, *Roma Christiana*, 2 vols., (Rome, 1976). For urban topography, especially for a later period, see F. Castagnoli *et al.*, *Topografia e Urbanistica di Roma* (Rome, 1958). For Roman administration, L. Halphen, *Etudes sur l'administration de Rome au Moyen-age 751–1252* (Paris, 1907). For the study of the Roman countryside, the topographical basis was long ago laid by G. Tomassetti, *La Campagna Romana, antica, medioevale e moderna*, 4 vols., (Rome, 1913); see also, yet again, Toubert (B3–*f*), which is now also the most up-to-date study of papal territorial politics after 900. The historiography for the Roman Church is immense, but these books, alongside those in the parallel English section, provide an introduction, and most of them have extensive bibliographies.

(c) Culture
Evidence here is more than usually diffuse. See, for a start, *Settimane di Studio*, above all XXII (1974) on culture in general, but also X (1962) on the Bible, XVII (1969) on historiography, and XIX (1971) on education. Education is also the subject of an important article by D. A. Bullough, 'Le scuole cattedrali e la cultura dell'Italia settentrionale prima dei comuni', in *Vescovi e Diocesi* (B6–*a*) pp. 111–43.
For literary culture, see also A. Petrucci, 'Scrittura e libro nell'Italia altomedievale', *S.M.*, x.2 (1969) pp. 157–213 for the sixth century, alongside A. Momigliano, 'Gli Anicii e la storiografia latina del 6s. d.c.' *Rendiconti dell'Accad.Naz. dei Lincei, classe di sc. morali, stor. e filol.*, VIII ser., 11 (1950) pp. 279–97, and, among many works on Boethius, P. Courcelle, *La consolation de philosophie dans la tradition littéraire* (Paris, 1967); Tjader (B3–*a*) gives many insights on this early period, too.
The best guide to the whole period up to 800 is P. Riché, *Education et culture dans l'occident barbare* (Paris, 1962). For Paul the Deacon, see B3–*b*. Tuscan culture is analysed in A. Petrucci, 'Scrittura e libro nella Tuscia altomedievale, ss. 8–9', *5° Congresso* (B3–*f*) pp. 627–43, with a good bibliography for eighth-century literature and writing in general. For Neapolitan culture, see Cilento in *Storia di Napoli* (B3–*e*); for Salerno, see Delogu (B3–*e*) and M. Oldoni, 'Interpretazione del *Chronicon Salernitanum*', *S.M.*, x.2 (1969) pp. 3–154.
Some major discussions of art and architecture are F. W. Deichmann, *Ravenna. Haupstadt des spätantiken Abendlandes* (Wiesbaden, 1969–   ); G. P. Bognetti *et al.*, *Santa Maria di Castelseprio* (Milan, 1948), from which Bognetti's great work on the religious history of the Lombards (cf. B3–*b*) also originated. For all problems of Italian art history 550–800, the best survey is H. Belting, 'Probleme der Kunstgeschichte Italiens im Frühmittelalter', *Frühmittelalterliche Studien*, 1 (1967) pp. 94–143, with full bibliography. The discovery of a ship, wrecked off the Sicilian coast, that contained the major architectural pieces for a prefabricated sixth-century Byzantine church, is discussed in G. Agnello, 'Il ritrovamento subacqueo di una basilica bizantina prefabbricata', *Byzantion*, XXXIII (1963) pp. 1–9.

ADDITIONAL NOTE

Tabacco (B1) is now available separately as a paperback, *Egemonie sociali e strutture del potere nel medioevo italiano* (Turin, 1979) with a new historiographical introduction. Montanari's articles (B5–*c*) have been expanded into a large book, *L'alimentazione contadina nell'alto medioevo* (Naples, 1979), which will for long remain the fundamental introduction to the subject. They both appeared too late to be used here. Many of Fumagalli's articles (B5–*c*) are also now collected, as *Coloni e signori nell' Italia settentrionale, ss. 6–11* (Bologna, 1978). Much is going on in Italian early medieval studies at the moment, and much has already been published in 1980; I close the list at about the beginning of the year.

References

INTRODUCTION

1. See bibliography (B6–c)
2. *Historia Langobardorum*, 2.14–24 (see chapter 2, note 1).
3. See bibliography (B3–f)

I. THE ROMAN LEGACY

1. Compare attitudes in Cassiodorus, *Variae* (*M.G.H. A.A.*, 12), 8.31, 33 (esp.8.33.4).
2. F. Braudel, *The Mediterranean and the Mediterranean World in the Age of Philip II* (Eng. trans. London, 1972) pp. 85ff.; P. Toubert (B3–f) pp. 269–73; F. Sabatini, *La regione degli altopiani maggiori d'Abruzzo* (Roccaraso, 1960).
3. Gregory the Great, *Epistolae*, 9.126 (*M.G.H. Epp*, 1–2).
4. Sidonius Apollinaris, *Epistolae*, 1.5.
5. *Variae*, 2.21, 32, 33.
6. Pliny the Younger, *Epistolae*, 5.6.1; Rutilius Namatianus, *De Reditu Suo*; eighth-century occupation of the Tuscan coast is seen in numerous charters in *Memorie e documenti per servire all'istoria di Lucca*, v. 2, ed. D. Barsocchini (Lucca, 1833).
7. L. C. Ruggini, *Economia e società (B5–c)*, Part II, *Passim*.
8. *Consularia Italica* in *M.G.H.A.A.*, 9. M. A. Wes's belief that the Roman senator Symmachus placed great weight on 476 (B3–a) has been countered by B. Croke, 'The chronicle of Marcellinus in its contemporary and historiographical context', Oxford D. Phil. thesis 1978, chapter 5.
9. Malchus, frag. 10 (*Fragmenta Historicorum Graecorum*, IV, ed. K. Muller, Paris 1851); cf. A. H. M. Jones, 'The constitutional position of Odoacer and Theoderic' (A3–a).
10. *Anonymus Valesianus* (*M.G.H. A.A.*, 9) 65–7; Cassiodorus, *Chronica* (*M.G.H. A.A.* 11) 1339.
11. *Variae*, 1.42–4.
12. Procopius, *History of the Wars* (Loeb, ed. H. B. Dewing) 5.1.
13. Petronius Maximus: Olympiodorus, frag. 44 (*Frag. Hist. Gr.*,IV). Faustus: *Variae* 1.35, 3.20, 27.
14. *Variae*, 4.51; A. Chastagnol (B3–a).
15. Ruggini, *op. cit.* is the basic study for northern Italy; pp. 330–5 for bishops. Ennodius, *Vita Epifani* (*M.G.H. A.A.* 7, pp. 84–109) for Epiphanius; *Variae*, 12.27 for Datius.
16. B. L. Twyman, 'Aetius and the aristocracy' (A3–a); but for some altercations in the details of the groups see F. M. Clover, 'The family and early career of Anicius Olybrius' (A3–a) pp. 182–92.
17. cf. E. Sestan (B1), pp. 202–3, A. H. M. Jones, *Later Roman Empire* (A3–a) p. 245. For all narrative to 565, *vd.* references in E. Stein (B3–a).
18. K. Hannestad, 'Les forces militaires d'après la Guerre Gothique de Procope', *Classica et Medievalia*, XXI (1960) pp. 136–83. The calculations are for the 530s, but the rough numbers are doubtless valid for the 490s.
19. *Anon. Vales.*, 60.
20. *Anon. Vales.*, 66, 69; Procopius, *Wars*, 6.6.
21. See, in general, J. Sundwall, *Abhandlungen* (B3–a) pp. 133–6; in particular, *Variae*

2.15, 16; Ennodius, *Epistolae* (*M.G.H. A.A.*, 7) 9.23. For Amalasuntha, Procopius, *Wars*, 5.3–4; for Samnium, *Variae*, 3.13.

22. In general, Sundwall, *op. cit.* pp. 106–7, 154–6; in particular, *Variae*, 1.3, 4; 9.24, 25 (and *passim*).

23. *Variae* 1.24, 38; *Anon. Vales.*, 61; Procopius, *Wars*, 5.2.

24. *ibid*, 7.40. For Cyprian and Opilio, cf. Sundwall, *op. cit.* pp. 110–1, 142–3; *Variae*, 8.16, 17, 21, 22; *Anon. Vales.* 85–6; Procopius, *Wars*, 5.4. For Cethegus, *Ibid,* 7.13.

25. ibid, 5.8–10; 6.7.

26. cf. V. Bierbrauer (B3–a).

27. Tax: Procopius, *Wars*, 7.1. Naples: *ibid*, 5.8–10. Rome: *ibid*, 5.20.

28. cf. Stein, *op. cit.*, II pp. 569–71 and *refs. cit*, following L. M. Hartmann, (B1), 1 pp. 305–6 and *refs. cit. Contra*: G. Tabacco, 'La storia politica e sociale' (B1) pp. 37–8, and Procopius, *Wars* 7.6, 13. Ranilo: J-O. Tjäder, *Die nichtliterarischen lateinischen Papyri Italiens*, 1 (Lund, 1955) n. 13.

29. Procopius, *Wars* 6.20; Pelagius in *M.G.H. Epp.*, 3 pp. 72–3.

30. L. Schiaparelli (ed.) *Codice diplomatico longobardo* (Rome, 1929–33, henceforth 'Schiaparelli') n. 228; cf. L. Schmidt, 'Die letzten Ostgoten', *Abhandlungen der Preussischen Akademie der Wissenschaft–, Philogische-historiche Klasse.* 1943, n. 10, pp. 3–15, though by no means all the people he lists are Goths.

31. In *Corpus iuris civilis*, III (ed. R. Schöll and W. Kroll, 6th ed. Berlin 1954), appx. 7 and 8; cf. T. S. Brown (A3–b).

2 THE KINGDOM OF ITALY, 568–875

1. Ed. in *M.G.H. S.R.L.* pp. 45–187; henceforth 'Paul, *H.L.*'.

2. Procopius, *Wars*, 7.34. cf. J. Werner, *Die Langobarden in Pannonien* (Munich, 1962), and *idem*, 'Die Herkunft der Bajuwaren . . .' in *Zur Geschichte der Bayern*, ed. K. Bosl (Darmstadt, 1965) pp. 21–43. For Lombard history to 590, *vd.* L. Schmidt (B3–b).

3. Procopius, *Wars*, 8.25, 33.

4. G. P. Bognetti, 'Santa Maria foris portas di Castelseprio e la storia religiosa dei Longobardi', (henceforth '*S.M.C.*') in *Età Longobarda* (henceforth *E.L.*; Milan, 1966–8), II, pp. 71ff; *idem*, 'Tradizione Longobarda e politica bizantina nelle origini del ducato di Spoleto', *E.L.*, III pp. 441–75; *idem*, 'La rivalità tra Austrasia e Burgundia . . . .', *E.L.*, IV pp. 559–82.

5. Paul, *H.L.*, 2.32.

6. Paul, *H.L.*, 3.5–7, 19; Menander, *Historia*, 25, 29 (ed. B. G. Niebuhr, *Corpus Scriptorum Historiae Byzantinae*, 1, Bonn 1829, pp. 327–8, 331–2).

7. Paul, *H.L.*, 3.16; P. Darmstädter (B3–b) p. 5.

8. Authari: Gregory the Great, *Epistolae* (*M.G.H. Epp.*, I–II) 1.17. Franks: Paul, *H.L.*, 3.17; Fredegar, *Chronicon*, IV 43, 68 (*M.G.H. Scriptores Rerum Merovingicarum* = '*S.R.M.*', III).

9. Dukes: Paul *H.L.*, 4.3, 8, 13, 18, 27; Gregory the Great, *Epp.* 2.33, 45; 13.36.

10. Paul *H.L.*, 3.16; 4.30; O. von Hessen, *Secondo contributo all'archeologia Longobarda in Toscana* (Florence, 1975) pp. 90–7; *E.L.*, III p. 525.

11. *S.M.C.*, *passim*, for this and Lombard history in general to 700.

12. Gregory, *Dialogi* (ed. U. Moricca, Rome 1924) 3.28; Jonas, *Vitae Columbani* (ed. B. Krusch, *M.G.H. S.R.M.*, IV 2.25; *Vita Barbati* (in *M.G.H. S.R.L.*) p. 567.

13. *Epp.*, 7.23.

14. Cf. O. Bertolini 'I vescovi del *regnum langobardorum* al tempo dei Carolingi' (B3–c).

15. *M.G.H. Epp.*, III p. 694.

16. Paul *H.L.*, 5.7, 18.

17. Ed. F. Bluhme in *M.G.H. Leges*, IV or F. Beyerle, *Leges Langobardorum* (Witzenhausen, 1962). Laws henceforth referred to under kings' names.

18. M. Gluckman, *Custom and Conflict in Africa* (Oxford, 1959) pp. 28ff, 43–7.
19. Cf. R. Schneider (B3–*b*) pp. 5–63, 240–58.
20. D. A. Bullough, 'Urban change in Early Mediaeval Italy: the example of Pavia' (A5–*b*); E. Ewig, 'Residence et Capitale pendant le haut moyen age', *Revue Historique*, ccxxx (1963) pp. 36–47; C-R. Brühl, *Fodrum, Gistum, Servitium regis* (henceforth '*F.G.S.*'; Cologne, 1968) pp. 368–75.
21. Schiaparelli 19, 20; C-R. Brühl (ed.) *Cod. Dip. Long.*, III (henceforth Brühl; Rome, 1973) nn. 12, 13. Officials: *F.G.S.* pp. 377–80.
22. Schiaparelli 137, 163, 255.
23. Mints: Rothari 242 (only Benevento minted independent coins). Price-fixing: *Memoratorium de Mercedibus Commacinorum, M.G.H. Leges*, IV pp. 176–80. City walls: V. Fainelli (ed.), *Codice Diplomatico Veronese*, I (Venice, 1940) n. 147.
24. Brühl 19, 27, 43, 44.
25. *M.G.H. Dipl. Kar.*, I n. 174; cf. P. S. Leicht, *Studi sulla proprietà fondiaria nel medioevo*, II (Padova, 1907) pp. 47–54 for all the material, though not the conclusions.
26. V. Fumagalli, 'L'amministrazione periferica dello stato nell'Emilia occidentale in età carolingia' (B3–*c*).
27. All documents conveniently together in U. Pasqui, *Documenti per la storia della città di Arezzo nel medioevo*, I (Florence, 1890).
28. Rothari 23–4.
29. Siena: Brühl 13; Brescia: Brühl 31, 33. cf. *F.G.S.* pp. 365–6.
30. Liutprand 44; Schiaparelli 19, 86, 184; E. Saracco Previdi, 'Lo *sculdahis* nel territorio longobardo di Rieti' (B3–*c*).
31. For eighth-century history, *vd.* L. M. Hartmann, (B1) II; O. Bertolini (B6–*b*).
32. Liutprand 1–6 and *Notitia de actoribus regis* 5; Schiaparelli 16, 18 (the only earlier gift is 14 of 710).
33. *M.G.H. Epp.*, III p. 694; Paul *H.L.* 5.37.
34. Liutprand 118.
35. D. A. Bullough, 'The writing-office of the dukes of Spoleto in the eighth century' (A3–*b*).
36. Rothari, prologue; Liutprand 59; Ratchis 1, 10, 11, 14.
37. Paul *H.L.* 6.51.
38. Ratchis 9, 12, 13; also Aistulf 4, 5. Cf. G. Tangl, 'Die Passvorschrift des Königs Ratchis' (B3–*b*).
39. For Aistulf, *vd.* biography *s.v.* 'Astolfo' in *Dizionario biografico degli Italiani*, IV (Rome, 1962) pp. 467–83.
40. Aistulf 7; Pasqui, n. 11; *Liber Pontificalis*, I (ed. L. Duchesne, Rome 1886) pp. 441–54; wills: Schiaparelli 114, 117.
41. Brühl 44, *Liber Pont.*, I pp. 495–6.
42. Rebels in *M.G.H. Dipl. Kar.*, I nn. 112, 187, 214; 776 capitulary in *M.G.H. Capitularia*, I n. 88; cf. E. Hlawitschka (B3–*c*) pp. 23ff, J. Fischer (B3–*c*) pp. 7–17. Hlawitschka and Fischer provide the best political analyses for the Carolingian period.
43. *M.G.H. Dipl. Kar.*, I nn. 81, 94; for Lombard parallels, cf. K. Schmid, 'Zur Ablösung der Langobardenherrschaft' (B3–*b*) pp. 6–29.
44. For details, O. Bertolini, 'Carlomagno e Benevento' (B3–*e*).
45. *Annales regni Francorum* in *M.G.H. Script. rer. Germanicarum, s.a.* 796, 801; cf. D. A. Bullough, '*Baiuli* in the Carolingian *regnum Langobardorum*' (A3–*c*).
46. Cf. T. F. X. Noble, 'The Revolt of King Bernard of Italy' (A3–*c*); H. Houben, 'Visio cuiusdam pauperculae mulieris', *Zeitschrift für die Geschichte des Oberrheins*, cxxiv (1976) pp. 31–42.
47. *F.G.S.* pp. 401–2.
48. Andreas, *Historia* (ed. in *M.G.H. S.R.L.* pp. 221–30) cc. 3–7.
49. *F.G.S.* pp. 421–51; *M.G.H. Dipl. Kar.*, I nn. 132, 134, and III n. 91 for examples of

rents and tolls; *Honorantiae Civitatis Papiae* in *M.G.H.S.S.* 30.2. pp. 1450–9 for a long tenth–eleventh-century list (*vd.* above, p. 89).

50. Darmstädter, *op. cit.* pp. 16–24. *M.G.H. Dipl. Kar.*, III n. 40 for a secularisation by Lothar.

51. *M.G.H. Capitularia*, II, 201–2.

52. V. Fumagalli, 'Un territorio piacentino nel secolo nono' *Q.F.*, XLVIII (1968) pp. 25–31 for the career of a local official; *idem, art. cit.* n. 26, and A. Castagnetti, 'Distretti fiscali autonomi . . .' (B3–c) for rural administrative units.

53. C. Manaresi, *I placiti del 'regnum Italiae'*, 1 (henceforth 'Manaresi'; Rome, 1955) n. 25; Paschasius Radbertus, *Epitaphium Arsenii*, 1.26 (ed. E. Dümmler, *Phil. und hist. Abh. der, Königl. Akad. der Wiss. zu Berlin*, II (1900).

54. D. A. Bullough, 'Leo *qui apud Hlotharium magni loci habebatur* et le governement du *Regnum Italiae* a l'époque carolingienne' (B3–c).

55. Schmid, 'Ablösung . . .', pp. 33–5.

56. Cf., apart from Fischer, Bertolini *art. cit.* n. 14, and G. Tabacco, 'La storia politica e sociale' (B1) pp. 88ff.

57. E.g. *Capitularia*, II 213 c. 4, 221 c. 13. For judicial powers of bishops, cf. H. Keller, 'Der Gerichtsort in oberitalienischen . . . Städten' (B3–c) pp. 5–40.

58. G. Porro-Lambertenghi, *Codex diplomaticus Langobardiae* (henceforth 'Porro', Turin 1873) n. 270. The surviving diplomas of Louis to Angilberga are for the same region: cf. below, n. 65. For the Supponids, Hlawitschka, *op. cit.* pp. 299–309; for Brescia, G. P. Bognetti in *Treccani Storia di Brescia*, 1 (Brescia, 1963) pp. 449–83.

59. For the marches in general, A. Hofmeister, 'Markgrafen und Markgrafschaften im italischen Königreich' (B3–c).

60. *Annales regum Francorum. s.a.* 828; H. Keller, 'La formazione della marca di Tuscia' in *Atti del 5° Congresso internazionale* (B3–f) pp. 117–33 and refs, and H. M. Schwarzmaier (B3–f), for the march of Tuscany in general.

61. For Louis, P. Delogu, 'Strutture politiche e ideologia nel regno di Lodovico II' (B3–c); H. Keller, 'Zur Struktur der Königsherrschaft' (B3–c) pp. 152–5.

62. *Capitularia*, II, 213; cf. also 209–12, 228.

63. Manaresi, 57, 65.

64. Fischer, *op. cit.* pp. 68–76.

65. Suppo: J. F. Böhmer and E. Mühlbacher, *Regesta Imperii*, 1 (2nd ed. Innsbruck, 1908) n. 1243; Angilberga, Brescia, Casauria: nn. 1183–1272 *passim*.

66. *Capitularia*, II, 218.

67. Andreas, *Historia* cc. 17–8.

68. *Annales Bertiniani s.a.* 872 (ed. G. Waitz, *M.G.H. Scriptores rerum Germanicarum*).

3. ROMANS, LOMBARDS, FRANKS AND BYZANTINES

1. Paul, *H.L.*, 2.4, 26; 3.23–4; Marius of Avenches, *Chronicon* (*M.G.H. A.A.*, 11) *s.a.* 569–71, 580; cf. Ruggini, *op. cit.* pp. 466–89, for a complete list of economic calamities to 700.

2. Paul, *H.L.*, 2.31–2; 3.16. For a typically deft pessimistic commentary, see Bognetti *S.M.C.*, pp. 110–41; as a counter, G. Fasoli, 'Aspetti di vita economica e sociale nell' Italia del secolo 7' (B5–c) pp. 109–16.

3. Gregory, *Epp.*, 2.33; 5.38; 9.205; 10.5.

4. So F. Schneider (B3–b) pp. 155–64, 177ff. (with surviving Romans); *S.M.C.* pp. 141–9 (without).

5. In Grancia (prov. Grosseto, Tuscany), out of eighty burials (about ten with 'Lombard' metalwork), only one weapon was found; if these were Lombards at all, they were at least not a warrior group. Cf. O. Von Hessen, *Primo contributo alla archeologia*

longobarda in Toscana (Florence, 1971) pp. 53–80. Pottery: I. Baldassare, 'Le ceramiche delle necropoli longobarde di Nocera Umbra e Castel Trosino', *Altomedioevo*, I (1967) pp. 141–85.
    6. G. Fingerlin *et al.*, 'Gli scavi nel castello longobardo di Ibligo–Invillino' (B3–*b*). Cemeteries in cities: *S.M.*, xiv (1973) pp. 1136–41; xv (1974) pp. 1118f., 1125.
    7. Paul, *H.L.*, 4.22; B. Migliorini, *Storia della lingua italiana* (Florence, 1958) pp. 79–80.
    8. Fortonato: Schiaparelli 16. Mixed names: Schiaparelli 287, *Chronicon Salernitanum*, c. 25 (ed. U. Westerbergh, Stockholm 1956). Slaves: cf., for example, Schiaparelli 154. G. Tabacco, 'Dai possessori dell'età carolingia agli esercitali dell'età longobarda' (B4) pp. 228–34.
    9. *Storia del diritto italiano. Il diritto privato*, iii, ed. P. S. Leicht, (Milan, 1948) pp. 193–4; cf. Rothari 175.
    10. Bognetti, *S.M.C.*, chap. 1.8; 'La proprietà della terra . . .', *E.L.* iv pp. 76ff. But *vd.* E. Levy (A4) pp. 87–99, 187ff. Exceptions: e.g. Schiaparelli 49 (730).
    11. Paul, *H.L.*, 2.32; 3.17; 5.38–9.
    12. *Romani*: Schiaparelli 206. Senator: Schiaparelli 18.
    13. Tabacco, 'La storia politica e sociale' *cit.* p. 62; cf. 'Dai possessori . . .' *cit.*
    14. Aistulf 2, 3.
    15. *M.G.H. Leges*, iv p. 595; cf. R. Bordone, 'Un'attiva minoranza etnica nell' alto medioevo (B3–*f*). Hlawitschka (B3–*c*) is fundamental for the Frankish settlement.
    16. Cf. brief summary in G. Rossetti, 'Società e istituzioni nei secoli 9 and 10: Pisa, Volterra, Populonia', *5° Congresso cit.* pp. 296ff.
    17. For the Exarchate: A. Guillou (B3–*b*), and esp. T. S. Brown, 'The Church of Ravenna and the imperial administration in the 7th century', and his forthcoming book (A3–*b*).
    18. Agnellus, c. 111.
    19. Gregory, *Epp.*, 2.12, 18; 3.1, 2, 60; 9.47, 76.
    20. G. Marini, *I papiri diplomatici* (Rome, 1805) n. 122.
    21. L. M. Hartmann (B5–*b*) pp. 123–4 for Comacchio; Manaresi 17 for Trieste; Schiaparelli 50 for Siena.
    22. Agnellus, c. 152.
    23. John the Deacon, *Gesta episcoporum neapolitanorum*, c. 42 (*S.R.L.* p. 425).
    24. Manaresi 17; summary and commentary in Guillou (B3–*b*) pp. 294–307.

4. CITIES AND THE COUNTRYSIDE

    1. Luni: B. Ward-Perkins, 'Luni', (A5–*b*); see G. Schmiedt, 'Città scomparse e città di nuova formazione in Italia', *Sett.*, xxi (1973) pp. 503–617, for much comparative data.
    2. *Versum de Mediolano civitate* in *M.G.H. Poetae*, I pp. 22–6; for Lucca, Barsocchini 965–6 (890). Cf. P-A. Février, 'Permanence et héritages de l'antiquité dans la topographie des villes' (B5–*b*).
    3. Porro 287 (879); *M.G.H. Dipl. Ottonis In.* 145 (952); C. Violante (B3–*f*) pp. 109–15 for prices.
    4. *Variae*, 7.5; *M.G.H. Capitularia*, ii 213 c. 7.
    5. D. A. Bullough, 'Urban change in Early Mediaeval Italy' (A5–*b*) pp. 99ff., 119–29; Barsocchini 1759 (818); Justinian, *Novella 67 (Corpus Iuris Civilis*, iii); cf. M. Mauss, *The Gift* (London, 1951), pp. 31–45; T. Veblen, *The Theory of the Leisure Class* (London, 1924) chapter 4.
    6. *Vd.* H. H. Schwarzmaier (B3–*f*) pp. 14–70, I. Belli Barsali, 'La topografia di Lucca nei ss. 8–11' (B5–*b*). Louis III: Liutprand of Cremona, *Antapodosis* (*M.G.H. S.S. rer. Germ.*, new ed. J. Becker) 2.39.

7. Schiaparelli 69 (739); Barsocchini 216, 221, 322 for Natalis. Ravenna: Agnellus cc. 126–9.

8. Schiaparelli 293; see also above, pp. 132–4.

9. *Variae*, 8.31; Ruggini, *Italia annonaria* pp. 301–11, 350–9.

10. John the Deacon, *Vita Gregorii*, 2.24–30 (Migne, *PL* 75); *Liber Pont.*, 1 p. 502; cf. *Papers of the British School at Rome*, XLVI (1978) pp. 173–7.

11. Rothari 367, Grimoald/Liutprand *Memoratorium de mercedibus magistri commacinorum*, Ratchis 13, Aistulf 4–6; *M.G.H. Capitularia*, 1 28 c. 4, 88, II 217 c. 10; cf. G. Duby (A5–a) pp. 48–70; K. Polanyi, C. M. Arensberg, H. W. Pearson. *Trade and Market in the Early Empires* (Glencoe, Ill., 1957) pp. 243–70.

12. Aistulf 3; L. M. Hartmann, (B5–b) pp. 123–4; *M.G.H. Dipl. Karol*, 1 n. 132; *Capitularia*, II 233–41.

13. *Honorantiae, M.G.H. S.S.* 30.2 pp. 1450–9; for crafts, U. Monneret de Villard, 'L'organizzazione industriale nell' Italia langobarda' (B5–b) is still basic; for markets, F. Carli (B5–a).

14. The text is lost; cf. F. Schneider (B3–b) p. 268n., and *idem*, 'Bistum und Geldwirtschaft', *Q.F.*, VIII (1905) pp. 81–2.

15. Manaresi 56.

16. *Honorantiae* c. 5; *Codice diplomatico Padovano*, ed. A. Gloria, (Venice, 1877) n. 7 (829); cf. G. Luzzatto (B5–b) pp. 4–16.

17. Violante (B3–f) pp. 115–34; G. Rossetti, *Società e istituzioni nel contado Lombardo* (B3–f) pp. 172–82; Porro 211 for Brescia.

18. General guides in the works of P. J. Jones in bibliography sections A5–a, B5–c; most recently, 'La storia economica' (B1) pp. 1555–1681.

19. Schiaparelli 194; cf. 218, 293; Barsocchini 231, 273; *Mem. de Merc. Com.* 5; *Liber Pont.*, 1 pp. 501–2; Caesar, *Gallic War* 7.17.

20. M. Montanari, 'Cereali e legumi nell'alto medioevo' (B5–c); V. Fumagalli, 'Rapporto tra grano seminato e grano raccolto nel polittico del monastero di S. Tommaso di Reggio', *R.S.A.*, VI (1966) pp. 360–2.

21. Rothari 284–358.

22. Forests: Brühl 41 (cf. also Brühl 24). Polyptychs: *Inventari altomedievali di terre, coloni e redditi*, ed. A. Castagnetti *et al* (Rome, 1979) Cf. M. Montanari, 'L'alimentazione contadina nell'alto medioevo' (B5–c) for figures. Archaeology will soon help to solve this problem; cf, for example, G. W. W. Barker, 'Dry Bones', *Papers in Italian Archaeology*, I (A5–c) pp. 35–49.

23. *Vd.* the works of V. Fumagalli in bibliography section B5–c; P. Toubert (B3–f) pp. 339–48 and *refs. cit.*

24. C. Klapisch-Zuber, 'Villaggi abbandonati . . .' (B5–c) pp. 317–26; *Archeologia Medievale*, V (1978) pp. 495–503; *Pap. Brit. Sch. Rome* XLVII (1979). Caesarius of Arles, *Sermones*, I, 67, ed. G. Morin, (*Corp. Christ. Ser. Lat.* CIII, 1953).

25. Tjäder, *Papyri Italiens* n. 3; Gregory, *Epp.* 1.39a, 42; 2.38. J. C. Percival, 'Seigneurial aspects of Late Roman estate management', *English Historial Review*, LXXXIV (1969) pp. 449–73 is a suggestive analysis of all the early material.

26. Liutprand 92; cf. Rothari 41–137 for the threefold social division.

27. Schiaparelli 137, 155, 226.

28. Schiaparelli 52, 54, 59, 60, 64, 79, 109, 129, 159, 291.

29. Porro 66, 105, 114, 117, 118, 120, 127, 128, 133, 135, 137, 172, 191, 197, 199.

30. Travo: *Inventari*, pp. 136, 157–8; *Codice diplomatico di S. Columbano di Bobbio* I, ed. C. Cipolla (Rome, 1918) n. 36. Teuprand: Schiaparelli 178.

31. *Vd.* Hartmann (B5–b) pp. 42–73; G. Luzzatto, *I servi delle grandi proprietà ecclesiastiche* (B5–c) esp. pp. 47ff., 70–4.

32. *M.G.H. Capitularia*, 1 93c. 5 (813); P. S. Leicht, 'Livellario nomine' (B5–c).

33. *Inventari*, p. 63 Porzano; Schiaparelli 192; W. Kurze, *Codex diplomaticus*

Amiatinus (Tübingen, 1974) and review by B. Andreolli, *R.S.A.* xvII (1977) pp. 139–40.
34. Schiaparelli 206, Manaresi 8, Liutprand 6.
35. Rothari 279–80.
36. Manaresi 110, 112 (Cusago), 49 (Trento), 89 (Oulx), 9, 34; cf. also data in B. Andreolli, 'Contratti agrari e patti colonici nella Lucchesia' (B5–*c*) pp. 125–7. For Limonta, see n. 38.
37. In Manaresi, but more completely in *Chronicon Vulturnense*, ed. V. Federici, (Rome, 1925–38) nn. 23, 24, 25, 26, 55, 71, 72.
38. Limonta: Porro 314, 417, 427 (Manaresi 117, 122), 625; cf. A. Castagnetti, 'Dominico e massaricio a Limonta' (B5–*c*); for European context, R. H. Hilton, *Bondmen Made Free* (London, 1973) pp. 66ff. Otto: *M.G.H. Constitutiones*, I n. 21.
39. Violante (B3–*f*) pp. 76ff., 91ff.; Andreolli, *art. cit.*; G. Rossetti, 'Società e instituzioni: Pisa, Volterra, Populonia', *5° Congresso cit.* pp. 259–72; P. J. Jones, 'An Italian Estate' (A5–*c*); G. Cherubini, 'Qualche considerazione . . .' (B5–*c*) pp. 55–63.
40. Prices: Andreolli, *art. cit.* p. 118, *M.G.H. Capitularia*, I 28 c. 4. Cf. K. Polanyi, *Primitive, archaic and modern economics* (New York, 1968) pp. 175–203; M. Godelier, *Rationality and irrationality in economics* (London, 1972) pp. 252–303; W. A. Christian, *Person and God in a Spanish Valley* (London, 1972) pp. 168–71; P. Grierson, 'Problemi monetari dell'alto medioevo', *Boll. della società pavese di stor. pat.* LIV (1954) pp. 67–82.
41. *M.G.H. Capitularia*, I 88; Porro 88.
42. Cf. C. Violante, *Studi sulla cristianità medioevale* (Milan, 1975) pp. 328–39; L. A. Kotel'nikova, *Mondo contadino e città in Italia* (Bologna, 1975) pp. 19ff.

5. SOLIDARITY, HIERARCHY AND LAW

1. Marius of Avenches, *Chronicon* (*M.G.H. A.A.* 11) *s.a.* 569; Paul, *H.L.* 2.9; Rothari 153, 177. Against *S.M.C.* pp. 39–40n., see H. H. Meinhard, 'The patrilineal principle in early Teutonic Kingship', *Studies in Social Anthropology* ed. J. Beattie, R. G. Lienhardt, (Oxford 1975) pp. 23–6.
2. M. Gluckman, *op. cit.* Chapter 1; J. M. Wallace-Hadrill, *The Long-Haired Kings* (London, 1962) pp. 121–47; cf. M. Hasluck, *The Unwritten Law in Albania* (Cambridge, 1954) for examples, and E. Gellner, *Saints of the Atlas* (London, 1969) pp. 104–25, for oath-helping.
3. Liutprand 13, 22, 61, 119.
4. *Summa Perusina* 6.35.10 (ed. F. Patetta, Rome, 1900); cf. P. S. Leicht, 'Vindictam facere', *Scritte Varie*, II.2 (Milan, 1949) pp. 363–6.
5. Liutprand, *Antap.* 2.48, 55–6; 3.7–8, 44–5; 5.32.
6. Paul, *H.L.* 4.37.
7. Rothari 167, Liutprand 70; Schiaparelli 161 (cf. 154), 249; cf. J. Davis, *Land and Family in Pisticci* (London, 1973) pp. 107–45.
8. Pasqui, *Arezzo cit.* 292–3, 240.
9. G. Salvioli, 'Consortes e colliberti' (B4); Manaresi 36.
10. Schiaparelli 163.
11. Schiaparelli 81.
12. Manaresi 76 (cf. 82, 84), 124.
13. Rothari 359, 227, Ratchis 8.
14. Liutprand 91, *M.G.H. Capitularia*, II 219 c. 5. For implications, cf., for example, L. Nader, *Law and Culture in Society* (Chicago 1969) pp. 69–91. For parallels, cf. C. P. Wormald, 'Lex Scripta and Verbum Regis' (A4).
15. From Barsocchini. The samples are in each case of over 300 witnesses from some 60 charters.
16. Everard will: P. Riché, 'Les bibliothèques de trois aristocrates laics carolingiens',

Le Moyen Age, LXIX (1963) pp. 96–101. Cf. D. A. Bullough, 'Le scuole cattedrali e la cultura dell'Italia settentrionale' (B6–*c*).

17. F. Brunetti, *Codice diplomatico toscano;* II (Florence, 1833) n. I, wrongly dated 774;F. Sinatti d'Amico, 'L'applicazione dell' Edictum . . . in Tuscia', *5° Congresso cit.* pp. 745–81.

18. *M.G.H. Capitularia*, II 213 c. 3.

19. Manaresi 64, Porro 208.

20. Compromise: Manaresi 97; compurgation: Manaresi 44. Cf. comments by J. Van Velsen in M. Gluckman (ed.) *Ideas and Procedures in African Customary Law* (Oxford, 1969) pp. 137–49;

21. *M.G.H. Constitutiones*, I n. 13 and commentary in *Liber Papiensis*, *M.G.H. Leges*, IV pp. 568–80. Cf. A. Visconti, 'La legislazione di Ottone I', *A. S. Lombardo*, LIII (1925) pp. 40–73, 221–51.

22. M. Bloch, *Feudal Society* (London, 1962) pp. 141–2, 233–5, 443; Rothari 177; J. Boissevain, 'Patronage in Sicily', *Man* New Ser. I (1966) pp. 18–33.

23. *M.G.H. Poetae*, I p. 48; cf. D. A. Bullough, '*Europae Pater*', *Eng. Hist. Rev.* LXXXV (1970) p. 76.

24. Rothari, Prologue and 48, 74; *Lex Baiwariorum* 3.1 (*M.G.H. Leges*, v.2); Aistulf 2.

25. Schiaparelli 293 for Taido (and perhaps Porro 80 for kinsmen); Schiaparelli 137, 155, 226 for Gisulf; Liutprand 59 and *Notitia* 5, Ratchis 10. Cf. the works of G. Tabacco in the bibliography, section B4, esp. 'La connessione fra potere e possesso . . .', pp. 146–64, 207–28.

26. Rothari 167; Brühl 31; Schiaparelli 28 for an apparent non-official.

27. Gregorius: *Dip. Kar.*, I 183. Gaidoald: Schiaparelli 203, Brühl 26 (p. 156).

28. Paul, *H.L.*, 5.1.

29. Liutprand, *Notitia* 5.

30. Ratchis 10, 11, Rothari 225. Revocable and nonheritable: Rothari 177, Schiaparelli 124.

31. Manaresi 66.

32. Liutprand 83, *M.G.H. Capitularia*, I 162 c. 3, II 218 c. 1. But in Kurze 67 (809) tenants served in the army (under their landlord).

33. *M.G.H. Capitularia*, I 93 c. 5; for private jurisdiction, see e.g. *Regesto della chiesa di Pisa*, I (ed. N. Caturegli, Rome 1938) nn. 23, 15, 16.

34. *Capitularia*, I 158 c. 8 (cf. 165 c. 2), II 224 c. 4, 225 c. 3.

35. Cf. G. Tabacco, 'Il regno italico' (B4) pp. 771–7.

36. Kurze 75. For Italian military feudalism, *vd.* P. S. Leicht, 'Il feudo in Italia nell'età carolingia' (B4).

37. Barsocchini 365.

38. Manaresi 25, 35, 43, 64 against Franks; 57 for Jeremias.

39. Schwarzmaier (B3–*f*) pp. 222–44; C. E. Boyd (A4) pp. 88–99.

40. Gerbert, *Epistolae* (*M.G.H. Briefe*, II) nn. 2, 3, 5; *Dipl. Ottonis III* n. 303; *M.G.H. Constitutiones*, I n. 23. Rather: *Dipl. Ottonis I* 348; cf. F. Weigle, 'Ratherius von Verona im Kampf um das Kirchengut', *Q.F.* XXVIII (1937–8) pp. 27–35.

41. Rather, *Praeloquia*, 1.23 (Migne, *P.L.* 136 c. 167).

6. THE SOUTH

1. *Chronicon Vulturnense, cit.* (henceforth *C. Vult.*) n. 61.

2. Erchempert, *Historia Langobardorum Beneventanorum*, ed. in *S.R.L; Chronicon Salernitanum, cit.* (henceforth *C. Sal.*).

3. L. Duchesne, 'Les évêchés d'Italie et l'invasion Lombarde' (B6–*a*).

4. *C. Sal.* c. 27.

5. Erchempert, cc. 15, 24–5, 56.
6. Cf. P. Delogu (B3–e) caps. 1 and 3.
7. R. S. Lopez and I. W. Raymond (A2) p. 54; *Honorantiae* c. 6.
8. *Codex diplomaticus Cajetanus*, 1 (Montecassino, 1887) n. 19. For Jews, *vd.* esp. *The Chronicle of Ahimaaz*, (A3–e).
9. C. *Vult.* 157, 177, 178, 181. For Byzantium, A. Guillou (A5–b).
10. C. *Vult.* 140 (Liburia), 9, 12, 70 (Appennines).
11. Slave *condumae*: Gregory, *Epp.* 9.71, 13.18; *C. Vult.* 22, 32, 38, 69; C. Troya, *Codice diplomatico longobardo* (Naples, 1852–5) nn. 430, 559, 568, 625, etc. Labour service and the end of slavery: cf. P. Toubert (B3–f) pp. 465–79. Southern agriculture in general: A. Lizier (B5–c).
12. *Cod. Dipl. Cajetanus* 100 (= Manaresi 250).
13. *Pactum Arechisi* (ed. M.G.H. *Leges*, IV pp. 213–5) and *Sicardi Pactio* c. 14 (*ibid.* p. 220); Troya *op. cit.* vol. V, 616ª; cf. the works of G. Cassandro, most recently 'Il ducato bizantino' in *Storia di Napoli*, II (Naples, 1969) pp. 129–56.
14. *Vd.*, for basic analyses, N. Cilento, *Le origini della signoria capuana* (Rome, 1966), J. Gay (B3–e), C. G. Mor (B1).
15. R. Poupardin (B3–e) p. v.
16. Cf. Gay (B3–e); V. von Falkenhausen (B3–e); A. Guillou, 'Italie méridionale byzantine ou Byzantins en Italie méridionale?' (B3–e).
17. *Vita S. Nili* c. 72 (Migne, *Patrologia Greca* 120 c. 124).
18. F. Carabellese, *L'Apulia ed il suo comune nell'alto medioevo* (Bari, 1905), pp. 109ff., 167ff.; F. Trinchera, *Syllabus Graecarum membranarum* (Naples, 1865) nn. 18, 20.
19. Cf. A. Guillou and F. Holzmann, 'Zwei Katepansurkunde aus Tricarico', *Q.F.* XLI (1961) pp. 1–28.
20. Cf. Poupardin, Cilento, Delogu *opp. cit.*
21. So, for example, *C. Vult.* 34, 41, 45, 62.
22. *C. Sal.* c. 54; cc. 42ff. for Sico's past history.
23. Erchempert c. 22, *C. Sal.* c. 58.
24. *Chronicon S. Benedicti* c. 14 (*S.R.L.* pp. 475–6); Erchempert cc. 40, 45
25. F. Ughelli, *Italia Sacra*, 2nd ed. (Venice, 1720–2), VI cc. 393–4, X Appendix c 471.
26. Erchempert c. 65.
27. Cf. Toubert (B3–f) esp. pp. 303–549, 960–1038; the best introductory narrative is P. Partner (A6–b). For S. Vincenzo, *vd.* M. del Treppo, 'La vita economica e sociale in una grande abbazia . . .' (B5–c).
28. *Regesto Sublacense*, ed. L. Allodi, G. Levi, (Rome 1885) n. 200; *C. Vult.* 109; cf. Toubert pp. 322–3 for a register of similar texts for Lazio.
29. C. *Vult.* 124, 115.
30. E.g. C. *Vult.* 92, 167.
31. E.g. C. *Vult.* 109, 110, 164.

7. THE FAILURE OF THE STATE

1. As G. Rossetti notes, 'Formazione e caratteri delle signorie di castello . . .' (B3–d) p. 308. General histories for 875–962: Hlawitschka (B3–c) pp. 67–94, Hartmann (B1) III. 2, Mor (B1, G. Fasoli (B3–d). Best analysis to 905: P. Delogu, 'Vescovi, conti e sovrani nella crisi del regno italico' (B3–d).
2. *Vd.* G. Fasoli, *Le incursioni ungare in Europa nel sec. 10* (Florence, 1945).
3. Liutprand, *Antap.* 3.39–41. Cf., for the decline of the bureaucracy, Keller, 'Konigsherrschaft' (B3–c) pp. 155–204.
4. Basic for this and later tenth-century developments: Rossetti, 'Formazione' cit. pp. 243–309; and Tabacco, 'La storia politica e sociale' (B1) pp. 113–37, a masterpiece of

compressed analysis; cf. also *idem*, 'La dissoluzione medievale dello stato' (B3–*d*) pp. 397–413.

. 5. *I diplomi di Berengario I* (henceforth '*D.B.I.*'),ed. L. Schiaparelli, (Rome, 1903) nn. 38, 84.

6. *D.B.I.* 65, 88, 117 (= Manaresi 125, 128); G. Tiraboschi, *Codice diplomatico Nonantolano* (Modena, 1785) nn. 78, 85; cf. Rossetti, 'Formazione' *cit.* pp. 270–86.

7. An indicative exception is *D.B.I.* 76, where twenty-nine proprietors from in and around Novara combine to build a *castello* on their own property and inhabit it.

8. Darmstädter (B3–*b*) pp. 5, 26–31.

9. V. Fumagalli, 'Vescovi e conti nell' Emilia occidentale' (B3–*d*); Rossetti, 'Formazione' *cit.* pp. 286–305; Keller, 'Gerichtsort' (B3–*c*) pp. 32ff.

10. *D.B.I.* 47.

11. *M.G.H. Dip. Heinrici II*, n. 278, cf. Tabacco, *Liberi del re* (B4) pp. 167–82. The Mantuans had trouble resisting Boniface of Canossa, though – cf. *Dip. Heinrici III*, n. 356.

12. Liutprand, *Antap.* 4.6–7.

13. Fumagalli, 'Vescovi' *cit.* pp. 182–9.

14. Liutprand, *Antap.* 5.33. The Ottonians collected the *fodrum*, a money commutation of royal hospitality rights, but it is doubtful how far this could be called a tax – cf. *F.G.S.* pp. 534–77.

15. Manaresi 132–44; only 140–1 are in Lucca (in Hugh's own presence), and 137 in Asti.

16. General history after 962: Hartmann (B1), IV; Mor (B1); after 1002, C. Violante in *Storia d'Italia*, I (B3–*d*).

17. Cf. *F.G.S.* pp. 502–14.

18. Piedmont, the stronghold of the irredentist lay aristocracy, may have been an exception, but here too public power declined; cf. G. Sergi (B3–*f*).

19. For Emilia: Fumagalli, 'Vescovi' *cit.* and *Terra e Società* (B3–*f*) pp. 80–123. *I diplomi di Ugo e di Lotario* (ed. L. Schiaparelli, Rome 1924) n. 78 (945) for gifts to the king.

20. Fumagalli, *Le origini di una grande dinastia feudale* (B3–*f*); R. Schumann (A3–*f*) pp. 55–8. The Obertenghi, a close parallel on the Emilian fringes, lack a published modern study; cf. Schumann, pp. 60–4.

21. Schwarzmaier (B3–*f*) pp. 193–261, and arts. by Schwarzmaier, Keller, Rossetti in *5° Congresso cit.* The Tuscan march only included north and central Tuscany.

22. Barsocchini, 1098, 1161; F. Bertini, *Memorie e documenti*, IV Appendix, n. 84.

23. Hugh: as n.21, with A. Falce, *Il Marchese Ugo* (B3–*f*); Peter Damiani, *De Principis Officio*, II 3–5, in Migne *P.L.* 145 cc. 827–30.

24. *M.G.H. Dip. Heinrici IV* n. 334.

25. *Cartulario della Berardenga*, ed. E. Casanova, (Siena 1927) n. 53; cf. P. Cammarosano (B3–*f*). The best general analysis of these developments is C. Violante, 'Quelques caractéristiques des structures familiales . . .', *Famille et Parenté* (B4) pp. 87–151, by contrast with a whole school of historians influenced by K. Schmid, esp. 'Zur Problematik von Familie, Sippe u. Geschlecht . . .', *Zeitsch. f.d. Gesch.des Oberrheins* 105 (1957) pp. 1–62.

26. E.g. for Tuscany, W. Kurze, 'Monasteri e nobiltà nella Tuscia altomedievale', *5° Congresso cit.* pp. 339–62. Only the greatest Frankish aristocrats like Adalbert I and Winigis founded monasteries in Tuscany in the ninth century.

27. Cf. works of Violante in bibliography, esp. *Storia d'Italia*, I pp. 80–6.

28. As, for example, in the *castello* of Brivio near Bergamo in 968 (Porro 706).

29. E.g. E. Conti (B3–*f*) pp. 154–6.

30. *M.G.H. Dip. Ottonis I.* 384, *II.* 291, *III.* 265, 268. Nonantola: L. A. Muratori, *Antiquitates Italicae*, III (Milan, 1740) pp. 241–3. Cf., in general, Tabacco, 'La storia politica e sociale' pp. 153–67 and *refs. cit.*; L. A. Kotel'nikova, 'O formakh obščinnoy organizatzii

severoital'yanskovo krest'yanstva v 9–12 vv', *Sredniye Veka*, xvii (1960) pp. 116–40 and *refs. cit.*

31. The best guides are the works of Fasoli in bibliography (B4); these give reference to individual city histories.

32. *D.B.I.* 90; *Dip. Ottonis II.* 312.

33. *Dip. Lotario*, 1 (contrast *D.B.I.* 12); *Dip. Berengario II.* 11 (ed. in same volume).

34. Rather: Migne, *P.L.* 136 cc. 679–86; Milan: Violante (B3–*f*); Cremona: *Dip. Ottonis III* 198, 222, *Conradi II* nn. 251–3. Wipo, *Gesta Chuonradi*, ed. H. Bresslau, (Hannover 1919) cc. 7, 12–3, 16, 34–7.

35. *Rerum Italicarum Scriptores*, vi. 2, ed. M. Lupo Gentile, 2nd ed., (Bologna 1936) p. 5.

List of Rulers

Roman Emperors

Honorius (393–423)
Constantius III (421)
John (423–5)
Valentinian III (425–55)
Petronius Maximus (455)
Avitus (455–6)
Majorian (457–61)
Libius Severus (461–5)
Anthemius (467–72)
Anicius Olybrius (472)
Glycerius (473)
Julius Nepos (473–80)
Romulus Augustulus (475–6)

Odoacer, King (476–93)

Ostrogothic Kings

Theoderic (490–526)
Athalaric (526–34)
Amalasuntha (534–5)
Theodahad (534–6)
Witigis (536–40)
Ildibad (540–1)
Eraric (541)
Totila (541–52)
Teias (552)

Lombard Kings

Alboin ((560) 568–72)
Cleph (572–4)

Authari   (584–90)
Agilulf   (590–616)
Adaloald   (616–26)
Arioald   (626–36)
Rothari   (636–52)
Rodoald   (652–3)
Aripert I   (653–61)
Perctarit   (661–2, 672–88)
Godepert   (661–2)
Grimoald   (662–71)
Garibald   (671–2)
Cunipert   (679–700)
Alahis   (c. 688–9)
Liutpert   (700–1)
Raginpert   (700–1)
Aripert II   (701–12)
Ansprand   (712)
Liutprand   (712–44)
Hildeprand   (735–44)
Ratchis   (744–9, 756–7)
Aistulf   (749–56)
Desiderius   (757–74)
Adelchis   (759–74)

Frankish Kings (E: Emperor)

Charlemagne   (774–814, E800)
Pippin   (781–810)
Bernard   (812–7)
Louis the Pious   (E813–40)
Lothar   (817–55, E824)
Louis II   (840–75, E850)
Charles the Bald   (875–7, E875)
Carloman   (877–9)
Charles the Fat   (879–87, E881)
Berengar I   (888–924, E915)
Guy   (889–95, E891)
Lambert   (891–8, E892)
Arnulf   (894–6, E896)

Louis III   (900–5, E905)
Rudolf   (922–6)
Hugh   (926–47)
Lothar   (931–50)
Berengar II ⎱   (950–62)
Adalbert   ⎰

German Emperors to 1039

Otto I   (962–73)
Otto II   (973–83)
Otto III   (983–1002)
Arduin, King   (1002–15)
Henry II   (1004–24)
Conrad II   (1024–39)

Princes of Benevento to 981

Arichis II   ((758), 774–87)
Grimoald III   (787–806)
Grimoald IV   (806–17)
Sico   (817–33)
Sicard   (833–9)
Radelchis I   (839–51)
Siconulf   (839–49) (Prince of Salerno   849–51)
Radelgar   (851–3)
Adelchis   (853–78)
Gaideris   (878–81)
Radelchis II   (881–4, 897–900)
Aio   (884–91)
Ursus   (891–2)
Byzantine rule   (892–5)
Guy IV of Spoleto   (895–7)
Atenulf I   (900–10)
Landulf I   (900–43)
Landulf II   (943–61)
Pandulf I   (943–81)

GENEALOGICAL TABLE I: LOMBARD KINGS (FROM 520) AND DUKES OF BENEVENTO (FROM 642)

CLEPH
572-4

Garibald
k. of
Bavaria
=

WACCHO
c. 520-40

Walderada

WALTHARI
c. 540-7

AUDOIN
c. 547-60

ALBOIN
560-72

X

Gisulf I
duke of
Friuli

Grasulf I

Gisulf II
of Friuli

AUTHARI = Theudelinda = AGILULF
584-90   590-616

Gundoald
duke of Asti

ADALOALD   Gundiperga   =   ARIOALD
616-26   626-36

= ROTHARI
636-52

RODOALD
652-3

RADOALD
duke of
Benevento
642-7

ARIPERT I
653-61

PERCTARIT
661-2, 672-88

GODEPERT
661-2

D = GRIMOALD   = Ita
     duke 647-62
     king 662-71

GARIBALD
671-2

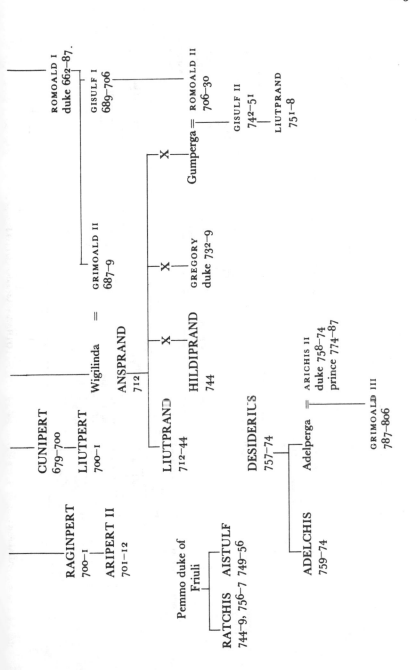

GENEALOGICAL TABLE 2: CAROLINGIAN AND POST-CAROLINGIAN RULERS OF ITALY

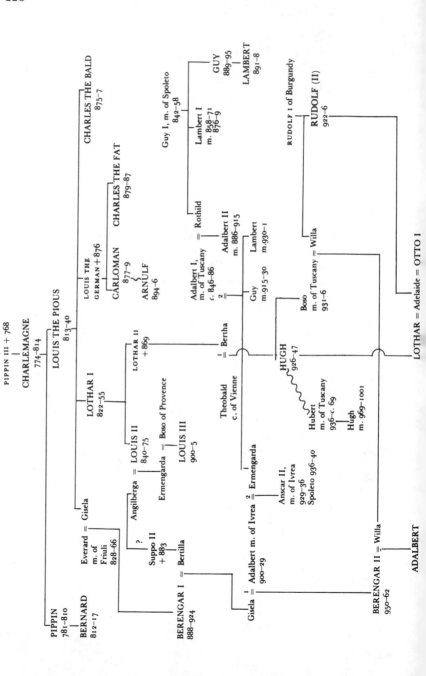

Index